Understanding systems failures

Victor Bignell and Joyce Fortune

Understanding systems failures

Manchester University Press

in association with the Open University

Distributed exclusively in the USA and Canada by St. Martin's Press

First published in 1984 by
Manchester University Press
Oxford Road, Manchester M13 9PL, UK
and Room 400, 175 Fifth Avenue, New York,
NY 10010, USA

Distributed exclusively in the USA and Canada by
St. Martin's Press Inc.
175 Fifth Avenue, New York,
NY 10010, USA

Reprinted 1985, 1989, 1991, 1992

British Library cataloguing in publication data
    Bignell, Victor
    Understanding systems failures
    1. System theory
    I. Title. II. Fortune, Joyce.
003 Q295

Library of Congress cataloging in publication data
    Bignell, Victor
    Understanding systems failures
    Bibliography: p.
    Includes index.
    1. System failures (Engineering) I. Fortune, Joyce.
    II. Title.
TA169.B4   1984   003   83–12016

ISBN 0 7190 0973 1

Printed in Great Britain by
BPCC Wheatons Ltd, Exeter

Contents

Preface

The spur that prompted the writing of this book was the need for a text to accompany a section of the Open University course T301: *Complexity, management and change*. However, the opportunity has been taken to produce something that will serve other purposes too. The aims of the book are set out in the Introduction, which also explains how and why this book should be read.

The general reader will find a more comprehensive account than the daily newspaper will have provided on the 'bad news' of earlier years. The student taking other courses that require the analysis of case studies will find in those presented here a challenge for the ways of thought that his or her present course of study adopts.

The book was written while the authors were in the employ of the Open University and has benefited from the University's services of typing and library work. The authors are grateful to members of the Open University Systems Group and in particular the T301 course team for discussions on the book, and accepting it as a recommended text for the course. Thanks must also go to students and tutors of a previous course, TD342 Systems Performance, who, over the years that course was presented, challenged many of the ideas about systems and failures and thus helped to sharpen up these ideas.

The case studies could not have been written without the unwitting help of the investigators and authors who had already worked on these stories and published the books and reports listed in the bibliography. Also listed there are some of the books on systems and related matters that the authors found useful. Chapter 6 was prepared with the help of notes collected locally by Barbara Morris of Sheffield City Polytechnic. Alan Stone provided much information for chapter 2.

Copyright acknowledgments

The publishers gratefully acknowledge permission granted for the use of the following copyright material: Fig. 2.1. The Open University; Fig. 2.2. source Figs. 2.3, 5.1, 5.4, 5.6; Associated Press Photo; Figs. 2.7–2.16 US Nuclear Regulatory Commission. *Three Mile Island: A report to the Commissioners and to the public*, Rogovin, Stern and Huge. Washington D.C., 1980; Fig. 2.7 GPU Nuclear, Three Mile Island Nuclear Station; Figs. 3.1, 3.2, 3.4, 3.5 The Humber Bridge Board, Ferriby Road, Hessle, North Humberside; Figs. 3.3, 3.6, 3.7 David Lee Photography Ltd., George Street, Burton-on-Humber; Figs. 4.1, 4.2 Her Majesty's Stationery Office; Figs. 5.2, 5.3, 5.5, 5.7, 5.9, 5.10, 5.11, 5.12, 5.14, 5.15 Ministry of Justice and Police of Norway, *The* Alexander L. Kielland *accident*, Oslo, 1981; Fig. 5.8 Rauma Repola, Snellmaninkantu B, SF-00170, Helsinki 17; Fig. 6.1 *The Independent Commission on Transport; Changing directions*, Coronet Books, 1974; Fig. 12.1 McGraw-Hill; Table 3.2, Her Majesty's Stationery Office; Tables 3.3, 3.5, The Humber Bridge Board.

Introduction

Failure has only rarely been selected as a subject for study in its own right. Books on failure usually concentrate on one area, such as aircrashes, financial failure or industrial management. However, in this book a wide range of failures from different areas of activity are brought together, and an attempt is made to present a way of studying failures that contains guidelines and particular recommendations aimed at improving our understanding of failures, their background and how they came about.

The starting point for the book is that we are, all of us, continually coming across what are called here 'failures'. This is discussed in the first chapter, but for the moment we can say that if the performance of some activity is noted to fall below standard, this is called failure. Thus shipwrecks, stock exchange crashes and even our own disappointing holiday will fall within the meaning of failure, even though a specific study of these cases may not occur here.

After the first chapter, on failure, the next six set out a number of case histories, each containing failures. Some of the histories are explained at length, others are much shorter. In every case a number of aspects are explored. At a first reading of this book the histories can be read simply as stories, but noting all the while how the meaning of failure, and the attributes of failure, as set out in summary at the end of the first chapter, recur in the case histories.

The subjects for the case histories were selected with the aim of providing suitable material for explaining the book's approach to failure, but certain constraints guided the choice. Thus the histories were selected from the public domain in order to give the reader the opportunity to find and add further information. Similarly, all the major case studies and most of the short ones are comparatively recent so that the context of the histories is more likely to be familiar, and those histories were preferred for which considerable documentation was not difficult to obtain. Finally, the case histories would cover a wide range of activities. In the event it was found that suitability for explaining the approach to failure was by no means a constraint on selection. It emerged that once significant failures had been identified, an analysis on the lines suggested could be undertaken and completed.

The chapters in the second half of the book set out the way that we as authors suggest that a failure case history should be studied. In explaining the approach a number of examples are drawn from the case histories in the first part of the book, and the reader should go back to the case histories where necessary to check on the analysis carried out by the authors. The same case histories, and others, can be returned to in order to extend the analysis, and the reader can also apply the approach to case histories and failures that particularly concern him or her.

In essence, the basis of the analysis is the suggestion that an approach be made to the understanding of the background to failure by using the idea of a 'system'. This idea is explained in chapter 8, but it has already found wide application and a considerable measure of acceptance in such diverse fields as biology, geography and organisational management.

The concept of system is employed in the following way. What might be called standard forms of system are selected, and comparisons are made between these and what can be found of 'systems' in parts of the case history. The comparisons are intended to reveal points of match or mis-match, that take the analysis back, stage by stage, through the many and successive causes of failure. The idea of system, the particular types of systems used here, and the way that comparison operates, are explained in these later chapters of the book. The comparison as presented in this book relies on the use of a limited number of concepts of how failure arises, but the approach is also capable of accommodating other concepts of the origins of failure. Some of these have been omitted for reasons of space but there will also no doubt be other possible candidates for inclusion that have not yet been considered.

Every chapter except the last one is concerned with the particular intention of this book, to give assistance in the understanding of failure. The meaning of 'understanding' in the context of this book is set out in chapter 8, and is regarded as a useful aim in its own right, as it enlarges our experience. However, if further objectives are needed, the final chapter outlines how the method for understanding can be used for repairing the systems that have yielded failure, can assist in forecasting failure and finally can help prevent future failure.

1

Failure

1.1 Failure and its nature

Strictly speaking it should be unnecessary to point out to someone who has taken the trouble to open this book that failure has a certain interest and fascination, but interest is an important part of our theme. In the failures studied here something is seen to have happened (or not happened); someone shows an interest in the change, and sees it as a failure. In a word, they are disappointed. Thus failure can most often be expressed simply as a shortfall between performance and standards. Brief though it is, this phrase embodies the basis of a complicated concept having a range of types and meanings; the remainder of this chapter expands upon failure as a label for what we are studying.

The change that is seen as a failure naturally needs someone to observe it, and the change may be one that affects them immediately and directly: bus fares going up, the no. 29 bus service is being withdrawn. It might be a future effect: local authority policy could lead to the local school ceasing to have a sixth form five years hence. The change might be one that does not involve us directly: massive floods on a distant continent break through neglected flood defences and highlight deficiencies in relief services. Here, we feel for the misfortunes of others, and the failure to prepare properly. But even that degree of involvement is unnecessary for an examination of a failure, as we can make a study of what someone else sees as a failure, provided of course that we can accept that their judgement might be valid. Whether it is valid will emerge from the analysis itself. Also, it is possible that although we may disagree with someone else's verdict as to failure, we may be looking out for some connection between the change that has been declared a failure and one for which our concern is more direct because it would be a failure to us.

The change that produces a verdict of failure might be reported in a newspaper or one of the other media, as indeed have all the case studies in this book in one guise or another. That is clear evidence of interest by the editor of, say, a newspaper, in expectation of interest on the part of both potential and regular readers. However, inclusion in a newspaper or other news medium is not a sufficient or necessary test for a failure, for the media deal with much more than failures, they tell of successes and they also seek to inform, instruct and entertain. Furthermore, although the topics of our case studies have appeared in the media the ways in which failure is studied are capable of application to matters that are not reported there.

A further group of failures with which we might be concerned are those that have not happened yet. They are the outcomes of situations analogous to those included in our half-dozen case studies except that the failure has not yet emerged and we are looking ahead to search for the possibility that it might do so. They are the future failures that one day could be bad news for someone. This book, we hope, will make a contribution to forestalling them.

Failures therefore can occur in the past, present or future; they will vary in duration too. One particular type of newsworthy failure has come to be called a catastrophe. It is sudden and overwhelming, as in an aircrash, and knocks all the other news off the front page, even though only a handful of people may suffer direct loss. Another failure might be long drawn out, like unemployment that affects millions, but is not always on the front page. The word catastrophe is also applied to natural disasters such as earthquakes, volcanoes and floods but these are not necessarily failures. The failure associated with them may lie more with our inability to cope with their effects, or our inability to predict them. The impact of some large mysterious object from space in the Taiga region of the USSR in 1908 was one of the largest natural catastrophes of recent years but no performance level was in anyone's mind so there can be no shortfall. Indeed, no people were involved at all.

A further distinction between types of failure takes us back to our interest and concern over failure. A major accident to an airliner is considered by all concerned to be a failure unless the loss was due to a terrorist bomb, and even then only an extremely small minority would see this as a success. Chapter 2 of this book concerns events in a nuclear power station. Although there was a possible danger that radioactivity might spread from the plant, and clearly this would be a failure, the view is now held by some people inside and outside the nuclear power industry that the events at the station can be regarded as a successful if unwitting test of nuclear safeguards, as very little radioactivity escaped the several lines of defence that had been deliberately built in. This view and the example of a terrorist bomb in an airliner are extreme ones and few people would disagree that on the whole these are examples of failure, but consider unemployment again. This is a failure to all who are unemployed, but to the government charged with managing the national economy, unemployment might seem to be a necessary evil, even a success if it brings about re-training of people in new technologies, breaks the power of the trade unions or leads to a 'better' distribution of industrial locations. So it seems likely that most items of news will be read as bad by some people and good by others; there will always be someone who sees success, as against someone who sees failure. Perhaps the most extreme examples of this arise in what can be called adversary situations, when by the very nature of the situation (a game, a court case or a war for instance) not all can win. Those who lose will usually see what happened as a failure unless, like the British retreat from Dunkirk, or the charge of the Light Brigade, the defeats are celebrated as though they were victories. More conventionally, a military study of an engagement in a battle can be made from the point of view of the loser as a study in failure, and at the same time it is a study of success for the winner. Nevertheless, even the winners would do well to study the failures of their adversaries, in order to be able to promote failure in the opposing ranks and avoid failure in their own.

So the designation of failure depends on the goals of the party concerned. If these are not achieved then there will be a failure and as observers we can see a failure there too. We can sympathise (or not) and go on to understand how the failure came about. If we are indifferent to the objectives of others, or if our objectives are in competition with theirs, we may not actually regard the outcome as a failure for us; it might even be a success. Now this difference is all very well in a game or a war when two sides differ, but if the two sides are required to come together to discuss what should be done as a result of the assessment it will be difficult for them to agree on what should be done if they already disagree about the effectiveness of what has gone before.

Other examples of disputes over failures occur when considering the performance of large enterprises such as the National Health Service. Indeed it could be said that one of the reasons for setting up such a scheme, or nationalising an industry like coal or steel, is that in the identification of failure in such cases there is too much that is open to disagreement for the assessment of performance and design of consequent changes to be carried out in private hands, which perhaps represent narrow or vested interests. It seems that only the elected or appointed representatives of the public can be trusted to judge whether a particular outcome in these areas is a success or a failure. Hence we have fierce debates on whether something like the health service is a success, although agreement is unlikely when the protagonists have different views on what would constitute success. Should performance of a health service be measured in terms of prevention, or cure? How should scarce resources be divided between helping the temporarily incapacitated and easing the last days of the dying? As a less morbid example, is public transport a commercial enterprise serving customers well able to pay, or is it a public service that should be available to all without hindrance, as the National Health Service was originally intended to be? Whether failure to reach one of these targets signals a failure depends on the viewpoint currently adopted by the observer, but if we are in good health, and own a car, we may not even think about the performance of these public services, let alone come to judge their performance as a failure or a success.

Whether a particular case is deemed to be a success or a failure is a matter of judgement, and in looking for failures the basic activity behind the idea of judgement is a comparison in which we compare an ideal or a goal with what we see as the output from an activity. Failure is judged to occur when the comparison shows a shortfall. This shortfall can take several forms: the first, which has already been described, is one in which a desired performance standard exists but where the current output is not up to that standard. This is the most common form of failure identification. In other cases the assessment extends over time, with the performance only occasionally falling below standard to give a brief shortfall that requires investigation. Maybe the performance actually rises above the standard, and the reasons for this could be just as tantalising as the reasons for a shortfall: if performance could be stabilised at the new, higher level that is perhaps only reached occasionally at present, standards for comparison could be raised. It might seem wrong to see this as a failure, but 'over-success' is a failure if it has made greater calls on people, equipment, materials and organisation than are warranted by the modest standard currently being aimed at, or if its unpredictability points to a lack of knowledge of the operating characteristics of the system. The failure in this context will be over-consumption of resources and wasteful expenditure.

In order to plan ahead, it is necessary to predict future performance and judge it against standards. There could be change in performance, or change in standards, or both. Performance could be increasing but if our standards are rising still faster then something that is predicted as a success appears to become a failure. Furthermore, not only might the numerical value used in a standard change, the very aspect of performance that is assessed might change entirely. A manufacturer might be increasing the output of a commodity and yet the demand from consumers outstrips supply. Availability has replaced quality and price as the measure of performance. The same kind of uncertainty and lack of knowledge that can accompany prediction characterises past failures in which unexpected and undesired side effects are produced. The side effects and after effects of certain drugs, such as thalidomide, provide good examples. They can also be seen as failures in which future hopes for success were thwarted.

The subjective nature of failure suggests that it would be unfair, and indeed untrue in the terms used here, to say for instance that a railway service is a failure within itself. What we really mean by failure is that someone judges something to be a failure. Failure is an observation about something, for the failure is not the thing itself, even though we will sometimes lapse into this shorthand. So, in any situation, the collection of hardware, people, ideas and so on that make up an activity cannot be a failure; the product is the failure, and failure applies to the collected items only in respect of their performance together in producing, or not producing, a result. The idea of failure as the product of many items and activities is taken up later when we see how what we call the systems approach is applied. For the moment we shall note several other aspects of failure.

It is not helpful to explain failure in terms of 'bad luck' although there can be an element of chance in failure. If an inspector of the steelwork for a bridge had happened to choose one girder rather than another for careful examination the bridge might not have broken. This is bad luck perhaps, but it is not helpful just to shrug off failure as if we were powerless in the face of chance. Better to learn from the incident by asking how the frequency and nature of the inspections were arranged. What was the inspection procedure for the finished girders just after they had been welded, or before they left the factory, or on arrival at the site for the bridge?

A catastrophe such as a bridge collapse can be the result of a host of small omissions which were not regarded as failures at the time. If we look into their circumstances and backgrounds failures are found to be multicausal, they arise from complicated, interactive and interdependent prior activities. It is also unlikely that a chain of events that precedes a major failure will be a simple linear one. Much more likely it will be found to be a branched one with the causes of the failure coming from several background areas.

Failures are outputs from a combination of prior conditions, circumstances and events, but must some person or persons be to blame? In the last century the chief engineer for a bridge project was regarded as responsible for all that was done (or not done) by those under him. Thus Thomas Bouch, the engineer of the ill fated first Tay bridge, in Scotland, was held by an inquiry to be 'wholly to blame' when due to bad design, construction and maintenance the bridge fell into the Tay estuary. Today the complication and interdependence of an activity such as building a bridge is recognised to a much greater extent so that when the West Gate Bridge in Melbourne, Australia, collapsed during construction, the inquiry blamed all concerned, even the financial promoters and the labour unions. There is now a greater recognition of multiple responsibility for failure. Indeed, even responsibility for failure due to the action of an individual behaving criminally would not be left laid entirely at his or her door today. Excuses or reasons, depending on your point of view, would be found for him or her.

Occasionally there is room for dispute about human responsibility. A classic case is when some new effect in technology or science emerges as a result of an investigation of a failure. An example occurred in the mid 1950s when two of the first jet airliners, Comet aircraft, suffered mysterious and total destruction by explosion of their pressure cabins, killing all on board. The common cause was traced to an unsuspected and surprising property of the metal of the fuselage. Under certain conditions it was likely to crack before many flying hours had been accumulated. No one was held to blame and it could only be regarded as unfortunate that a discovery new to the science of materials had to be made at the expense of so many human lives. It is not expected, the argument went, that standards need be set out and met in respect of unknown phenomena. Yet the absolution of the engineers from blame must be regarded as debatable in that fully representative testing was not carried out. Today's new aircraft undergo tests that simulate real service to a much greater extent, and the hope is that even unknown and unexpected eventualities will have been covered.

1.2 **Failure, in outline**

From the discussion so far it is possible to suggest several key aspects of failure:

A failure is said to occur when disappointment arises as a result of an assessment of an outcome from an activity.

Failure can be a shortfall of performance below a standard, the generation of undesirable side effects or the neglect of an opportunity.

The assessment of an outcome as failure is dependent upon the values held by the person making the judgement. These values affect how much of the performance of an activity is included for the assessment, what quantities or qualities are regarded as significant, and what standards are adopted. The values are liable to vary from individual to individual, and group to group. They are liable to change with the time and the occasion of the judgement, and the viewpoint taken.

Failure can occur in a variety of forms, namely: catastrophic or minor; overwhelming or only partial; sudden or slow.

Failure can arise in the past, present or future.

Failure will be found to be multicausal, and to have multiple effects.

In the case studies that follow this chapter, these many dimensions and attributes of failure will reappear, and later in this book the notion of failure is taken up again, in order to seek an understanding of failure.

2

The accident at Three Mile Island nuclear power station

2.1 Significance of the accident

On 28 March 1979 a maintenance mishap at the Three Mile Island nuclear power station in the United States of America led to an emergency that could have had catastrophic consequences for the station and the people on site, and indeed over a wide area of countryside around the plant. During the emergency the staff failed to comprehend all that was happening in the damaged power plant and neglected to take the correct steps to deal with it. Unforeseen problems arose and small quantities of radioactive material entered the atmosphere. On several occasions the authorities on and off the site recommended measures that could have affected hundreds of thousands of people in the surroundings, and at one point certain members of the public who were thought to be particularly at risk received advice to leave their homes and seek safety.

This accident at the no. 2 reactor of the Three Mile Island nuclear power station near Harrisburg in Pennsylvania was a crucial event in the history of the peaceful use of atomic energy. High hopes had been held out that this type of power plant would be effective in meeting demands for electricity until at least the end of the century; on the other hand nuclear power in any form has had a vociferous opposition lobby, whose members had been very critical of these plants.

Great efforts had been made to ensure an acceptable level of safety but during this accident there even arose the threat that the entire neighbouring population would have to leave their homes. Actually, this proved unnecessary but public confidence suffered a severe set back. The nuclear power plant and the equipment in and around the building housing it were damaged so severely that at the time of writing the plant is still out of commission and may remain so for ever. Cost figures are difficult to gauge in a case like this but the lowest estimates are put at one thousand million dollars, and insurance on the station is inadequate to cover all the costs.

The designers of a nuclear plant or any piece of equipment for that matter can only give assurances that they have faced up to the known dangers. To cope with problems beyond these they depend upon general and detailed care being taken during the building, inspecting, operation and maintenance of a system. In addition they rely upon the intelligence, training and wits of those who are present when the unexpected occurs. In the Three Mile Island accident the malfunctions proceeded in a largely unexpected manner, and, after an initial flurry of events, progressed comparatively slowly so that correct human evaluation of what was happening, followed by timely intervention, could have stopped the incident at an early stage. As far as mechanical operation was concerned every item of equipment (except for one valve) worked as it had been intended to. Also, no new phenomenon of physical science emerged; it was the way the behaviour of equipment was presented to operators and the way they reacted that almost turned a malfunction into a disaster.

2.2 The plant

To understand what happened it is necessary to know something of how the equipment worked. At the heart of such a plant is the nuclear reactor. Here is the source of power, tens of thousands of fuel rods, each a long narrow tube of zirconium metal alloy, packed with pieces of uranium oxide material containing 2.6 per cent of the metal uranium 235. On its own a small bundle of fuel rods would not do very much. It would emit radioactive particles that are smaller than atoms, but these pass any adjacent uranium without much release of energy. However, if the rods are immersed in water its atomic structure slows down or moderates the particles so that now when they strike nearby uranium they will produce heat. The impacts also liberate more particles, which are in turn slowed by the water and they too produce heat by an impact somewhere else in the uranium. This sequence is an example of a chain reaction, and is the source of heat in the reactor.

The bundle of fuel rods is called a core and, together with the moderating water, is enclosed in a thick steel vessel about four metres across and ten metres high. The water is under pressure, so the unit is called the pressure vessel and, strictly speaking, this is the reactor. The use of pressurised water as a medium for transferring heat away from the core for use in generating electricity gives the name pressurised water reactor (PWR) to this layout. The water in the pressure vessel could be allowed to boil and the resulting steam used to drive turbines coupled to electric generators. However, this would send radioactive steam into the atmosphere around the power station, so the water is circulated in a closed loop called the primary circuit (see figure 2.1) and through a steam generator in which the hot radioactive water heats up a second lot of water before being returned to the pressure vessel. This second body of water (in the secondary circuit) is allowed to boil; it turns into steam which drives the turbo-generators to produce electricity. Most of this steam is condensed back to water which, together with a little make-up water, is pumped back to the steam generator for further steam raising.

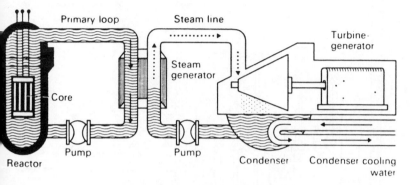

2.1 Basic layout of pressurised water reactor

Rods of the metal cadmium are suspended above the banks of fuel rods in the pressure vessel. Cadmium absorbs the sub-atomic particles so that lowering the cadmium rods into the core slows down the reactor. This is how the power of the reactor is controlled, and also forms part of the safety system. If the flow of water in the primary circuit is slowed down or stopped, or the water boiled off and drained away, this would be called a loss of coolant accident (LOCA). In a severe LOCA the temperature and pressure in the reactor would rise and cause the pressure vessel to give way by leaking from joints distorted by the heat, or cracks in the vessel. In an extreme case the vessel might explode, damaging the power station and injuring or killing staff. More terrifyingly, the explosion would release clouds of radioactive dust and steam which in small doses would increase the likelihood of cancer or genetic damage, and in large doses would cause radiation sickness and eventual death.

Great precautions are taken to prevent escapes from the primary circuit but the consequences that would follow such an escape are so terrible that designers take the further precaution of enclosing the entire reactor in a larger containment building (figure 2.2). If problems occurred this would seal off the area around the reactor vessel and the primary circuit so that nothing could escape. Any build-up of air pressure in the containment building would be released in a safe way by filtering out radioactive debris as the air left. Meanwhile emergency cooling systems would have come into play and if this cooling water became radioactive it could be dealt with safely too.

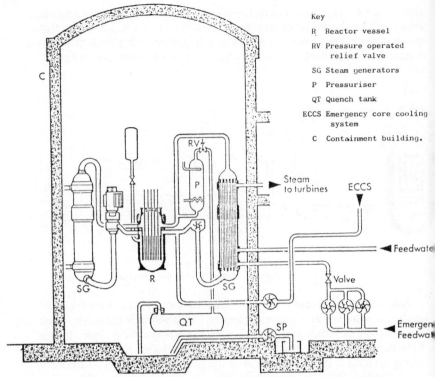

2.2 Pressurised water reactor at Three Mile Island (simplified)

2.3 **The accident**

The Three Mile Island incident of 28 March 1979 commenced with a maintenance crew trying to renew resin that was used for the special treatment of water for the plant. In order to remove the old resin the crew used air injection to clear it out but they allowed some water to enter an air circuit that opened and closed certain valves. This mistake had been made at least twice before at the plant but the operating company had not installed preventive measures. The affected valves shut off and the pumps in the same circuit closed down in quick succession. One of the pumping circuits affected was the feedwater line to the steam generator in the secondary circuit so the safety system shut down the steam turbine and the electric power generator it drove.

Deprived of an outlet for the heat still entering it from the reactor core the water in the primary circuit increased in temperature and pressure. A relief valve on top of the pressuriser opened as was intended and steam and water began to flow out to a drain tank on the floor of the

containment building. To reduce the production of heat in the reactor
core the control rods automatically descended into it, stopping the
nuclear process in one second. However, the arrival of the rods in the core
does not stop all the nuclear activity, for spent fuel continues to give off
about six per cent of full power, so this residual heating had to be dealt
with.

The control rods dropped down only eight seconds after the first pump
had cut off and in that time each automatic response of the equipment in
the plant had been monitored and displayed on the operators' control
panel. In some cases, such as pumps cutting out, the display was
accompanied by the sounding of alarms. It was 4 am; the four operators
in the control room were about to try to take in what had happened,
understand it and its significance, grasp the pressing but ever changing
state of affairs, decide on courses of action and take them. Later they
would be in contact with outside experts, and others would be coming to
the site. Meanwhile, within the circumstances in which they were then
working, and having regard to factors that we shall examine later the
operators could not reasonably have been expected to achieve more than
they did.

When the pumps supplying water to the steam generator stopped,
three emergency pumps for the feedwater started. Fourteen seconds
after the accident began an operator in the control room noticed that
these pumps were running but he did not notice two particular warning
lights on a control panel. They signalled that valves were closed on each
of the two emergency feedwater lines and so were preventing water from
reaching the steam generators, which soon boiled dry. One light was
covered by a tag, rather like a tie-on luggage label. The tag hung from a
nearby switch and carried a maintenance warning. It is not known why
the other light was not seen. Not until almost eight minutes later did the
operators notice the closed valves and open them. Running the plant
with these valves closed amounted to a violation of the operating licence
for the plant and they might even have been in the closed position since
the last checklist surveillance two days earlier, as no systematic checks of
them were called for at shift changes.

The combined effects of lowering the control rods and opening the
relief valve brought the pressure in the vessel down to normal in about
fifteen seconds, at which time the relief valve should have closed. But
instead of doing so it remained open. This was the only malfunction of a
piece of equipment that occurred throughout the entire incident, but it is
highly significant that its failure remained undetected for two and a half
hours. One reason for this must be that the state of the valve, whether it
was open or closed, was not sensed directly. Instead, the corresponding
indicator lamp on the control panel merely signified that the electrical
solenoid operating the valve had functioned. The position of the solenoid

was erroneously taken to indicate the position of the valve but the solenoid had withdrawn alone, leaving the valve open. Through this valve more than one third of the contents of the primary water circuit escaped. If the operators had detected the open valve they could have closed a back-up valve.

Relief valves of this type had given trouble before, and almost precisely the same thing had occurred in a similar plant, Davis-Besse, near Toledo, Ohio. Here too the operators misinterpreted the signs, but realised what was happening after twenty minutes, and closed their back-up valve in time. After this earlier incident separate analyses were performed by the plant manufacturers, the operating company and two groups of officials from the regulatory agency. However the analyses were not co-ordinated and the knowledge gained was not shared with the industry.

Two minutes into the TMI-2 accident two high pressure pumps started automatically, triggered by a lowering of the pressure in the primary circuit. They began injecting water into the circuit to make up the deficiency. By now over one hundred alarms were operating in the control room and the operators became confused as to what was happening. They did not realise the need for water to be pumped in, indeed from indications in the pressuriser they believed the circuit to be full already so that any extra would be too much. If the circuit became completely full any small increase in temperature would give such a large increase in pressure that something would burst. It was their aim to maintain a 'bubble' in the pressuriser, so that the elasticity of the bubble would cope with pressure variations.

The water level in the pressuriser was rising now, not because there was too much water in the system, but rather because the relief valve was still open, the water temperature was going up and the high pressure injectors of emergency water coolant were still running. The operators had been trained to maintain a certain water level in the pressuriser so they reduced the inflow of water by switching one pump off and reducing the flow from the other to ten per cent. The let-down valve was opened to release what was believed to be an excess of water. The original fall in pressure and the failure of the injection to bring down the temperature should have alerted the operators that LOCA was under way but it did not. This mistake persisted for four hours.

Meanwhile, concern remained that the primary system would become over-full. This impression came in part from the rapid filling of a tank in the base of the containment building, but this was due to the relief valve being open, and not to the system being full. The tank overflowed into the sump in the floor of the building and an automatic pump came on to transfer the radioactive water to a waste tank in the adjacent auxiliary building.

Steam bubbles formed in the pressure vessel and forced water round the primary circuit to the pressuriser so that operators again received the impression that the whole circuit had plenty of water. In fact, the reactor core had been uncovered and steam was insufficient to cool it. The fuel rods became overheated and began to break up, releasing radioactive iodine into the primary circuit.

Pressure was still falling, so much so that the pumps in the primary circuit had to be switched off because the steam bubbles caused such severe vibrations that the operators feared the pumps would be damaged. Warnings that the vibration was about to exceed safe limits added even more to the total of alarms that went off that morning. Not until two and a half hours into the incident was the relief valve line finally blocked off so that pressure increased. Half an hour later however a site emergency was declared because of the radioactivity detected in the overflow from the primary circuit. This it will be remembered had reached the auxiliary building; radioactive steam was emitted from there through the chimney.

One of the pumps in the primary circuit was tried again but it still vibrated too much and so switched itself off, signalling the fact just as radiation alarms were received. Again these competed for the attention of operators and the colleagues who had joined them. Meanwhile, unbeknown to the control room staff, the reactor core had been uncovered, probably by two thirds, allowing the zirconium metal alloy of the fuel cladding to react with the steam in the primary circuit. This produced hydrogen, most of which collected at the top of the circuit but some escaped into the containment building itself, where a cloud is believed to have been the cause of a mild explosion.

After fifteen hours one of the primary circuit pumps could be restarted and this time it stayed running, allowing a flow of water to the steam generators. The main danger now seemed to be the hydrogen. It had formed a bubble at the top of the primary circuit and it was feared that lowering the circuit pressure would expand the bubble and thus impair water circulation. If the bubble came to contain oxygen too, the mixture could explode, destroying the reactor and endangering the integrity of the containment building. For several days media across the world speculated whether the bubble would explode before it could be removed. In the event it was eased out safely. Attention could now turn to investigation, clearing up and making safe, and learning the lessons.

2.4 Outside

Many words have been written on TMI-2, many official and unofficial inquiries made and reports filed. We shall focus on aspects highlighted by the comments of two of the largest inquiries. The US President's

Commission, headed by J. G. Kemeny, concluded that the accident was caused by 'people-related problems and not equipment related problems'. The US Nuclear Regulatory Commission's report by M. Rogovin stated that 'the principal deficiencies in commercial reactor safety today are not hardware problems, they are management problems'. The remainder of this account will focus on human and management aspects, both at the plant and elsewhere.

Among the areas of activity that enabled lessons to be learned from the Three Mile Island incident was the handling of communications between the plant and the outside world, including the role of the media. As time went on, an increasingly wide variety of agencies took part in this process. They will be described as the account proceeds, but the story again will begin in the TMI-2 control room.

The accident had started at 4.00 am on Wednesday 28th March 1979, when the feedwater shut off. The requirements and procedures devised for the event of an emergency laid down certain conditions that would call for authorities outside the plant to be informed, but not until 7.00 am were these conditions satisfied. When detection monitors began to show a likelihood of a release of radioactivity the operators, in accordance with their instructions, informed certain authorities. First amongst these was the Nuclear Regulatory Commission (NRC). This is the US Government's regulatory body for nuclear activities. It had supervised the design and construction of TMI-2 and other power stations, set and implemented standards covering a wide variety of aspects of such stations, and was required to take a role in preparing the contingency plans to deal with accidents, and, if necessary, to step in and help with implementation. The NRC was expected to provide expertise from within its own ranks or from other agencies such as national laboratories and international contacts.

Next came the Pennsylvania Emergency Management Agency (PEMA). At 7.02 the officer on watch there learned that an emergency had been declared at Three Mile Island. In accordance with standard operating procedures he notified the duty officer at the Bureau of Radiation Protection (BRP) in the Department of Environmental Resources, officers in neighbouring counties of Pennsylvania and his own operations officer. By 7.20 the bureau had contacted Three Mile Island and could then report that there should be no off-site consequences of the emergency. But at 7.35 the Three Mile Island plant supervisor notified the agency that conditions were worsening, a general emergency should be declared, and the agency was recommended to give instructions to evacuate nearby areas. The agency alerted the counties again, informed the state governor and lieutenant governor, and passed the news to the Bureau of Radiation Protection. However the bureau checked back and discovered that the conditions which demanded the

2.3 The Three Mile Island plants

notifications and evacuations had actually occurred around 4 am. After this the reporting was to become more timely. The 7 am communication also went to the external managers of the plant, Metropolitan Edison (Met-Ed) in the first instance, and from them to the General Public Utilities Corporation (GPU), the parent company of Met-Ed.

The incident had already been under way for three hours but from 7.00 am until 8.00 pm the operators found it very difficult to know what was going on in the plant. How might it behave if certain control operations were or were not carried out? What conditions in the plant should be sought? How could they be achieved? The plant was behaving in a way so far removed from normal that the operators could not understand what was going on and therefore could not be confident of regaining control.

Despite the uncertainty which must have reigned at the plant the lieutenant governor somehow found it possible to announce at 10.55 am on Wednesday 28 March that he had been advised that everything was under control and that there was, and would be, no danger to public health and safety. Also, at around lunch time that day, Jack Herbein, vice president of Met-Ed spoke to press reporters, who wrote up what they heard. They emphasised that the main safety system in the almost brand-new plant had worked well enough to prevent a very serious accident. Evacuation was never discussed. On the other hand the Rogovin inquiry into the accident concluded that by 9 am on Wednesday the information available to those in the control room contained so many uncertainties that the state officials should have been advised on the following lines:

● The reactor core has been badly damaged and has released a substantial amount of radioactivity.

● The plant is now in a condition outside the range of previously analysed cases. Although water for cooling might be available portions of the core could melt and radioactivity be released outside the site in a few hours if the cooling systems do not work.

● If the cooling systems do work, evidence of their success should be available in a few hours.

● A precautionary evacuation of people in the first few miles around the plant should begin, these people being taken at least twenty miles away. In a radius of ten miles people should be alerted that an evacuation might follow.

The emergency plans called for the plant staff to inform PEMA and local government of the levels of radiation outside the plant so that these authorities could then make decisions about evacuation, based on 'scientific' data. However, this was inadequate for giving the authorities a wide enough picture. No message style existed for saying that there was uncertainty, the plant might become vulnerable to damage, and releases of radioactivity might become more likely: shades of meaning could not be expressed. For example, it might have been found necessary to release a quantity of radioactive gas deliberately in order to avoid a more dangerous condition, such as an explosion. The arrangement lacked the finesse necessary for transmitting 'unscientific' information on likelihoods, possibilities and vague probabilities. Figure 2.4 shows the communication paths as they existed in the first few days, and figure 2.5 shows them at a later stage.

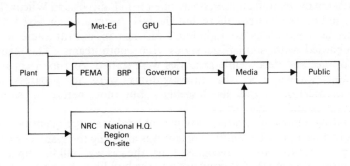

2.4   Communication paths, Wednesday–Friday

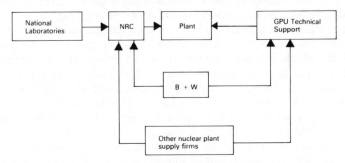

2.5   Communication paths after Friday

As we have seen, the NRC received notification early on the Wednesday morning. A team of inspectors from the NRC regional office arrived at the plant at 10.15 and a large technical staff gathered in NRC's Washington office. This second group tried to monitor what was happening on site by direct phone lines, and to give technical guidance by the same route. Communications were still inadequate and a team of half a dozen specialists assembled and went to the plant on Thursday morning. Things were quiet there. Teams from the Department of

Energy were monitoring conditions in the air and on the ground; the NRC staff of eleven already on site had a mobile van within which to analyse environmental samples for radioactivity. Radiation levels gave no cause for alarm and the reactor circuits seemed stable despite the gas bubble in the primary circuit. Even in this lull, though, the communication services at the site were overtaxed, severely hampering NRC staff.

Meanwhile, the utility assembled its own back-up team for the plant staff but each new member became absorbed in two-shift, round the clock, technical support. The NRC team therefore did not realise that in effect the GPU had a team on site equivalent to their own. The GPU team contacted the manufacturers, steam plant firm Babcock and Wilcox (B & W), and other plant suppliers, but the NRC team also contacted these firms as consultants so individual officials in a firm came to be bombarded with similar questions from both teams. This caused annoyance and delay while priorities were settled. As time went on it became known that the investigations were in progress and communication problems lessened, but not before a serious misunderstanding had arisen.

During Thursday and the early part of Friday a large quantity of gas that had been dissolved in the coolant was affecting the plant's external support circuits. No one recognised that the gas was building up in the exhaust tanks, and then leaking out into the buildings during transfer to waste tanks. A major release of this radioactive gas occurred at 8 am on Friday 30 March, through the chimney of one building.

The release was anticipated by plant staff, who called in a helicopter to measure the radioactivity in the plume above the chimney. The reading was one which, if it had occurred at ground level on the site boundary, would have suggested a serious plant failure such as the rupture of a waste gas tank. Intense exchanges ensued as to the relationship between measurements made at the chimney and the site boundary, and between air and ground readings. Meanwhile the existence of this single reading triggered various actions that would have been unnecessary had both NRC in Washington and the state authorities been told clearly that although the emission would be intense, it would also be so brief as to cause no problem outside the site.

At 8.40 am the same day the PEMA received two simultaneous telephone calls from Three Mile Island reporting a general emergency due to the chimney radiation reading. Non-essential personnel were to leave the site, and the agency was recommended to clear people from down-wind of the site. As a result, the counties received an alert and the State Emergency Operations Centre was activitated. At 9.15 am the NRC office at Bethesda, Maryland, confirmed the evacuation, adding that it should extend to a radius of ten miles (sixteen km). The report added that senior personnel of the NRC supported this. However, further discussion between various parties downgraded the governor's action to one of recommending that people within ten miles of the Island remain indoors until further notice. Two hours later the advice was added that pregnant women and pre-school-age children within five miles should leave. The Pennsylvania National Guard, state police and emergency services had been alerted to assist. At 10 am a telephone overload occurred in the area, and a thirty to forty minute delay was experienced on all calls through the Harrisburg exchange. The Pennsylvania Emergency Management Agency Emergency Operations Centre had over one hundred telephone lines in use but the media and public saturated them, and the Defense Civil Preparedness Agency installed a radio system instead.

To continue the chronology of the evacuation saga, at 8.30 pm on the Friday the NRC advised that plans be made for evacuation from within a twenty mile radius. Three quarters of a million people would have been involved and no plans had been made for such a large scale operation. Apart from the daunting task of dealing with so many people it would have been impossible to deal with individual requirements as special cases; rather, provision had to be made on a routine basis for removal of seriously-ill patients, those on a life support system, newborn babies, pets and livestock, continuous process industries, prisoners and inmates of institutions and (last but not least) the seat of local government.

That Friday has been called the day of panic, but if there was panic it originated away from the vicinity of the reactor, as many of those who passed on pieces of news added their quotas of gratuitous urgency. The previous night both Met-Ed and the NRC knew that a large bubble of hydrogen gas had collected at the top of the reactor vessel. However, the degree of danger it posed and how to remove it were matters of disagreement. Met-Ed proposed to reduce pressure in the vessel in order to ease out the bubble. NRC on site feared that to do so would uncover the core and could lead to partial or complete melting of the fuel. The director of their Division of Systems Safety recommended to the NRC chairman that a precautionary evacuation be undertaken. The NRC concern was expressed to the Pennsylvania governor, the White House press secretary and the energy secretary. Meanwhile, the NRC's public stance was that a meltdown would not occur. At the site nothing was known about the evacuation scares until the afternoon.

Then, during a press conference on Friday afternoon, two of the NRC Bethesda staff admitted that a meltdown was possible, but only in the unlikely event of the reactor depressurising, the hydrogen bubble expanding enough or all the cooling systems giving out. The press reported this accurately but Met-Ed responded that reports of a meltdown were unfounded; the NRC commissioners issued a release saying there was no imminent danger of a core melt, but added later in the text that if the gas bubble expanded then some of the fuel would fail to cool and further damage to that fuel could occur. The conclusion formed by David Rubin, of the New York University journalism department, the Task Force on the Public's Right to Know, and the President's Commission on TMI-2, is that the authorities were trying to counter one report with another, diminishing the impact of the first without specifically denying the possibility of a partial melt down. Rubin goes on to point out the difficulty of maximising public understanding but minimising their alarm when in fact the scientific community must admit uncertainty. None of the parties involved, from Met-Ed to the public, knew how to seek, give or receive information in the case of a nuclear incident whereas a set of agreed phrases lead to more adequate understanding in the case of natural disasters such as hurricanes.

A notorious illustration of the problem of teaching and learning about the status of a nuclear emergency comes from a popular CBS television programme which was broadcast on the Friday evening. Walter Cronkite introduced a series of reports with the following:

The world has never known a day quite like today. It faced the considerable uncertainties and dangers of the worst nuclear power plant accident of the atomic age. And the horror tonight is that it could get much worse. It is not an atomic explosion that is feared, the experts say that is impossible. But the spectre was raised of perhaps the next most serious kind of nuclear catastrophe, a massive release of radioactivity. The Nuclear Regulatory Commission cited that possibility with an announcement that, while it is not likely, the potential is there for the ultimate risk of a meltdown at the Three Mile Island atomic power plant outside Harrisburg Pennsylvania.

This statement was compiled from what was known by the press, and in factual matters it was accurate. Only a few words were added to give colour and drama. It can only be speculated what Cronkite would have said if his staff had known that complete evacuation over a ten mile radius had been recommended early that morning and plans had begun for the enormous task of a twenty mile evacuation. The media were also unaware that NRC's concern was greater than they had expressed, and that their Director of Systems Safety had advised evacuation.

One final incident in this saga of media relations over TMI-2 concerns the bubble again. At 9.02 pm on Saturday 31 March, NRC officials in Bethesda said that the bubble of hydrogen contained oxygen too, and that the mixture could well explode. Relayed by Associated Press, the story not only alarmed residents, it upset the reporters and NRC officials on site too. There, it was known that oxygen was not collecting; the bubble could not explode. On orders from the White House the Bethesda press office was closed and all NRC information on TMI-2 was issued from the site. Associated Press had checked the story with public affairs officials and senior staff of NRC, while indirect confirmation was received from the Systems Safety Director and chairman. On these mistakes, David Rubin (see earlier) has since written that the public has a right to know what responsible officials are saying, even if (especially if) these sources turn out to be incorrect.

The initial accident had knocked out various support systems for the plant's main coolant circuits, and other services now had to be reinforced. For example, operation of the pumps was vital, and so was the supply of electrical power to them. Supplies of extra power from outside needed to be assured, so extra transmission lines were brought in and arrangements made for them to be coupled into the electrical supply to the plant. Extra ventilation arrangements were acquired, complete with the special filters needed. Questions were then asked about the ability of the water circuits to cope with the radioactive primary cooling water. The measuring equipment in some pipe runs had been overloaded and failed or became suspect; new devices were inserted to measure pressure, temperature and water level. Staff undertaking these tasks were assembled into a Plant Modifications Group. Task-oriented groups such as this replaced the previous structures which had been based on the parent organisations of the staff. A Radioactive Waste Management Group was also formed which took charge of the use of existing waste tanks and arranged for back-up tankage for effluent which had to be kept on site instead of being discharged into the river.

Advisers from those organisations further from the centre of operations, such as other utilities, national laboratories and other suppliers of equipment, were formed into an Industry Advisory Group (IAG). Over 110 people contributed directly to this group's work over the five weeks of its formal existence. The IAG began its work by examining basic problems that could be separated from the current day-to-day work of the other groups. It tackled such questions as the later stages of cooling the plant, the likely state of the damaged core of the reactor, medium-term problems over the need for continued filtering of effluents, and future modifications to the plant.

The groups were linked by the structure shown in figure 2.6 and their work was co-ordinated by the Joint Working Group shown there. This last group focused the efforts of the other groups, established priorities and watched to see if the allotted tasks were being done. In particular, this new structure that came into being in the first few days of April gave the NRC a clear place at which to insert its views. The GPU president said later that, while his organisation's relationship with the NRC was reasonably cordial prior to the formation of the Joint Working Group, there seemed to be 'a little more stand-offishness' afterwards. This was expressed by the NRC demanding that whatever was to be done had to receive their approval first. The new arrangement gave the NRC direct access to what was going on, and the NRC representative now reported back properly to all the NRC staff.

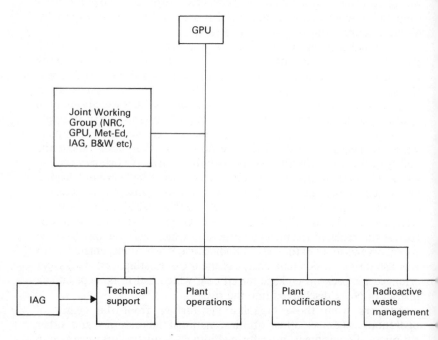

2.6   TMI recovery organisation, 4 April 1979

This question of approval in the case of a developing emergency demands special attention here. In normal operation the plant is operated in the context of a package of prior approvals of equipment, staff and procedures. In contrast to this the running of a plant during an emergency can involve proposals that are not covered by prior examinations, and a decision to act must be made, and the action completed, before there has been time for complete checks. All that can be done is to rely as much as possible on the results of prior control of design, material quality and staff skill, but also bear in mind that there must always be fall-back procedures in case a novel operation is unsuccessful or counterproductive. Possible contingencies must be anticipated but there must also be a readiness on the part of the regulating authority to judge the trade-offs between quality and time. In an emergency the effectiveness of an action is to be judged in terms of timeliness and speed as well as its approach to technical perfection.

2.5 **Human factors**

Any human intervention, whether a routine one or one carried out in an emergency, will have as key features the nature of the people concerned, the details of the equipment they use, and the way these react with each other. During the investigation of the TMI-2 accident several factors came to light concerning the interface between man and machine, and some of these discoveries and revelations were important in explaining the events that led to the failure of the plant and which allowed that failure to cause severe damage.

First, the operators themselves; each of the four on duty in the TMI-2 control room had had at least five years experience in the US nuclear navy. Many civilian nuclear reactor staff have served in the navy, and these four had longer lengths of service there than the industry average. Their special posts in the navy had included duties as electronics or communications technician, electrician and machinist. The navy produces highly-disciplined operators at these levels who are well trained to operate a specific part of the US navy's nuclear reactors, but other well-experienced personnel on each watch supervise the individual operators and have a better understanding of the operation of the plant as a whole. The officer in charge of each naval reactor watch is a commissioned officer and graduate engineer. He has been trained for each operator station but acts as a supervisor to integrate the operating system of men and machines.

For a commercial reactor such as TMI-2 the supervision was in the hands of a senior reactor operator. He would have been promoted from licensed operator after showing competence on duty and passing a special examination. The NRC required only three licensed operators on site, only one of whom needed to have been in the control room. The four TMI-2 operators had completed American high school but had not graduated. After navy service and training for commercial reactors they had all qualified with good grades in the necessary examinations set by the NRC but a study made for the accident inquiry cited several deficiencies in their training.

The training programme had consisted largely of listening to lectures, conducting classroom studies and working on a reactor simulator. This failed to develop operator skills for dealing with emergencies and mainly dealt with starting, stopping and running a reactor with 'normal' readings on the dials. Presentation of the training needed better organisation and its documentation lacked attractive formats that would have maintained the student's interest. Little provision existed for evaluating the effectiveness of the training for dealing with emergencies. Instructors and trainees alike lacked feedback on their performance.

Our attention will next centre on the control room, where the majority

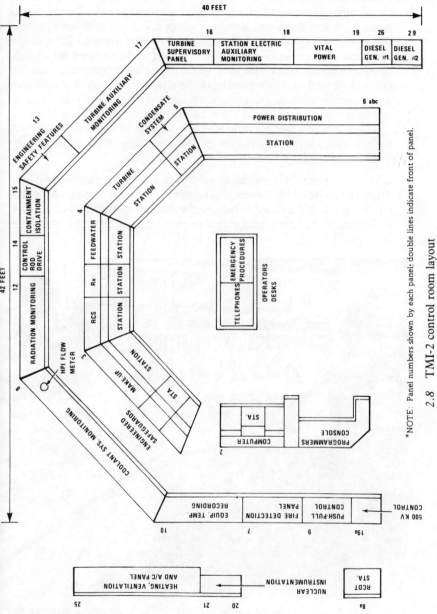

2.8 TMI-2 control room layout

*NOTE: Panel numbers shown by each panel; double lines indicate front of panel.

of plant functions were both carried out and monitored. The room was large, with consoles and panels carrying on their surfaces a multitude of controls, instruments and alarms. Figures 2.7–2.17 show the layouts of the controls and details of the instrumentation. Despite its size and complexity, the control room was intended to be manned by a single operator during normal operation so the central desk contained what was considered vital to the overseeing of the steady state, together with start and stop controls and emergency warnings. During abnormal running conditions extra staff could come in and man the remaining panels.

The layout of a work station should both ease an operator's tasks and make it less likely for errors to occur. However, reports compiled for the TMI-2 inquiry found much amiss in this respect:

● For one piece of equipment in the plant, the pressure in it was displayed on panel 10, the temperature of the contents on panel 8, but the control that could be used to halt undue changes in these was on panel 4. Indication of the flow of make-up water was on panel 8 but the control for it on panel 3.

2.9   Visual scan necessary for operator (on left) controlling make-up to monitor make-up flow (operator on right)

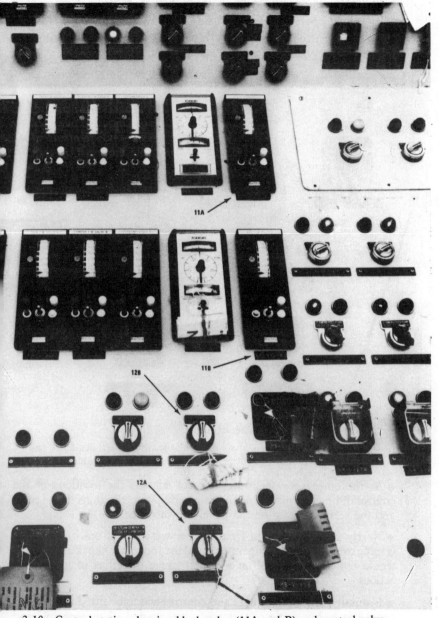

2.10 Control station showing block valve (11A and B) and control valve
(12A and B) layout

● Indicator lights associated with particular controls were placed variously above, below or to one side of them.

● On some controls a clockwise turn switched operation from manual to automatic; on others the reverse was the case.

2.11   Pressuriser heater control showing the right to left sequence and inconsistency of control movement to auto and manual

● At the emergency feedwater control station, the locations of the control did not mimic the actual valve and pump positions in the plant and the relative layout on the panel was inconsistent.

● Nearly seventy items in frequent use were out of reach so that in leaning over for them the operator could inadvertently knock a switch, or would not be able to see on a distant gauge the effect of his control actions.

● Naturally, the many gauges and controls had to be fitted into limited panel space, but some of this space was wasted. Some controls and displays were unnecessarily large whilst others were too small in relation

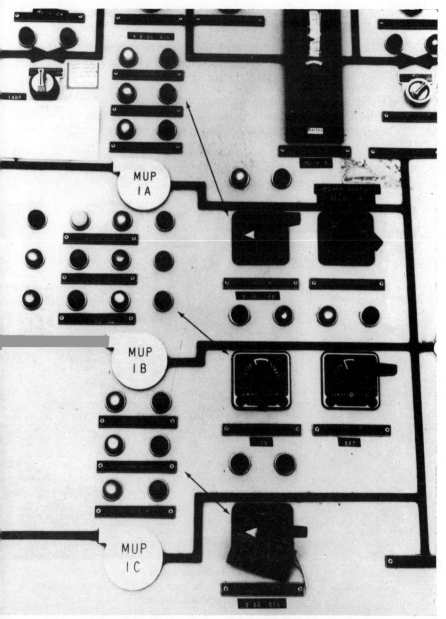

2.12 Relationship of make-up pump controls and indicator lights

to their importance. The pressuriser water level is an important example of this.

● Other necessary indications were entirely absent: emergency feedwater flow, and flow in the discharge line from the pressuriser relief valve were two that proved significant.

● Other displays were out of the easy view of the operator, or badly sited relative to their associated controls. The indicators that showed whether the reactor coolant pumps were vibrating badly or were out of balance lay on the rear of panel 4.

● Only the top half of sixteen rows of certain indicator lights could be seen from the normal operating position.

2.13   Indicator board.
1. Indication below this line cannot be seen by a 6 ft operator standing at the ESF operating station

2. Indication below this line cannot be seen by a 6 ft operator from the closest position in front of the control consoles

● Reactor coolant tank instrumentation was on panel 8A, outside the main operating area. If read and interpreted properly this display could have given the clue that the pressure operated relief valve was still open. This valve had been leaking slightly for months and had been opened briefly very early on in the accident, so high temperature and continual flow from it was to be expected, but not so high or so persistent. No continual readout was provided to draw attention to the continuing state of affairs.

● Critical alarms were not colour coded or graded in priority. Legends were excessively wordy or used inconsistent abbreviations.

● Coloured lights were used for many purposes but a colour did not carry a specific meaning so, depending on the application, a red light could mean any of fourteen different states

● Some lights flashed white on a white background, or were in poor contrast against neighbouring lights.

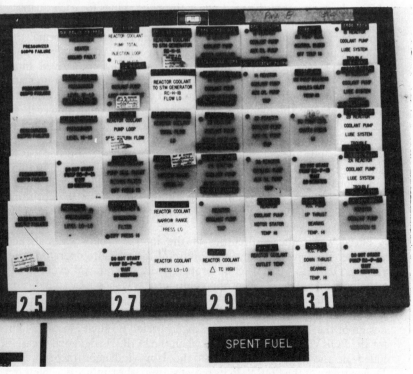

2.14   Typical TMI-2 alarm panel

● The effect of a multiplicity of flashing lights obscured the effect of each and reduced confidence that a correct picture of system state had been deduced.

● Some gauges did not have the pointer and scale in the same plane (i.e., the pointer was not against the scale edge or as nearly so as possible). An operator not directly in front of the pointer and the scale could easily make an incorrect reading. Well over one hundred meters in the TMI-2 control room could be faulted on this.

For a plant installed so recently, surprisingly little use was made of computers in control. In fact only two computers were used, and these only for monitoring alarms, logging plant performance data and carrying out simple calculations. The computers' outputs went mainly to two automatic typewriters. One of these would print alarms, and the second the general data. The alarm printer produced a record when an alarm signal arrived from its computer. This sampled quantities under constant measurement such as certain temperatures, pressures and levels of liquid; it compared the readings with preset values for each quantity and printed alarms if the reading lay outside acceptable limits. The computer also arranged that when conditions returned to normal this would be printed out too. However the alarm printer could only produce one line of message every four seconds so if alarms arrived more frequently than this their printing was delayed and the computer and printer could only be made to print current events by ignoring what still lay unprinted in the memory. The second printer could, however, be requested to give current values and summaries of groups of values or trends in their movement. Some critical quantities were recorded continuously in the computer for later printing. The computer was an efficient recorder and indicator of conditions during normal running conditions of the plant, but in an emergency its siting away from the central console, its slowness in giving readings and the delay in printing made it nearly useless as a prime diagnostic tool in the rapidly changing conditions of an emergency.

There were other difficulties at the interface between man and machine. We have seen that the failure of the pressure operated relief valve (PORV) to 'seat' or close properly was a significant event in the sequence and yet the status of this component was shown by an indicator light whose labelling suggested that it signalled the state of the valve, not just the supply of electric current to it. Curious to relate, the original design of the TMI-2 control room incorporated no such indicator light for the PORV at all. Only in 1978, when the PORV had on one occasion failed in the open position, was the lamp indicator incorporated. Downstream of the PORV, in its outlet system, the rupture disc blew out on the tank that the PORV outlet pipe led to. The disc is a deliberately

2.15 Indicator light and controls for the pressure operated relief valve

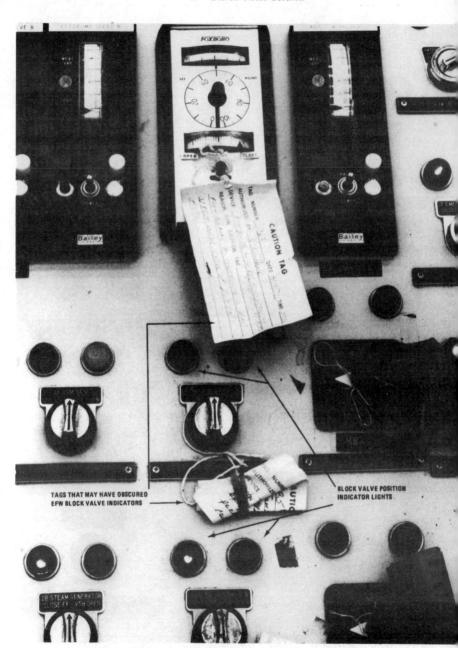

2.16   Valve controls and indicator lights showing caution tags

2.17 Maintenance tags on TMI-2 control panel covered one of two lights indicating that the two emergency feedwater valves were closed

weakened panel that fractures under a given excess of pressure and thus protected the main body of the tank. When it fractured, releasing water into the containment building, the pressure in that enclosed space increased rapidly and an alarm sounded. That the disc had ruptured was surmised correctly by the supervisor and the duty operator but again they attributed the over-filling of the tank to the brief operation and leaking of the same pressuriser valve. Not only did the operators misinterpret these signs of the open valve, they also failed in relation to the temperature indicated in the line from the valve to the tank. Because the valve had been leaking, the temperature had been at 180°F (83°C) for months. They expected that an open valve would push this up to well over 300°F (149°C), but in fact the flow constriction due to the valves would keep the outlet pipe temperature below or only just above 300°F. The operators were not aware of this; it was not included in their training or the emergency procedures.

Then, on two occasions during the accident the operators misread a reading of 285°F as 235°F. Only when a different supervisor came on duty was it noticed that the outlet pipe temperature downstream from the pressuriser relief valve was 229°F, 25°F above that in the safety code instructions. He closed the valve properly. There seem to have been other fixed ideas in the minds of the operators:

● High temperature in the pressuriser would be accounted for by the long standing leak and the brief opening of the valve.

● If anything was amiss, it would be in the secondary circuit; this was always the culprit.

● High pressure injection had happened before and did not imply a loss of coolant.

● The reactor could be controlled from the level of water in the pressuriser. Indeed it was newcomers, without recent experience of the quirks of this plant, that made the most perceptive diagnosis and initiated the vital actions that prevented further disaster.

The training of the operators included instructions for emergency procedures but several criticisms have been made of these:

● They failed to tell the operator what level of leak from the circuits or loss of function they would be able to cope with and what demanded extra help from outside. Too many valuations of a subjective nature were demanded, e.g., 'becoming stable after a short period of time'.

● The procedures referred to a four step emergency action that would occur within two minutes, while elsewhere they stated that the fourth step 'can be allowed to take five minutes'.

● Nomenclature in the written procedures differed from that on some control room panels.

● The procedures tested for symptoms of an emergency but did not help with diagnosis.

● Operators were told to monitor certain conditions in the reactor, the containment building and in various circuits but were not told acceptable levels for the data they collected, nor what to do in the event of strange combinations of these readings occurring, as happened from two until 150 minutes after the accident began.

● It was not clear whether one, several, or all of a set of stated symptoms needed to be present if a particular problem was to be diagnosed.

● A procedure given in one section demanded monitoring of a particular valve, a similar procedure elsewhere omitted this.

Investigators felt that these procedures failed to identify in clear and concise terms what decisions the operators were required to take, what information they needed to make the decision, what actions needed to be taken to implement the decision and how the connectedness between decisions and actions was to be verified.

A year before the TMI-2 accident one operator had written:

The alarm system in the control room is so poorly designed that it contributed little in the analysis of a casualty. The other operators and myself have several suggestions on how to improve our alarm system – perhaps we can discuss them sometime – preferably before the system as it is causes severe problems.

No significant changes were made and we now know what the result was. The scene was set for errors and misinterpretation on the part of operators who were poorly equipped in several respects. They lacked the experience and training to cope with the abnormal conditions in the plant, and the control room facilities made their task all the more difficult. Even the 'experts' who flocked in could not fully comprehend what was going on. When the accident threatened to become a major disaster that would affect neighbouring areas the handling of public relations was piecemeal and muddled.

Nuclear engineers are inclined to regard the Three Mile Island accident as a partial success because the several lines of defence against major releases of radioactivity held intact. However, it is likely that in years to come TMI-2 will remain famous as the accident which provided a focus for fears over the likelihood of an even more serious failure, and will serve to delay further building of this type of reactor, if not others.

3

The Humber Bridge

In this chapter we shall study a civil engineering project that was completed very late, cost much more than was estimated originally, perhaps even should never have been started, and yet stands as a show-piece of British engineering skill. We shall look at the building of the Humber Bridge.

A major civil engineering exercise such as the building of the world's longest span suspension bridge is a non-routine, non-repetitive, one-off undertaking that has financial, temporal and technical measures of performance associated with it. Projects such as this obviously require careful planning, management and control in order to try to make sure that the targets set for them are realistic and are met. The major hazards that threaten the success of most projects of this type are delay and cost escalation. Delay is simply the gap between the expected time of completion of the various stages of the project and the actual dates when they are finished. Cost escalation is defined as the difference between the final cost, or latest estimate of final cost, and the original definitive estimate. On smaller projects cost escalation of ten to twenty per cent is relatively common, whereas on larger, longer projects, particularly those with a high development content or considerable uncertainty at the earlier stages, huge increases are possible. Cost escalations of fifty per cent have been reported on petrochemical projects, 140 per cent on North Sea oil projects, 210 per cent on nuclear power stations and 545 per cent on the Concorde aircraft project.

The major factors that lead to cost escalation are inefficiency, inflation, poor information on which to base estimates, changes to the contract and even the form of the original contract. Delay and cost escalation are not independent, of course, because the longer a project takes, the higher the costs are going to be. We shall see that all of these causes contributed to the cost escalation in the building of the Humber Bridge, and shall encounter many delays, but first of all let us set the construction project in its context.

The river Humber, which drains one fifth of all England's river water, is one of Britain's largest estuaries and commercial waterways. Until

1974, when the county of Humberside was created in a far reaching reorganisation of local government, the northern bank of the river lay in Yorkshire and the southern in Lincolnshire. There had been talk of building a bridge across the river Humber near Kingston upon Hull since the last century and indeed designs for both a multi-span road bridge and a suspension bridge were prepared in the 1930s by Sir Douglas Fox and Partners (now Freeman Fox and Partners). In the 1970s though, the formation of a new county that would incorporate land on both sides of this great river was seen as being dependent upon the existence of a link across the river. J. Haydon W. Glen, clerk to the Humber Bridge Board and chief executive officer and town clerk to Kingston upon Hull, stated in an article, 'The Humber Bridge: the realisation of a dream' (1973), that 'without the bridge the creation of the new county of Humberside would have been impossible'.

A bridge became a possibility when the Humber Bridge Act was passed in 1959. The Act was promoted by Kingston upon Hull Corporation and led to the formation of the Humber Bridge Board. The board is now made up of twenty-two representatives of the local governmental authorities which are shown on the map in figure 3.1. The number from each council is

Hull City Council	12
Humberside County Council	2
Lincolnshire County Council	1
Scunthorpe Borough Council	1
Beverley Borough Council	3
Glanford Borough Council	3

Under the terms of the Act the board was empowered to construct, operate and maintain the bridge and approach roads, to acquire the necessary lands, to borrow the money needed and to collect tolls from bridge users.

In November 1965 the death occurred of Henry Solomons, then Labour member of parliament for the constituency of Hull North. Labour had gained the seat from the Conservatives in 1964 with the rather small majority of 1,181, so a voting swing of only a little over one per cent in the next election would have been enough to return the seat to the Conservatives. Newspaper reports on the by-election that followed the death of the MP were suggesting, right up to the eve of the poll on 27 January 1966, that Labour were likely to lose the seat. However, a good by-election result was crucial to Labour because throughout the 1964–66 government the Labour majority over the Conservatives and Liberals was always less than five. Labour were, therefore, ready to pull out all the stops to secure a victory and so a major election campaign was launched. At a by-election meeting in Hull on 18 January the then

Minister of Transport, Mrs Barbara Castle promised, 'you will have your Humber Bridge'. This pledge seems to have had a persuasive effect on the voters, for at the by-election Labour increased its majority to 5,351 on a swing of 4.5 per cent: the largest swing to a governing party in any by-election in a marginal seat since May 1924. In his diaries, Richard Crossman made no attempt to disguise Mrs Castle's promise as anything other than a by-election ploy.

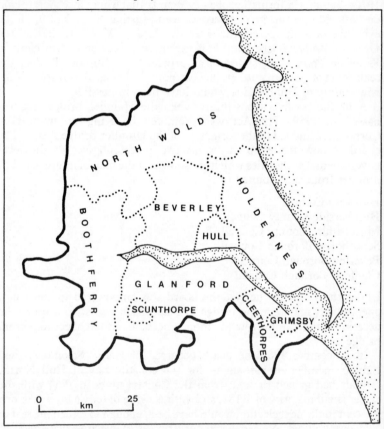

3.1   Map of region showing councils with representatives on Humber Bridge Board

In 1971 the Minister for Local Government and Development in Edward Heath's Conservative government announced in parliament that a bridge over the Humber would be built. His announcement came two years after a government report 'Humberside – a feasibility study' had been published by the Central Unit for Environmental Planning. This group had been set up in 1966 within the Department of Economic Affairs though it drew also on the resources of other governmental departments. Its first task was to carry out a study of the Humberside area in order to examine the possibility of accommodating a large increase in population there. This study was to form part of a wider examination of national problems of locating a growing population up to the end of the century and was thought necessary because of a prediction that the population was expected to increase nationally by nearly fifteen million between 1969 and the year 2000. For the purpose of the feasibility study the assumption was made that the population in Humberside would rise by between 300,000 and 750,000 before the end of the century.

The main recommendation of the report was that a major growth in the population of Humberside should not be planned to take place before 1980, but that steps should be taken in order to prepare the area for the possibility of major development. The steps suggested were as follows:

1. the area's roads should be improved during the 1970s;
2. sub-standard housing should be replaced at an increasingly faster rate;
3. the economic growth prospects of the area should be maintained;
4. the Humber Bridge should be built so as to be in use by 1976.

The report did not neglect to mention the divisive effect that the Humber would continue to have between the north and south banks even if a bridge were built near Hull. It pointed out that the south bank would still need its own large-scale central area facilities and with a caution that now, with hindsight, seems ridiculous, warned that development on the south bank should not be so close to Hull as to overload the bridge. Once the announcement had been made in parliament that the bridge should go ahead, a detailed design was begun immediately by Freeman Fox and Partners in consultation with the Humber Bridge Board.

3.1 The situation and design of the bridge

The Humber Bridge is the world's longest single span suspension bridge and has been built about five miles west of Hull city centre where, although it narrows, the river Humber is still more than a mile wide and is used frequently by small seagoing cargo ships and inland waterway traffic. The bridge is sited between Hessle on the north bank and Barton-upon-Humber on the south. The map in figure 3.2 shows the wider setting of the bridge.

The bridge has dual two-lane carriageways and a pathway on either side for pedestrians and cyclists. The bridge deck is suspended from two massive steel cables that pass over a tall tower on or near each bank and are then anchored firmly to the ground. For the first time in a large

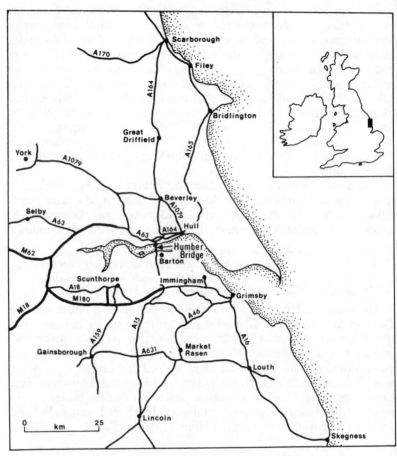

3.2   The wider setting of the Humber Bridge

suspension bridge the towers have been built of reinforced concrete instead of steel. The bridge deck is made up of 124 hollow steel boxes, each weighing 140 tonnes and 18 metres long that have been welded together. Each box consists of stiffened steel panels that have been welded together to form a hollow box section 22 metres wide and 4.5 metres deep. The upper surfaces of the boxes form the carriageway. Figure 3.3 shows a box being placed in position and illustrates its shape. The boxes are suspended from the main cables by slimmer cables. Special arrangements have been incorporated in the design to allow for movements of the deck due to changes in temperature, traffic loads and wind forces.

3.3 A box section being positioned

The structural data are as follows:

Main span between piers	1,410 m (4,626 ft)
Side span, north	280 m (919 ft)
Side span, south	530 m (1,739 ft)
Height of towers above piers	155.5 m (510 ft)
Clearance over high water level	30 m (98 ft)
Total weight of concrete	480,000 tonnes
Total weight of steel	27,500 tonnes

Main cables:

(i) Two, each consisting of 14,948 five millimetre diameter wires, with an additional eight hundred similar wires in each cable in the northern side span.

Total length of wire: 44,000 miles (approx 71,000 km)

(ii) Diameter of main cables   0.7 m (27 inches)

As a measure for comparison the main span between piers of the Forth Road Bridge is 1,006 metres and of the Severn Bridge is 988 metres. The second largest span is to be found in the Verrazano-Narrows, New York, which is 1,298 metres long.

3.2 **The builders**

The designers and consulting engineers for the project were Freeman Fox and Partners of London. Seven main contracts were let, the details of which are shown on the diagram of the bridge and of its immediate surroundings (figure 3.4). British Bridge Builders Ltd. was a consortium comprising the Sir William Arrol branch of Clarke Chapman-John Thompson Ltd., the Cleveland Bridge and Engineering Co. Ltd., (part of the Cementation Group), and Redpath Dorman Long Ltd., (part of the British Steel Corporation).

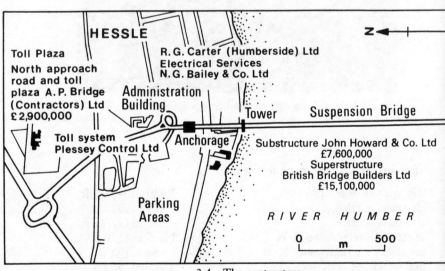

3.4   The contractors

3.3 **The building of the bridge – A calendar of events**

May 1971 Detailed design commenced.

July 1972 Work began on the embankment for the southern approach road.

April 1973 Work started on the substructure.

May 1974 The north tower reached full height.

June 1975 Work began on building the box sections for the deck at Priory Yard, a disused railway sidings at Hessle.

November 1975 The south tower pier caissons were finally sunk into place. The anchorages for the main suspension cables were completed.

September 1976 The south tower reached full height. The site was handed over to British Bridge Builders.

November 1976 Work began on the administrative and control building.

November 1976 So that the towers would be vertical when the bridge structure was complete, the towers were pulled back at the top before the suspension cables could be erected. The deadweight of the superstructure when it was finally completed would bring the towers back into the vertical.

February 1977 The first strand of steel rope was winched across the river in preparation for the building of the catwalks that were to be used during the spinning of the main cables.

September 1977 Cable spinning began. Each cable consists of 14,948 parallel galvanised drawn wires which are divided into thirty-seven strands of 404 wires each for the purposes of erection and anchorage.

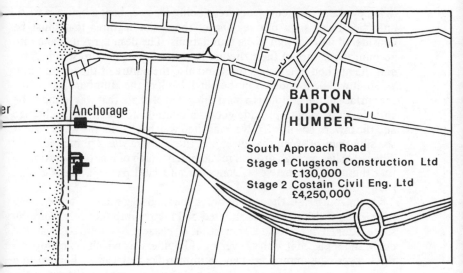

In addition, on the Hessle side span between the anchorage and the tower there are a further eight hundred wires in each cable, divided into four strands. The cables were formed from the wires by a process called 'spinning' and then compacted into a circular shape.

October 1979 First deck section erected in the Hessle side span.

April 1980 The joining together of the deck sections began.

September 1980 Laying of the asphalt road surface began.

December 1980 Joining together of the deck sections completed.

June 1981 Bridge opened to traffic.

July 1981 The Humber Bridge was opened officially by Her Majesty the Queen.

This outline calendar of events fails to reveal a long story of delay. When work began in 1972 it was announced that the bridge would be ready in 1976. Thus the construction actually took more than twice as long as was originally intended. Many reasons can be cited for this massive delay, which started with the building of the south tower. To illustrate the nature of the hold-ups, two examples will be looked at in detail here. The first concerns the construction of the afore-mentioned south tower and the second is a hold-up in the laying of the final carriageway surfaces.

3.4 Geological problems and a shortage of steel

Whenever a permanent structure is being erected, be it a house, a road, an office block or a bridge, one of the major features that must be considered in its design is the foundations. The designer must take into account the nature of the structure in respect of its design, weight, size and the method of construction, and also the nature of the ground into which it will be founded. On the north bank of the Humber, just below the surface of the ground is a hard thick bed of chalk that was found to be sufficiently strong to provide good foundations for both the anchorage and the tower. The north tower was sited well back from the water so that the side span between the tower and the anchorage is 280 metres long. The latter lies on high ground immediately north of a railway cutting so that the main line between Doncaster and Hull passes under the side span of the bridge.

On the south side, the span between the anchorage and the tower is 530 metres long with the tower situated 500 metres into the river from the south bank. On this shore the action of glaciers has scoured away the chalk and replaced it with a covering of boulder clay which lies on top of a thick layer of Kimmeridge clay. Kimmeridge clay can be likened to a book that has been soaked in water and then squeezed until most of the water has been removed. During the squeezing the material shrinks and becomes what is called 'consolidated'. The Kimmeridge clay under the south side of the river and its bank was found to be over-consolidated which means that if the load on it is removed (that is if it ceases to be squeezed by the land above it) the clay will spring back and crack. The river has deposited alluvial material on top of the boulder clay but preliminary soil investigations showed that neither the boulder clay nor the alluvial deposits would provide good foundations because of their variable natures, and so a decision had to be taken to sink the foundations of the southern tower and anchorage into the Kimmeridge clay. It was realised that this would be no easy matter because construction would be taking place in the river and because of the nature of the clay. Careful plans would therefore have to be drawn up if the foundations were to be able to support such mammoth structures and in order to draw up these plans it would be necessary to carry out further tests. Figure 3.5 shows the geological conditions at the site.

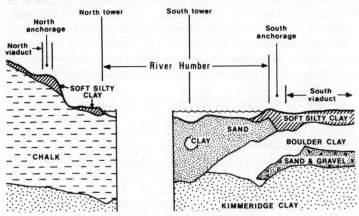

3.5   The geological conditions

In order to find out whether the Kimmeridge clay would be able to hold the weight of the bridge a test piling scheme was devised and carried out in 1971. This was done in the following way. Two forty-metre long thirty-ton stressed concrete piles were driven into the ground and 'bridges' built over the head of each pile by placing blocks on each side and balancing a crossbeam on them so that it was above, but not touching the pile. Steel ingots, called by the technical name of kentledge, weighing eight-hundred tons, were then stacked onto each bridge and a jack positioned between each pile and the crossbeam above it. The pressure exerted by the jacks was increased in stages until the steel ingots were just about to be lifted, at which points the pressure on each pile was equivalent to eight-hundred tons. At each stage the downward deflection of the piles was plotted onto graphs. The load was then decreased in stages by releasing the jack gradually and the upward deflection of the piles was plotted. The differences between the pre- and post-loaded heights of the piles were also noted and checks made to ensure that the differences were within acceptable limits.

As further tests were carried out into the nature of the Kimmeridge clay a major problem came to light that would have to be solved before any excavation work could be carried out. Laboratory tests showed that the Kimmeridge clay would quickly turn to soft mud if it came into contact with water. The lowest point of the foundations for the south anchorage and the tower would be well below the surface of the river, so water under a high head of pressure would continually be trying to enter any cracks in the Kimmeridge clay. On the other hand, if the Kimmeridge clay was allowed to dry out whilst excavation was under way it would cease to be over-consolidated and would thus crack badly. The cracking would in turn weaken the clay so much that the foundations would not then be strong enough to support the weight of the bridge. It was thus vitally important to prevent the Kimmeridge clay from becoming either too dry or too wet for this might have eventually caused a disaster to occur, perhaps many years later when the bridge was fully loaded with traffic.

The foundation of the pier on which the south tower was to stand was to be located in water with a maximum depth of 7.6 metres, a tidal range of 7 metres and a current that can run at a speed of up to six knots. It was recognised that these would be difficult conditions to work in but the site for the foundations could not be moved onto dry land because the span of the bridge would have had to be lengthened beyond the maximum that was thought to be practicable. Therefore some other more feasible solution to the problem had to be found. A decision was finally made to use two caissons to support the 16 metre deep pier on which the tower was to be built. Caissons can be likened to giant shoe boxes made from concrete but in this case they were to be circular in shape. They were to be positioned with their bases about 33 metres below the river bed and penetrating into the Kimmeridge clay to a depth of eight metres. The solution sounded reasonably straightforward to the civil engineers involved but unforeseen problems were to appear almost immediately.

In order to reach the site where the caissons were to be sunk it was necessary to build a temporary steel jetty, five hundred metres long, from the shore. At the time (1973), Britain was in the grip of an industrial dispute and, in order to save energy, factories were working a 'three day week' on a rota basis. This led to a severe shortage of products such as steel which required a high energy input for their manufacture. In order to be able to make use of whatever steel sections could be obtained, the design of the jetty was constantly amended. As a consequence the overall final cost of the jetty and the time taken to build it were increased.

Before the building of the caissons could begin it was necessary to build a watertight wall around the site and to pump out the water inside so as to allow concrete to be poured in to form the walls of the caissons. It was not practical to form the watertight dam by sheet piling around the site of the pier because of the variable depth of the deposits above the Kimmeridge clay so it was decided to build an artificial sand island in plan like a figure 8. A picture of the coffer dams is shown in figure 3.6.

3.6   The coffer dams

Sheet piles, fourteen metres long, were driven into the river bed and the area within filled with sand. High tensile steel hoops were then placed around the structure to prevent the sand from bursting outwards. However, another problem was hovering just around the corner. Whilst the dam was being built, the fast flowing Humber scoured material from the continually shifting river bed to a far greater extent than the contractor, John Howard and Co. Ltd. had envisaged and so it became necessary to dump twelve thousand tons of chalk boulders around the outside of the dam in order to try to prevent the scour. At last work could now begin on the construction of the caissons.

The cutting edges of the caissons were formed side by side on the sand island so that excavation of sand from the centre of the caissons could begin. As material was excavated from the river bed the caissons sank so that new sections of the caissons could be constructed on top by using a steel framework and then encasing the framework in concrete. In order to reduce the friction between the caisson and the Kimmeridge clay a layer of bright yellow clay called Bentonite mixed to a slurry with water was pumped around the caissons so that it formed a layer about 75 millimetres thick. On 11 March 1975, when the west caisson had been sunk about thirty metres, disaster struck. In just twenty minutes, approximately one million gallons of water gushed into the west caisson. It was unfortunate in one way that it was not sea water for that would have risen to the level of the tide and then stopped, but this present influx reached more than six metres above high tide level. The contractors had fallen into a natural trap that was lying in wait for them. With luck they might have discovered it whilst carrying out the test borings and pilings and thus have been forewarned, but as it was it came as a total surprise. They had struck artesian water. Most of the Bentonite layer around the caisson was washed away and considerable subsidence was caused to the sand island around the caissons. The dead weight of the caisson of 11,500 tons was insufficient to move it without the Bentonite as a lubricant and so it became stuck. Attempts to replace the Bentonite layer were unsuccessful.

To make the caisson heavier and so encourage it to sink, the permanent design was changed by the engineers so that the outside walls of the caissons were 1.7 metres thick instead of 1.2 metres as originally proposed. The caissons had to remain flooded whilst sinking was carried out because the pressure on the Kimmeridge clay had to be maintained. Thus all excavation work had to be carried out under water and this made it very difficult for an accurate check to be kept on the ground levels inside the caisson as digging proceeded. Monitoring by taking soundings was carried out, but the conditions under the walls could only be checked by divers working by touch as the water inside the caissons was so muddy.

The engineers discovered that the only effective way to cut away the clay under the caisson walls was to use water jets at pressure. A number of jets set to point in different directions were lowered down each of the caisson cells by crane.

Originally the pier had been designed so that each of the two caissons was 29 metres deep, with extensions above, to form the support for the tower, that were smaller in plan area than the caissons themselves. Sheet steel walls were to be built on top of the caisson walls so that the support for the tower, or the cut-water, could be built inside it, but the problems caused by the loss of the Bentonite layer when the artesian water was released meant that the caisson walls had to be extended anyway in order to add weight and thus help the caissons to sink. The final design of the cut-water had therefore to be amended so as to add four thousand tons to the weight of each caisson. In addition to this, three thousand tons of steel ingots, or kentledge, were placed temporarily into each caisson in order to sink it. At each change of plan the costs and delays increased as materials had to be selected, purchased, transported and placed into position.

Finally the many efforts made to sink the caissons were successful and the foundations for the south tower were in place by September 1975. The next job was for divers to clean up the Kimmeridge clay manually and for each caisson to be plugged with deep concrete slabs in order to minimise the possibility of heave, or rising of the ground due to water penetrating the Kimmeridge clay. The tops of the caissons were capped at estuary level and a concrete 'bridge' formed between the two caissons to complete the pier on which the tower itself could be built. The pier which is shown in figure 3.7 was finished in March 1976, which, it must be remembered, was the year in which it had been planned that the bridge itself would be completed.

3.5 An accident and its effects

The box sections that form the carriageways of the bridge have been described already. In order to form the deck from the individual boxes, they were floated downstream from their construction site at Priory Yard to the bridge site on pontoons and hoisted into position using gantries travelling on the main suspension cables. This work started on 9 November 1979, and, despite the winter weather with its high winds and strong tidal currents all went well until March 1980 when one side of the carriage that carried one of the gantries came adrift, ran back and then came off the suspension cable. The 30-ton gantry fell between the two main bridge cables and onto the road deck underneath. The joint between the two box sections that were hit was badly damaged and the

3.7 The south tower

damaged areas had to be replaced. Some of the soft steel galvanised wire that had been wrapped around the suspension cables to protect them was torn from the upstream cable when the gantry slipped. In addition, lengths of wire catwalk were ripped away. Two of the cables that had been hung from the main suspension cable ready to support the next box were also damaged and had to be replaced.

In addition to the damage that was caused to the fabric of the bridge, three of the men working on the bridge were injured during the accident. Because of this the Department of Health and Safety had to be notified immediately and they placed a temporary ban on the use of the gantries until the cause of the accident could be determined and they could be satisfied that the gantries could be used with safety. Obviously with work halted the problem of determining the cause of the accident became a pressing one and so immediate steps were taken to investigate the matter.

The inspectors found that a simple clip connecting the tow wire ropes of the gantry had come apart and thus allowed it to run off the main suspension cables. They were not satisfied that a similar incident would not occur again and so a revised method of working had to be devised before work could be allowed to start up again. It was decided that in future the twin beam gantries would be moved one beam at a time using hauling wires connected to auxiliary winches on top of the towers instead of to the main winches. It obviously took time to set up and then implement this new method of working so this relatively minor accident contributed considerably to the final delay in the completion of the road surfacing of the bridge. The road surfacing had been planned to finish in December 1980, for asphalt can only be laid in dry, frost-free conditions, but because the start of the work was delayed it was interrupted by the winter weather. It was therefore March 1981 before the laying of the road surface could be completed.

3.6 The cost of the bridge

In 1959 the estimated cost of the bridge and its associated works was £15,750,000 plus the cost of purchasing land, easements and rights of way under the powers of the Act, payment (out of capital) of interest on money borrowed to cover building costs and the payment of the costs, charges and expenses of the Act.

At the early stages of the project there were strong hopes on Humberside that the government would meet a large part of the bill for the building of the Humber Bridge but these hopes were to be dashed. No grants from the government were forthcoming. In September 1969, Mr Peter Shore, the Labour economics minister, announced that the government would give no grant towards the project and that the money to build the bridge would have to be raised through loans, possibly direct from the government.

Despite such disappointments, local politicians continued to seek grants from the government and were encouraged in November 1970 when Mr Michael Heseltine, Conservative Under-secretary at the Department of the Environment told the House of Commons that the government had not categorically turned down the possibility of a grant for the Humber Bridge and that 'the question of government grant must depend on decisions on the financing of the bridge. It would still be possible, if the bridge were to go ahead, for it to be completed according to the original timetable' (that is by 1976).

In May 1971 the Conservative government finally dashed all reasonable hopes of a grant by announcing formally that it would loan the Humber Bridge Board seventy-five per cent of the total cost of the project at special low interest rates. The remaining twenty-five per cent of the cost was to be repaid from toll income. The size of the loan was then estimated at £18,500,000 but we shall see later how this sum was to rise before the bridge was completed. The Bridge Board is not required to start to repay its loan from the government until 1994, however. The breathing space is to allow the income from tolls during that period to be used to repay the loans which were raised on the open market in order to fund the remaining twenty-five per cent of the cost of the project. All of the loans are due to be paid back before 2041 but the time scale for repayments could be extended by the government if it so wished.

A report that had been presented to the Bridge Board in February 1970 estimated that if a bridge that cost £20,000,000 were opened in 1976 and it was used by even a relatively few number of vehicles each year it could be making a profit only sixteen years after it had opened. The report assumed that the charge for goods vehicles would be double that of private cars and light vans and estimated that if a five shillings (25p) private toll was charged the gross revenue each year from 24,000 daily trips would be £2,500,000. A 7s 6d (37½p) toll would cut the estimated use of the bridge to sixteen thousand daily trips, and thus give the same financial return. Yearly maintenance costs were estimated at £200,000.

When the loans were negotiated, the agreement included the arrangement that if the revenue from tolls was not large enough to meet the loans then the Humber Bridge Board could levy a precept on the ratepayers of the areas surrounding the bridge, that is on the district councils of Beverley and Glanford and Hull City Council. In the case of the first two the precept would be limited to 1⅔p in the pound and so Hull City Council ratepayers would have to find the remainder.

Clearly, when considering the financing of a major long-term project the economic conditions that might prevail in the future are at least as important as the conditions existing when the decision to go ahead with the project is made. The arrangements for the financing of the Humber Bridge were settled at a time when it was estimated that the total cost of the project would be approximately £24,000,000 but soon after the bridge was finally opened in 1981 the debts stood at roughly £145,000,000. This figure was made up of £91,000,000 construction costs and £54,000,000 interest owing on the money that had been borrowed whilst the work was in progress. Opinions always differ as to what will happen financially over a long period of time and there was no exception to that rule in this case. On the one hand it had been forecasted by Dr Eric Evans, Senior Lecturer in Economics at Hull University, that after sixty years the debt could be as high as £500,000,000. On the other hand, a public inquiry into toll charges that was held in March 1980 heard an estimate from Mr Peter Clay of the Halcrow Fox and Associates planning and transportation consultancy that if the optimum toll was used, the debt should be cleared before the fortieth year and that the maximum debt of £395,000,000 would appear in the twenty-sixth year. Even he warned, though, that if the forecast of economic growth turned out to be optimistic or the future population and employment levels significantly lower than anticipated, or if long-term rates of interest were substantially higher than expected, then there was a risk that the bridge debt would never be paid off from the toll income alone.

Throughout the project the estimated and actual costs rose alarmingly as the following table will show.

Table 3.1   *The cost of the bridge*

Date	Estimated Cost	Comments
1969	£23,000,000	
1974	£30,000,000	Includes a 25% increase in steel prices
June 1975	£43,000,000	£11,000,000 of increase attributed to inflation and £3,000,000 to additional work involving approach roads, toll buildings and equipment
January 1976	£45,000,000	
January 1977	£54,400,000	British Bridge Builders announced that the backlog of work on the roadway box sections might lead to another 'slight increase' in cost
June 1977	£58,556,000	Inflation-related wages and higher material prices blamed for the price-rise spiral
January 1978	£60,035,000	Figure does not include capitalised interest
February 1979	£67,000,000	
December 1979	£71,000,000	It was also revealed that the project was costing £25,000 per day in interest
March 1980	£75,000,000	The total debt for which the ratepayers would be responsible was estimated at £124,400,000. This figure includes interest on loans of almost £50,000,000
August 1980	£80,500,000	
August 1981	£145,000,000	Final debt

During the period of the Humber Bridge project inflation was running at unprecedently high levels, as table 3.2 will show. It must be borne in mind however, that if the project had been completed in a much shorter time then the actual cost of construction and the capitalised interest

would not have suffered in the same way from the effects of the inflation
that occurred during the later years.

Table 3.2   *Annual inflation figures 1970–81*

Year	Annual average index of inflation*	Equivalent of £23,000,000 at 1969 prices
1970	140.2	£24,465,857
1971	153.4	£26,769,347
1972	164.3	£28,671,472
1973	179.4	£31,306,525
1974	208.2 (Reset to 108.5)	£36,332,322
1975	134.8	£45,139,143
1976	157.1	£52,606,523
1977	182.0	£60,944,540
1978	197.1	£66,000,928
1979	223.5	£74,841,235
1980	263.7	£88,302,611
1981	295.0	£98,783,733

* The base level for calculations of the index was set at 100 on 16 January 1962.
It was reset to 100 on 15 January 1974.
Source: CSO Annual Abstract of Statistics, H.M.S.O.

It might have been expected that the effect of inflation upon the
construction costs would be mirrored by a similar effect upon the
estimated income from tolls, provided that traffic levels remained
roughly the same as those forecast. However the relationship between
toll income and construction, interest and operating costs does not seem
to have turned out to be what was hoped for, at least at the present time.
Increases in the costs of construction were far greater than anyone had
ever envisaged and, at the same time, the level of traffic and hence the toll
income were overestimated. Thus there was a greater gap between
income and expenditure than had been hoped for.

Inflation was not the only factor that contributed to the increases in
construction costs. Some of the other factors that proved important were
the unexpected geological problems, low productivity and poor
industrial relations in connection with the construction and splicing of
the roadway box sections and the cable spinning, and far greater
problems from high winds and cold weather than were anticipated.
There were also difficulties with contracts, one of which will be discussed
next.

In 1974 John Howard and Co., holders of the contract to build the
towers, had started losing 'substantial money' on the contract. They
were reimbursed for some basic material cost rises but were not covered
for others such as timber and scaffolding which had risen enormously in

price. Neither were they reimbursed for increased bonus payments so in January 1975 they announced that, as an economy measure, they were dismissing fifty night-shift workers. They also sought changes so that more items that were subject to price increases could be brought within the term of the variations of their contract. It was announced at the beginning of September that the Humber Bridge Board would give financial aid to John Howard and Co. in order to compensate them for the 'very substantial' losses on the contract. The aid was however said to be 'dependent upon completion of the contract with due diligence and without delay'.

3.7 **Toll income**

The tolls which came into force when the Bridge opened are shown in table 3.3.

Table 3.3 *Humber Bridge tolls*

Class of Traffic[1]	Actual Toll as from the opening of the Bridge[2]
Pedestrians	Nil
Pedal cycles	Nil
Motor cycles with or without side-cars	50p (70p)
Cars including 3 wheeled cars Light vans up to 30 cwt. capacity	£1 (£1.50)
Light commercial vehicles (30 cwt. to 3 tons) Cars and light vans with trailers	£2 (£2.90)
Heavy commercial vehicles (over 3 tons):	
Class A (2 axle)	£4.50 (£5.20)
Class B (3 axle)	£6.00 (£6.60)
Class C (4 axle)	£7.50 (£8.00)
Mini-buses with a seating capacity of more than 8 but not more than 16 passengers	£2.00 (£2.90)
Buses and coaches with a seating capacity of 17 and over	£4.50 (£5.20)
Disabled drivers in receipt of a mobility allowance	Nil
Ambulances	Nil

Notes

[1] A discount of 5% will be given in respect of all classes of user who purchase a minimum of 20 tickets in advance.

[2] The amounts shown in brackets are the maximum tolls approved by the Minister of Transport.

Guildhall
Kingston upon Hull
September, 1980.

J. Haydon W. Glen
Clerk to the Board

The estimates of toll income will be considered in relation to population, employment and traffic.

3.8 Population

The 1969 report, 'Humberside – a feasibility study', recommended the construction of a Humber bridge as part of the preparations for growth in the local population of between 300,000 and 750,000 by the end of the century. This predicted increase in population was arrived at in the context of an overall population increase of nearly fifteen million that was expected to take place throughout the country in the thirty years between 1969 and the end of the century. There is now no sign that such an increase will be seen on Humberside, and indeed in the nine years between 1971 and 1980 the population of the whole of England and Wales rose by only 389,400. Since 1971 the population of Humberside itself has risen by only 0.5 per cent to reach 843,282 in 1981. Six of Humberside's nine districts did show an increase in population between 1971 and 1981 but this growth only ranged from 3.5 per cent in Cleethorpes to a maximum of sixteen per cent in Holderness, whilst, at the same time, the populations of Great Grimsby, Kingston upon Hull and Scunthorpe (the three major areas of industry which account for two thirds of the county's population) decreased by four, seven and eight per cent respectively.

The 'Humberside structure plan – background studies', which was prepared in 1976, pointed out that its projections of population levels were much lower than those predicted in 1969 and thus large scale government investment in response to big population expansion was unlikely. On this basis it would seem clear that a decision to start the bridge project would not be taken today on the evidence that is now available.

3.9 Employment

The forecasts made in 'Humberside – a feasibility study' obviously failed to predict the oil crisis that was then imminent and to take into account the decline of Hull as a port and of the steel industry in Scunthorpe. At the time of the study the unemployment rate in the Yorkshire and Humberside region was 2.2 per cent, but since then unemployment in the region has risen dramatically. For the Yorkshire and Humberside region the numbers unemployed (excluding school leavers and adult students) expressed as a percentage of the appropriate mid-year estimate of total workforce (employed and unemployed) are shown in table 3.4.

Table 3.4   *Yorkshire and Humberside unemployment 1969–81*

Year	% Unemployed
1969	2.2
1970	2.8
1971	3.7
1972	4.1
1973	2.8
1974	2.6
1975	3.8
1976	5.1
1977	5.3
1978	5.6
1979	5.3
1980	7.0
1981	11.1

Percentage figures for the month of June alone at a more local level

Year	National Figure	Humberside	Hull (North)	Grimsby (South)	Scunthorpe (South)
1971	3.2	4.7	4.7	4.4	3.6
1976	5.3	6.9	7.5	7.0	5.2
1980	6.2	8.6	9.2	5.4	8.5

The economy of the county of Humberside is underpinned by agriculture and this sector of employment has continued to thrive. The Wolds is a big grain area and there is an extensive glasshouse market gardening industry. South Humberside, and the coastal area of the north, are very important vegetable and potato growing areas but the picture of the non-agricultural economy is not as rosy. Although the four ports of Hull, Grimsby, Immingham and Goole together account for almost a tenth of all the United Kingdom's seaborne trade, the fishing industry has been decimated and has lost in the region of five thousand direct jobs. Hull has been hardest hit by this loss because it was the heart of the country's deep sea trawler fleet. The middle sea fleet which is based in Grimsby has been hit less badly.

Steelmaking in Scunthorpe has suffered large cutbacks too. Over ten thousand steel jobs have been lost in the last decade and the jobs of the remaining nine thousand workforce are by no means assured. Although development areas have been declared on both banks of the Humber there are, as yet, no signs of widespread recovery.

3.10 **Traffic**

In 1969 the estimates of traffic were that, at the optimum toll for private vehicles, (a toll producing the maximum revenue) the bridge would be used by about 24,000 vehicles per day in 1981. Taking into account only the expected natural increase in population, the traffic was forecast to grow to about 34,000 vehicles per day by the end of the century. If the overall growth of Humberside that had been predicted was included the maximum traffic expected by the end of the century would be about 58,000 vehicles per day.

The actual traffic during the first year was approximately 6,500 vehicles per day which generated a toll income of approximately £9,000. This figure has to be set against daily interest payments of £52,000. Detailed traffic figures for the period up to 2 May 1982 are shown in the traffic report, table 3.5. Eighty-five per cent of the vehicles that use the bridge are cars and seven per cent are heavy vehicles, although the percentage of heavy vehicles increases to seventeen per cent on weekdays.

The bridge is known locally as the 'bridge to nowhere'. Dr Eric Evans, Senior Lecturer in Economics at Hull University was quoted in a *Sunday Times* article, 'Super-span', by Martin Leighton, as saying that 'nobody in particular wants to go from Grimsby to Hull, nor in the reverse direction. Nor can I see much of a take-up outside the people of Humberside for use of the Bridge as a shoppers' or tourist route'.

In conclusion, hard facts have to be faced. The bridge does not lie on any major north–south route and unless there is a major economic revival on Humberside, which, to say the least, appears extremely unlikely at the present time, the Humber Bridge would seem to be an engineering triumph and a memorial to a dream that died. Unfortunately it is a very costly memorial. The price may end up by being too high for the people of Hull to bear.

Table 3.5 Humber Bridge Board; Traffic report for period 1 April 1982 to 2 May 1982

Vehicle classification	Total number of vehicles for financial year ending 31.3.82	Number of vehicles during previous periods from 1 April 1982	Number of vehicles during current period	Total traffic to 2 May 1982	% traffic 1981–82	% traffic current period	% traffic since 24 June 1981	% of income from 24 June 1981
Motor cycles	50,734	0	7,067	57,801	2.2	2.8	2.3	0.8
Cars and light vans	1,904,508	0	210,377	2,114,885	83.6	82.1	83.5	58.0
Cars and light vans with trailers	23,261	0	2,594	25,855	1.0	1.0	1.0	1.4
Heavy commercial								
2-axle	63,822	0	8,032	71,854	2.8 ⎫	3.1 ⎫	2.8 ⎫	8.9 ⎫
3 axle	24,176	0	3,129	27,305	1.1 ⎬ 7.9	1.2 ⎬ 9.5	1.1 ⎬ 8.0	4.5 ⎬ 34.7
4-axle	90,553	0	13,070	103,623	4.0 ⎭	5.1 ⎭	4.1 ⎭	21.3 ⎭
Light comm./mini-buses	35,338	0	4,105	39,443	1.5	1.6	1.6	2.1
Coaches	13,735	0	1,100	14,835	0.6	0.4	0.6	1.8
Exempt	62,878	0	5,906	68,784	2.8	2.3	2.6	—
Humberlink	8,482	0	918	9,400	0.4	0.4	0.4	1.2
Total	2,277,487	0	256,298	2,533,785	100.00	100.00	100.00	100.00
Recorded toll income	£3,212,212	0	£383,532	£3,595,744				

Remarks: The report as presented will be produced on a 'monthly' basis to the nearest Sunday, midnight, to the end of a calendar month.

The Bank Holiday periods continue to generate tourist traffic, and have an adverse effect on the heavy commercial traffic, although the numbers have not fallen below 5,000 vehicles per week since settling down after Christmas.

4

Crisis at
Normansfield Hospital

At 7 o'clock in the morning of 5 May 1976 a strike began that was unprecedented in the history of the National Health Service. Some members of the union COHSE (the Confederation of Health Service Employees) walked out of the wards of Normansfield Hospital, Teddington and mounted pickets at the hospital gates. They left 202 mentally handicapped patients, including children, elderly people and many with multiple handicaps, some to the point of helplessness, in the care of only a skeleton nursing staff and a few other members of staff and relatives. To make matters even worse, some of those providing this minimal level of care were withdrawn at about 10 o'clock leaving a total nursing staff of seven in the hospital. With the nursing cover thus reduced to well below danger level the health and welfare of the patients was put at serious risk. Later that day the Consultant Psychiatrist in Mental Subnormality at the hospital, Dr Lawlor, was suspended from duty and the nurses returned to their wards shortly after half-past three.

This account will look at the events that led up to the strike and will use details taken from the official report: *Report of the Committee of Inquiry into Normansfield Hospital*, presented to parliament by the Secretary of State for Social Services by command of Her Majesty, November 1978, published as Command 7357 by Her Majesty's Stationery Office, London.

That report examines in depth not only the events that led to the strike but also the personalities of many of those involved and the shortfalls in the care being provided at the hospital. The report found that

the standard of nursing care was generally extremely low and the quality of life of many of the patients suffered accordingly. For long periods of time the hospital buildings were in poor repair and the standards of hygiene were often extremely low too. The patients were often dressed in ill-fitting, inappropriate dirty clothing and there were general shortages of bed linen and towels.

We, however, shall concentrate upon the strike and the events leading to it rather than upon these and the many other criticisms levelled at the hospital. We shall see that these events did not just take place over a matter of weeks, or even months, but over years. A situation that was seen by many to contain serious problems was allowed to deteriorate further and further until the lives and safety of some of those belonging to one of the most vulnerable sections of our society, the mentally handicapped, were put at risk.

Where possible we shall look at the events in roughly chronological order but first it is necessary to gain some knowledge of how the National Health Service (NHS) is organised and managed. In 1974 the NHS underwent a major reorganisation which was intended to improve the planning and provision of effective health care through an integrated approach to the problems of ill-health and the prevention of illness. The period we are interested in spans the reorganisation so we shall look at the arrangements as they existed both before and after 1974.

4.1 The administration of the NHS – pre-April 1974

Prior to 1 April 1974 Regional Hospital Boards (RHBs) were responsible for controlling the planning, conduct and development of hospital services in their regions and Hospital Management Committees (HMCs) administered the hospital services on their behalf. The RHBs and HMCs functioned through their officers who each had responsibility for a different sphere such as finance, administration and so on. This two tier structure is shown on the organisation chart (figure 4.1).

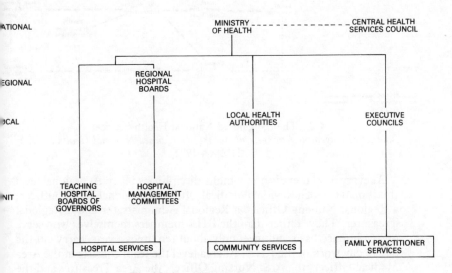

4.1 The National Health Service 1948–74

4.2 **The administration of the NHS – post-April 1974**

The RHBs and HMCs were abolished and replaced by a three-tier
structure. Area Health Authorities (AHAs) were created as the lowest
level of statutory authority with full planning and operational
responsibility for the hospitals in their areas. Regional Health
Authorities (RHAs) link the AHAs to the Department of Health and
Social Security and are responsible for planning and developing services
within their regions, allocating resources, reviewing and approving AHA
plans and controlling the performance of the AHAs in relation to these
plans. Each area contains one or more districts. A district is defined as a
population served by community health services supported by the
specialist services of a District General Hospital. Figure 4.2 illustrates
this new organisational tree.

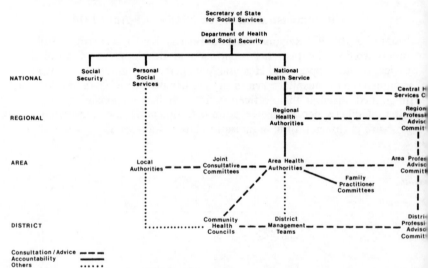

4.2   The reorganised National Health Service;
source: *Management Arrangements for the Reorganised National Health Service*
(HMSO, 1972)

At every level there is now a multi-disciplinary team. At regional level
this is made up of a Regional Medical Officer, a Regional Works Officer,
a Regional Nursing Officer, a Regional Administrator and a Regional
Treasurer. They, rather than the RHA members themselves who serve
on a voluntary basis and meet only about ten times a year, carry out the
day to day work of the RHA. At area level the team consists of the Area
Medical Officer, the Area Nursing Officer, the Area Treasurer and the
Area Administrator. In areas with more than one district there is also a

district team but in single district areas the Area Officers, together with the Chairman and Vice-Chairman of the Area Medical Committee, form the Area Management Team (AMT) in order to assume the district responsibilities.

4.3 Reorganisation and Normansfield

As a result of the reorganisation in 1974, Normansfield Hospital was transferred from the North West Metropolitan Regional Hospital Board and the Staines Hospital Management Committee to the South West Thames Regional Health Authority and the Kingston and Richmond Area Health Authority, which has a single district within it.

4.4 The events leading to the strike

The appointment of a consultant

Normansfield had been founded as a private institution for the mentally handicapped in 1868 by Dr John Langdon-Down, after whom, incidentally, Down's syndrome is named. It was sold to the NHS in 1951 but maintained its connection with the founder's family in that his grandson, Dr Norman Langdon-Down, remained as Medical Superintendent. When he retired in 1970 it was decided to appoint a Consultant Psychiatrist in Mental Subnormality and to establish tripartite management of the hospital by the Consultant, the Matron and the Hospital Secretary rather than appoint another Medical Superintendent. The Consultant took up his post in December 1970.

4.5 The Hospital Advisory Service reports

As part of a programme of visits to all hospitals for the mentally handicapped, a team from the NHS Hospital Advisory Service visited Normansfield in August 1970 in order to suggest how the management of patient care could be improved. Their major recommendation advocated a multi-disciplinary management approach which would require senior officers, including heads of departments, to meet on a regular basis with a pre-arranged agenda in order to plan and lay down the policies of the hospital and generally to coordinate these activities. The HMC accepted this recommendation but the newly appointed Consultant disagreed with the concept, and neither the HMC nor the RHB were able to get multi-disciplinary management operating fully before they themselves were abolished in April 1974.

The Hospital Advisory Service visited the hospital again in August 1972. In addition to describing two of the wards as serious fire risks and generally unsuitable for patients' accommodation, they found that the multi-disciplinary management that had been recommended was not taking place. They criticised the emphasis that was being placed on 'authority and decision taking' rather than on discussion and agreement, and the lack of machinery for joint consultation with all sections of the staff. They made recommendations about what should be done to establish the multi-disciplinary management approach but these were in direct conflict with the Consultant's view of his own role and when such a management team was finally set up in January 1973 it did not meet regularly, the consultant did not always attend when it did meet and, partially as a result, it was largely ineffectual.

4.6 Reports to the new Area Management Team

At the time of the reorganisation the Area Management Team commissioned three reports on Normansfield in order to enable them to assess the situation there. One concerned the catering services, the second the nursing service and the third an Organisation and Management report. We shall look at the last two of these.

The Organisation and Management report was accompanied by a letter to the Area Administrator from the leader of the team that prepared it in which he made clear that the hospital could not be managed properly unless all of the senior staff accepted multi-disciplinary management and changed their attitudes towards it and towards each other.

The report on the nursing service was sent to the Area Nursing Officer. It had been prepared by the Principal Nursing Officer (Psychiatric Division) who in March 1975 became the Divisional Nursing Officer, Psychiatric Division. The crux of the report was that 'the nursing staff at Normansfield would appear to have lost their way'. It severely criticised the accommodation in which more than half of the patients were kept and drew attention to shortcomings in the methods of care used, the lack of organised activities for the patients and the low level of morale in some wards. The report put forward numerous proposals that were designed to improve the situation but these were destined to be ignored. The Area Nursing Officer dismissed the report as too sweeping and informed the Area Management Team (AMT) to that effect. Furthermore the Senior Nursing Officer at Normansfield was not even allowed to see the report on the grounds that it was confidential.

After studying the reports the AMT agreed that their first priority was to recreate the multi-disciplinary management team at the hospital to comprise the consultant, the Senior Nursing Officer and the Hospital Administrator. This team was to be called the Senior Management Team

(SMT) and was intended to manage 'the service as a whole' within Normansfield. After initial difficulties the SMT was set up and then met regularly with a representative of the Area Administrator in attendance. This system of management was still in operation at the time of the strike.

4.7 The Community Health Council

In April 1974 a Community Health Council (CHC) was established in each district to represent the local community's interest and make its views known to the AHA. The CHC became involved in the affairs of Normansfield when the hospital's dental hygienist wrote to them because she felt her services were being wasted. As a result of this and a growing concern expressed by some members of the CHC who had 'personal experience of Normansfield', the Chairman and three other members of the CHC visited the hospital in November 1974. They were very worried by what they saw and decided that 'Normansfield was to receive priority for the attention and effort of the Council'. They made their views known to the AHA and after two further visits wrote to the chairman of the RHA explaining their concern. The Regional Administrator replied with an explanation that most of the matters raised were the concern of the AHA. After some discussion with the CHC, the Area Administrator sent a point-by-point reply to the CHC's criticisms. It would appear, however, that despite this exchange of letters the grounds for the CHC's complaints remained.

In 1975 the CHC set up a working party to consider the care of the physically and mentally handicapped. As a result of visits to both Normansfield and a number of other units they produced a report in June that made a number of recommendations for improvements. The report was sent to the Regional and Area Administrators but, as before, it did not lead to any major improvements and there was no real attempt to adopt many of the suggestions made.

The working party continued to visit Normansfield at regular intervals, noting any improvements and shortcomings and reporting these to the CHC. They also made a number of suggestions from time to time and these were always passed on to the Area Administrator. In April 1976 they presented a further report to the CHC but any action that might have been taken was forestalled by the strike. As a sad footnote to the involvement of the CHC at Normansfield, they found when they paid a further formal visit to the hospital in February 1977 that the situation which had appeared to be improving had returned to what it was like in November 1974. They found 'the place was dirty, uninspired, the patients seemed resigned and without the spark of friendliness which is so common normally with this type of patient'.

4.8 **In-service training**

Despite the obvious need for it as evidenced by the poor standard of nursing care, in-service training was neglected at Normansfield. There was a need to update the approach of the trained staff, train nursing assistants in their tasks and explain appropriate nursing care attitudes to them.

In 1974 the Regional Training Project Officer visited the hospital to give advice on in-service training for enrolled nurses and it was later decided that it would become the responsibility of one of the Nursing Officers. The individual chosen can hardly be described as an ideal candidate for the post. She and the consultant had quarrelled within a month of her joining the staff and as a result of the quarrel the consultant refused to speak directly to her about any matter concerning patients.

In her new role she was to be directly responsible to the Senior Nursing Officer but he was not given any say in the appointment. The desperately needed in-service training was thus put in the hands of a Nursing Officer with no formal training experience and unfortunately the outcome was that virtually no effective in-service training was given.

4.9 **Complaints from the nursing staff**

At the end of October 1974 the Senior Nursing Officer at Normansfield wrote to the Divisional Nursing Officer setting out in some detail some of the complaints of the nursing staff about the consultant. This letter was shown to both the chairman of the Division of Psychiatry and the Area Nursing Officer but no action was taken. In April and May of the following year the Area Nursing Officer received further confirmation that a problem existed in the relations between the nursing staff and the consultant but still took no action.

The confirmation came in the form of two reports, one a three-monthly report by a comparatively new Nursing Officer at the hospital and the second a report by a Senior Nursing Officer who had been seconded to Normansfield for three weeks. Both drew attention to complaints similar to those referred to in the letter mentioned above. The former catalogued a whole series of problems and concluded that 'Normansfield has certainly lagged behind and there are many societies outside the hospital who note this, parents are concerned, rightly so, encouragement is lacking and support zero'. The latter drew attention to 'the need of each member [of the SMT] to be accepted as an equal partner . . . [which] is a basic pre-requisite for better management'.

4.10 **The Department of Health is involved**

During 1975 the Department of Health received several inquiries about

Normansfield from two members of parliament and the CHC. These led to a visit to the hospital on 9 September 1975 by the nurse member of the Department's Regional Liaison Team, Mrs Twohig, who then wrote an internal memorandum that was extremely critical of what she had found. She was 'greatly concerned that management was failing in its duty to patients' and that 'serious embarrassment to Ministers might occur if there was further deterioration in standards of care at the hospital'. She gave detailed descriptions of her findings in her report and immediately after her visit spoke on the telephone to both the Area and the Regional Nursing Officers about her disquiet. She left them in no doubt as to the unhappy state of affairs she had found but the Area Nursing Officer still took no action other than to ask for a letter which she could show to the Regional Team of Officers to support her claim for direct assistance with the problems of Normansfield. It is worth adding here as evidence of the state of affairs at Normansfield that Mrs Twohig was so disturbed by what she saw that she was not prepared to leave the hospital until she was satisfied that every patient had sufficient blankets and bed linen.

4.11 More letters exchanged

On 19 November 1975 the Area Administrator, on behalf of the AMT, sent a highly critical letter to each member of the SMT. In it he pointed out that the hospital, patients and staff had suffered from 'the ravages of time and lack of overall management success', no significant improvements in service and management had taken place and, even more disturbingly, the 'SMT had not been able to create the necessary atmosphere for change from which many expected improvements should spring'. He threatened 'to advise the AHA and the RHA of the situation and ask them to take any remedial action that is within their power' unless a more constructive relationship between the members of the SMT was established in the immediate future from which a steady improvement in the quality of care could flow. The Consultant's reaction to this letter was to claim that he did not understand it and to ask for details and definitions. The Hospital Administrator failed to see what the Area Administrator was getting at. The third member of the SMT, the Senior Nursing Officer, accepted the failures of the SMT and replied to this effect.

At around the same time as this correspondence was taking place a letter from the Regional Administrator to a Deputy Secretary at the Department of Health showed that the former realised that there were serious problems at Normansfield. He wrote

Normansfield is a problem. I think we shall be able to deal with the physical deficiencies . . . The question of management is much more difficult. There is a clear indication of incompetence by the Consultant-in-charge and his colleagues (the nurse and the administrator) on the SMT. The Area are making strenuous efforts to come to grips with an extremely difficult problem but they are almost at the end of their tether . . . I am firmly of the view that something must be done before an unfortunate incident occurs rather than afterwards.

Despite this realisation he still adopted an attitude of wait and see. The price of waiting was being paid for by the patients.

4.12 The 'one-to-one' project

Throughout 1975 and the first few months of 1976 the resentment of the nursing staff, particularly at nursing officer level, increased steadily but in March the level of discontent rose dramatically as a result of conflict surrounding a 'one-to-one' project that was proposed by the Voluntary Service Organiser at the hospital. A 'one-to-one' project is a scheme by which individual members of the public are invited to 'adopt' individual patients as friends and is initiated by an open day at which the public meet the patients.

The SMT agreed in principle to the project, and a project advisor was invited to the hospital to discuss the scheme on 9 March 1976. In situations where the project had been run successfully it had been found that staff involvement at an early stage was very important and so after discussion between the Senior Nursing Officer and the Voluntary Service Organiser at a meeting of Nursing Officers the latter invited the Nursing Officers to be present at the meeting on 9 March. Arrangements were also made for a BBC reporter to attend.

Shortly before the meeting was due to start the Consultant learned that the Nursing Officers had been invited. He objected to their proposed presence and to that of the BBC reporter and made this clear by calling the Senior Nursing Officer and the Hospital Administrator into his office and informing them that neither the latter nor he himself would attend the meeting if the Nursing Officers were to be present. The Consultant then telephoned the Divisional Nursing Officer, Psychiatric Division, explained the situation and persuaded that officer that his objections to the Nursing Officers' presence were justified. The Divisional Nursing Officer, Psychiatric Division, then telephoned the Senior Nursing Officer to say that he accepted the Consultant's view. The Senior Nursing Officer passed the gist of the phone call on to a Nursing Officer who told his fellow Nursing Officers that they were not to attend the meeting, which went ahead without them.

If any one event can be said to have united the Nursing Officers in opposition to the Consultant it was this. They decided to make their protests known and, as a first step, sought advice from their union, COHSE. At the same time as their protest was getting under way, the Senior Nursing Officer wrote to the Divisional Nursing Officer,

Psychiatric Division, setting out his complaints about the way in which the matter had been handled.

4.13 Advice from the union

The Nursing Officers contacted the District Branch Secretary of their union and met him that day and again the following week. Following the first meeting the District Branch Secretary informed either the Area Personnel Officer or the Area Administrator that he had been called in to advise at Normansfield and asked that representatives of the area should meet him and some of the Nursing Officers. One of the Nursing Officers made a written complaint about the Divisional Nursing Officer, Psychiatric Division's role in the matter and a copy of this was left with the Area Nurse (Personnel). The Union Secretary also drew the attention of the Sector Administrator (Hospitals) to what had occurred.

The opinion of the Sector Administrator (Hospitals) was that the Nursing Officers should not have been invited to the meeting unless the SMT was unanimous in wanting to invite them but he did realise that 'this complaint is only a symptom of a particular difficulty at Normansfield' and as a result of this he suggested a meeting between himself, the Area General Administrator and the Divisional Nursing Officer, Psychiatric Division, pointing out that he thought 'some action must be taken, otherwise the position will worsen'. However, this suggestion of a meeting was not pursued and before long his prophecy came true.

As a response to the written complaint by a Nursing Officer referred to above, the complainant was invited to meet the Area Nurse (Personnel) and the Divisional Nursing Officer, Psychiatric Division at Area Headquarters. They sympathised with his point of view and then persuaded him to rephrase his complaint whilst giving him to understand that the matter would be raised with the Area Nursing Officer. No formal note was made of the meeting despite the fact that a formal grievance was being discussed.

4.14 The petition

At the second meeting between the Nursing Officers and the District Branch Secretary which was held on 15 March, a petition was drawn up against the Consultant. It read (according to the Report of the Committee of Inquiry)

We the undersigned object to the behaviour displayed by Dr. Lawlor, Consultant Psychiatrist at Normansfield Hospital in regard to the following specific points:

(i)   Attitude;
(ii)   Harassment;
(iii) Interference in Nursing duties;
(iv)   Objections regarding Union Membership

and we fear that if appropriate action is not taken we may find ourselves unable to cooperate any further with Doctor Lawlor.

The drawing up of the petition was solely the work of the Nursing Officers, whose names headed the list of signatures, and the District Branch Secretary of COHSE. As such it was contrary to the rules of the union which state that petitions must be discussed and approved at a general meeting of the branch before being signed or circulated.

It was also decided at the meeting that the Nursing Officers would only deal with the Consultant in pairs. Twenty-two signatures to the petition were collected in addition to those of the Nursing Officers and among them appeared the names of the majority of the more experienced nurses, sisters and charge nurses. The officers of AHA received copies of the petition on or about 19 March. The delivery seems to have been treated in a less than formal manner by both sides. The District Branch Secretary sent no covering letter with it, none of the Area Officers made any notes or records regarding it and no copies were sent to the Regional Authority who was the employer of the Consultant.

4.15 The Senior Nursing Officer complains to the Area Administrator

On 15 March the Senior Nursing Officer referred his complaints to the Area Administrator. In a letter he related the events surrounding the 'one-to-one' project meeting on Tuesday 9 March and pointed out that 'at the present time the morale of senior nursing staff at the hospital has reached its lowest level. Dr. Lawlor displays an autocratic attitude towards the Nursing Staff in general and myself in particular'. The Area Administrator sent a brief acknowledgement of this letter of complaint and said he would write again in a few days. He never did so.

4.16 Responses to the petition

At the request of the Area Administrator the Sector Administrator contacted the Consultant on 18 March and asked him if he would be prepared to attend a local inquiry into the allegations against him and to accept the findings. After discussing the matter with the Medical Defence Union the Consultant refused.

The following day a meeting was held at the request of the District Branch Secretary between himself, two Nursing Officers and four members of the AMT. The AMT was prepared, in principle, to pass the matter to the region but pointed out that further evidence in support of the complaints would be required. It was agreed that no further action would be taken by the AMT until it heard from the union representative again.

The additional evidence was prepared and delivered to Area approximately one week later but around this time the consultant took a step which in the words of the official report

was to aggravate the position considerably. Two high-grade former patients were employed as members of the domestic staff of the hospital . . . both were members of COHSE. Dr. Lawlor questioned the two men about their membership of COHSE on 25 March.

This led to an allegation by the union that the Consultant was trying to persuade them to leave COHSE and join NUPE, the National Union of Public Employees. The significance of this episode is that the petition had complained of the Consultant's objection in regard to union membership. Evidence for this complaint was sparse, to say the least, at the time at which the petition was drawn up but the Consultant's behaviour with the two former patients greatly strengthened the complaint.

It is surprising in view of all that had happened to date that when a joint meeting of the AMT and SMT was held on 30 March no reference was made to the industrial trouble or to the nurses' complaints. The person at the centre of the controversy, the Consultant, was not present at the meeting because he was still refusing to attend these joint meetings.

4.17 **More union action**

Union meetings were held on 31 March and 8 April. At the second of these meetings elections were held for Branch Officers and the lack of progress was discussed. A further meeting on 21 April was attended by the Regional Secretary of no. 13 Region of COHSE so that he could hear the nurses' grievances. The union members, particularly the Nursing Officers, emphasised their anger and growing impatience and encouraged the Regional Secretary to pursue the complaints to regional level. As a response to this he first telephoned and then wrote to the Regional Administrator, enclosing statements of complaint against the Consultant and stating that he was 'under a great deal of pressure to take all out strike action in order to have this Doctor removed'. He asked the RHA to investigate the complaints and to inform him what course of action it was going to take. In fact no mention of a strike had been made by the nurses at that stage.

The Regional Administrator asked the Regional Personnel Officer to investigate the matter and sent a copy of the letter to the Department of Health. The letter was not, however, shown to the other members of the Regional Team of Officers although they were told of it, nor to the chairman. The Regional Secretary of COHSE received no reply until 4 May which was the day the next union meeting was to be held. At that meeting the members were angry and impatient at the apparent lack of activity or interest on the part of the authorities. There is much doubt and confusion about what exactly happened at that meeting but although it is not clear whether it was decided that there should be a strike in twenty-four hours if the consultant was not suspended or that the Regional Secretary of COHSE would report back in twenty-four hours, many were convinced that they would be consulted again at a further meeting before the strike threat was implemented. Some of the confusion arose because not all of the staff concerned were able to attend the meeting at once because of ward duties and so it was held in two parts with those present at the second part being asked to endorse the views of those who had been present earlier.

4.18 The AHA meets

At the same time as the union meeting was in progress the AHA held one of its regular meetings. They had proposed to discuss whether to recommend that the RHA set up an inquiry but before they could do so the Area Administrator, as a result of a telephone call he received from the Area Personnel Officer, circulated a note to the AMT informing them that 'COHSE have met at Normansfield. Unless Dr. Lawlor is suspended forthwith there will be a withdrawal with effect from 9 am 5 May at Normansfield.' The Area Administrator, the Chairman and the Consultant Member of the AMT left the meeting and spoke to a union deputation comprising the Regional Secretary, the District Secretary and the Secretary of COHSE Long Grove Branch. There are a number of conflicting accounts of this discussion but the gist of it would appear to be that the union side demanded the suspension of the Consultant and were told that the AHA had no power to do this but would discuss recommendations for an inquiry that had been put forward by the AMT. They expected the discussion to last for approximately twenty minutes but the union delegation did not wait; they left as the AHA meeting reconvened.

4.19 Eleventh hour exchange of calls

The Regional Secretary of COHSE rang the Regional Personnel Officer at around 7 o'clock on the eve of the strike to inform him that he had been

given twenty-four hours to obtain the suspension of the Consultant and
that unless this happened there would be industrial action. He then
telephoned first to the Regional Administrator and then to the union's
District Secretary and discussed the matter with them. The latter
understood him to say that a decision had already been made by Region
that the Consultant would not be suspended, so he, in turn, almost at
once, telephoned this outcome to one of the Nursing Officers and from
there it spread rapidly through the hospital.

4.20 **Final strike meeting**

The members of the night staff were disappointed and angry and some
suggested an immediate walk-out. Fortunately for the patients though,
they were persuaded against this idea by their colleagues. Very soon an
informal meeting was called and staff who were off duty but available
were asked to gather at a staff residence. The night duty nursing staff
shop steward and the recently elected Branch Chairman also attended
but the District Secretary refused to attend and, indeed, finally took his
telephone off the hook so that he would not be disturbed again that night.
However, he did telephone the Senior Nursing Officer at another
hospital, Long Grove, to inform him of the state of affairs at
Normansfield. After some hours discussion it was decided by the
meeting that they would go on strike from 7 o'clock next morning and
that picketing would begin one hour before that.

Whilst the meeting was in progress the acting Senior Nursing Officer
(Night Supervision) at Long Grove who had been informed what was
going on by a late night call from the District Secretary of the Union, and
the Principal Nursing Officer, Psychiatric Division, had arrived at the
hospital. The latter had been prepared to address the meeting but had
not pressed to do so in case it inflamed matters even further. The Senior
Nursing Officer was informed at 5.30 am that there would be a
withdrawal of labour at 7.00 am but despite this he did not arrive at
Normansfield until the strike had begun.

4.21 **The strike**

According to the Report of the Committee of Inquiry, the Regional
Secretary of the Union arrived at 8.30 am and at 10 o'clock a COHSE
meeting was held, by which time the Area General Administrator and the
Area Personnel Officer had arrived at the hospital. The former addressed
the meeting and proposed that the strike be called off in return for the
Consultant staying away from the hospital for a day or two but he could
not give a categorical assurance that the Consultant would in fact stay
away. The meeting decided to step up the pressure by calling out those

few of their members who had been allowed on the wards, thus putting the patients at even greater risk.

The remainder of the AMT decided not to go to the hospital but to remain at area headquarters. At noon the Area Nursing Officer, acting on the basis of information she had received from the hospital, expressed great fears for the safety of the patients to the Area Administrator. He passed her views to the Regional Administrator who, in the light of these fears, decided to recommend the Consultant's suspension to' the Chairman. The Chairman acted in accordance with the recommendation, directing that the consultant be suspended until after the next meeting of the RHA which was to be held on 12 May.

Despite the fact that the decision to suspend the consultant was taken between noon and one o'clock and that the Consultant himself was informed of the decision at 2.30 the staff who were on strike at the hospital were not told until after 3 o'clock so the patients were deprived of their care for far longer than was necessary, given that the strike had to take place at all. Indeed, the staff did not return to their wards until about 3.45.

4.22 **In conclusion**

Very few of those concerned with Normansfield Hospital's management emerged from the inquiry without any blame for the problems there being attached to them. Some of the outside bodies and individuals associated with the hospital tried very hard to focus attention on the difficulties and to do what they could to improve the lot of the patients but they were battling against enormous odds. There was a lack of cooperation between senior medical, nursing and administrative officers and an extremely low level of morale. Area's policy of seeking to improve the situation by non-intervention and persuasion and Region's attitude of 'wait and see' had proved ineffective and on top of all this, when it came to the final crunch, on the day of the strike most of the nursing staff were prepared to abandon their patients, many of whom were helpless.

5

The capsizing of the
Alexander L. Kielland rig

5.1 **Introduction**

In the early evening of 27 March 1980 a floating hotel, the *Alexander L. Kielland* rig, broke up, heeled over and capsized whilst at its station in the Norwegian oil and gas fields of the North Sea. Out of 212 men aboard at the time only eighty-nine were rescued. In terms of loss of life it was the worst accident to date involving a North Sea rig, but although the casualty figures were horrifying they were not the only reasons for the full-scale Norwegian inquiry that followed, nor indeed for the inclusion of the disaster in this book. For example, the *Alexander L. Kielland* incident fanned the flames of distrust that had been smouldering within the minds of Norwegian fishing interests. Only three years earlier the offshore engineers operating the Ekofisk Bravo platform had lost control of an oil well and allowed 20,000 tons of oil to spill into the sea. Not until the Texan expert Red Adair had arrived could the flow be staunched. Those concerned with fishing had breathed a sign of relief that no damage had been done to their traditional industry by that oil spillage, but with their next breaths they sought assurances that all possible steps were being taken to see that the new bonanza did not destroy the old.

Speculation during the immediate aftermath of the *Alexander L. Kielland* disaster led to many guesses as to the cause. Had a ship struck the rig? Had a freak wave that could only be expected to arrive every hundred years demolished it? Had a mysterious metallurgical problem arisen? Was there yet another surprise influence at work in the cold, stormy and corrosive environment of the continental shelf offshore from Norway? In the event the immediate cause proved to be a good deal more prosaic than any of these. It was found to have derived from the rig's earliest days, when it comprised only schemes on paper and stacks of steel tubes in a French shipyard. And now the explanations by the builders were heard alongside the stories of the eighty-nine survivors. The commission of inquiry set up by the Norwegian government found that the survivors and their rescuers had had to improvise, adapt and use great resource. Added to the concern generated by the disaster was the view of some observers that these misfortunes on Norwegian rigs might signal a setback to the whole venture of collecting fossil fuels from under the North Sea.

One such observer, O. Noreng, in a comparative study of the way the United Kingdom and Norway were handling their oil riches, stated that for several years the latter nation would be extremely dependent upon the smooth operation of its two oilfields and one gas field for foreign exchange, and if the loss of a rig led to a loss of production whilst it was being replaced or whilst causes were examined and new lessons put into practice, this would damage the national economy as well as being a blow to Norwegian pride. Naturally other countries operating in the North Sea also watched with concern as the broken pieces of the *Alexander L. Kielland* were studied. What had gone wrong?

5.2 **The *Alexander L. Kielland***

Conventional conceptions of a North Sea rig concentrate upon the process of drilling for oil. Drill pipes are unloaded from a barge onto the open platform of the rig and assembled below a gantry. Helicopters pass overhead, and beneath the sea divers carry out work on the sea bed. This picture bears little relation to the *Alexander L. Kielland*, which was a place of peace and quiet compared with a drilling rig or production platform. It had been built for drilling by French manufacturers in the mid-1970s and delivered in that form to its owners, Stavanger Drilling, on 5 July 1976. Fitted out for drilling it was chartered to the Phillips Petroleum Company of Norway but during its entire life it was only used as an accommodation rig and as such was not employed directly for prospecting, drilling, or collecting oil or gas. It simply housed workers from other rigs nearby and provided eating, sleeping, resting and entertainment facilities such as would be found in a hotel or hostel ashore. The needs of the rig's 'hotel guests' were served by a permanent crew, rather as on a troopship. In March 1980 the rig was in service on the Ekofisk oilfield, almost equidistant from the Norwegian, British and Dutch coasts. The original provision of accommodation for the eighty workers needed to run the rig for drilling had been increased on four separate occasions so that by 1978 348 people could be housed.

The staff and their 'guests' (as we shall refer to them here) were housed in a complex of rooms on three decks, one above the other, rather like a ship and also having a recognisable bow and stern. However (Figure 5.1), unlike a ship these decks were supported so that the lowest was raised some fifteen metres above the sea by five hollow columns, thirty metres long. These stood on five massive flotation pontoons submerged below the sea's surface. Cables 1100–1500 metres in length ran from the upper part of the rig, down the sides of the columns, round pulleys just above

5.1 The *Alexander L. Kielland* 'hotel' rig, right, alongside its production rig

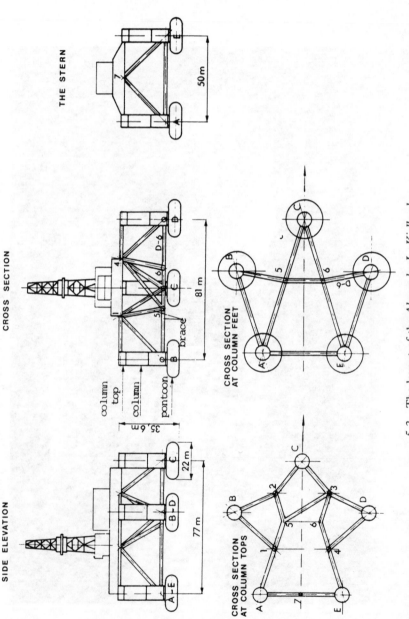

5.2 The layout of the *Alexander L. Kielland*

the pontoons, and out to anchors set in the sea bed. By slackening off the cables on one side and reeling in on the others the rig could move a little without the aid of tugs, and three of the pontoons each had a motor and a propellor to be used to halt the rig or assist in moving it when under tow. The forces needed for manoeuvring, together with the effects of sea and wind, the weight and inertia of the upper structure and decks, plus any forces due to work in progress on the rig (such as loading from vessels alongside) would have produced sideways pressures on each column. In order to oppose this, and to generally stiffen the structure, the designers had provided horizontal and diagonal bracing in the form of massive tubes that ran from leg to leg and up to the platform; figures 5.2 and 5.3 show the layout. The brace labelled D-6 was to be the trigger for the disaster.

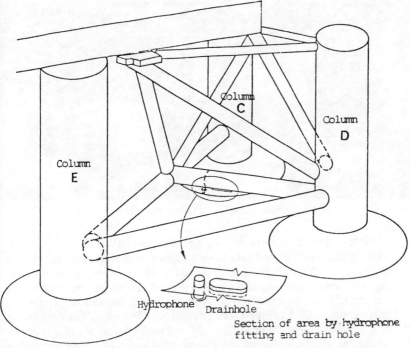

5.3   Location of the hydrophone fitting on brace D-6, and associated crack (shown dashed)

On 27 March 1980 there were 212 people on board this floating hostel, nearly all of them guests from other rigs. Just before 6.30 pm an impact was both heard and felt. It resembled a heavy wave striking the steelwork but actually had a much more sinister significance. The rig was starting to break up at bracing tube D-6 in the submerged part just above pontoon D. After the disaster the investigators proved that there had been a crack in the metal of the brace ever since the rig was manufactured. The crack, whose origin will be explained later, had worked its way around half the circumference of the bracing tube and weakened it until the next wave to hit the rig was sufficient to sever the brace completely. The structure shuddered as other bracing bars around column D broke under the unaccustomed load thrown onto them. The buoyancy of pontoon D then took over. It lifted and twisted the whole of column D about a point somewhere at deck level, where these bracings also broke so that the entire column and pontoon came away and floated off (figure 5.4). The rig slumped over by 30°–35°.

5.4   Leg D, detached and afloat

Most of the men were in the cinemas, the mess hall or the kitchen area. The sudden lurch to one side hurled them across whichever room they were in, and the contents of those rooms tumbled across with them. The rig still floated though, and came briefly to rest at its new inclination (figure 5.5). But now the tops of columns C and E were awash, and water entered column C by three doors that had been left open. The decks were also dipping below water at one side and water began to enter through several openings, reducing the buoyancy still further. The rig settled lower and lower in the water, keeling over to an ever-increasing degree until, some twenty minutes after the initial fracture, the remains of the rig suddenly lurched over and turned upside down (figure 5.6). Meanwhile the men aboard had been able to launch only one of the rig's seven lifeboats successfully. Although there were also twenty liferafts only four are known to have saved any lives, and two of these probably

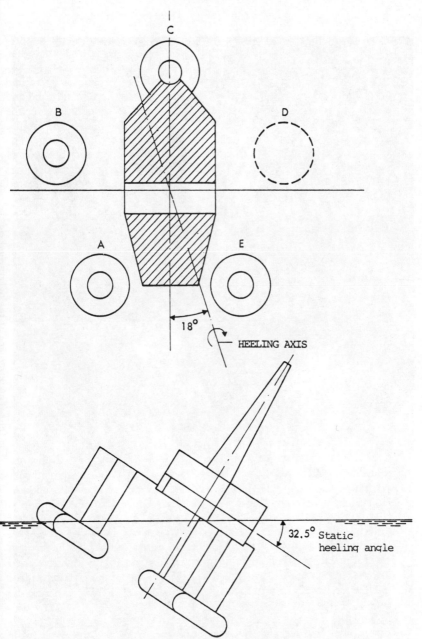

18°

HEELING AXIS

32.5° Static
heeling angle

5.5 Platform in heeled position

5.6 The four remaining legs of the overturned rig

came from Edda 2/7C platform. Of all the men in the *Alexander L. Kielland,* none was picked up by the statutory standby vessel provided for just such an eventuality.

On the day after the disaster the Norwegian government set up a commission to investigate the causes of the accident, to evaluate the performance of the lifesaving equipment and the rescue services, and to make recommendations for change. It began its task by interviewing many of the men involved in the incident and tracing much of the history of the rig back to its earliest days; witnesses and documentary evidence were examined, tests and calculations were made. Our version of the disaster is based on the commission's work and highlights failures at several stages in the story of the *Alexander L. Kielland* rig. However, many other features will not be covered here. Even the commission could not find out everything. Vital documents could not be traced and memories proved short or became shorter in the face of fears that blame might be attached to wrong decisions.

5.3 The fracture

As will emerge in what follows, the break in the bracing tube did not occur at a spot engineers would normally regard as critical, such as a welded joint at a junction with a column. Indeed the fracture location was more reminiscent of instances where pieces of domestic equipment have broken prematurely at the exact spot where a proud manufacturer had embossed a name, the part number or the phrase 'pat pending'. Like many of these failures the fatal break in the rig was for the most part what engineers call a 'fatigue' fracture, that is a progressive weakening of metal due to repetitions of comparatively modest loadings. As a result of fatigue the strength of the metal is reduced to such an extent that it falls below that needed to sustain even normal working loads and the material begins to crack. Fatigue failure then proceeds by progressive advances of the crack with each application of load until the uncracked portion is so small that it cannot withstand even one more loading and it breaks right through. A pre-existing split hastens the onset of fatigue failure and this was the case on the *Alexander L. Kielland.* Next we shall see how the rig's bracing bar D-6 came to contain such a split.

It was mentioned earlier that this rig was moored by cables attached to anchors set in the sea bed; reeling these cables in and out provided fine adjustment of the rig's position. This would have been particularly important when drilling for oil, and although the rig had not yet been used in this way it had originally been built for it and was equipped to take many of the fittings that would be necessary for drilling, such as the devices called 'hydrophones', which would be housed in the horizontal bracing bars to face downwards. Each hydrophone would pick up sound waves sent out by a device placed on the sea bed below the rig's intended site. By comparing the times at which signals arrived at each hydrophone the precise position of a rig could be found. The hydrophones were not fitted directly to each brace; instead, a hole was cut in the brace and special tubes made up and welded in as a lining around the edge of the hole (figure 5.7). The lining stood proud of the surface of the brace, and next a ring-shaped plate was welded to the lining's projecting outer end so that the hydrophone could later be placed in the lining tube and fastened to the plate. Metallurgical examination after the disaster revealed several faults in and around the tube. Its steel was of inferior quality for the job and liable to split and peel away in layers; in fact there had been no requirement that the strength of the metal be considered with this 'de-lamination' in mind. The welding deposit that fastened the lining to the brace was thin and badly shaped which resulted in low strength and poor 'give' here so that during manufacture or shortly afterwards the welding had given way and the plates had split. The finding of paint on the crack surfaces exposed by the final fracture confirmed the early date of these breaks because the paint colour was one only used during manufacture of the rig.

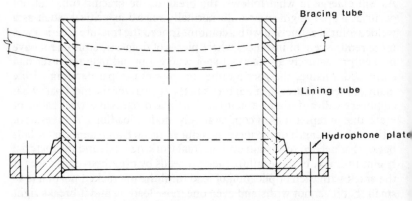

5.7   Sectional elevation of the hydrophone fitting

The mechanism by which it is possible for steel structures to fracture so early in their life, indeed almost before that life has begun, can best be explained by following the manufacturing process stage by stage. First, the basic tube for the bracing bar would be made by welding shorter tubes together, and then later the hole for the hydrophone and its support would be cut out with a flame torch. This heats the metal to melting point along the desired line of cut and virtually blows and burns it away. However, the metal on each side of the cut would also become hot and expand. The heat in the cut edges would dissipate to the surroundings but thermal contraction of the cooling metal would be restrained by the much cooler and more massive parts further away. Thus when the cut edges cool down, their contraction is restrained, leaving them in a permanently stretched state. Also when the lining tube comes to be welded in place both it and the main tube are reheated, and again cool off under restraint. The result is that parts of the structure start life with a built-in tension. The existence of these locked-in effects is hard to predict. Other features such as complex shapes of the steelwork and the sub-zero temperatures of the North Sea environment could help to cause cracks. Much can be done to help prevent cracking, by careful design of the shapes and sizes of the plates, selection of suitable material and by careful attention to the welding, but in the construction of the *Alexander L. Kielland* scant attention was paid to these considerations. The welding used here was the lowest of the three quality classes used on the rig, the run of weld metal was too narrow and it did not extend into the surrounding steel in the way it ought.

It is not known at which precise stage of manufacture these defects caused the first crack; it might have been during the welding itself, or during transport of this sub-assembly to the shoreside yard where final assembly took place. Perhaps the cracking began when the structure was still incomplete and temporary supports were in use. It is known that the rig was put together in stages by first setting out two of the pontoons and the lower parts of their columns afloat on the water of the assembly area. Next, a bracing tube was floated out on a barge and the barge ballasted to bring the tube to the right height for welding. This was repeated for the other pontoons and bracing tubes, each barge and pontoon having its ballasting changed repeatedly to suit the ever-growing assembly (figure 5.8). To give some idea of the sizes involved, a typical brace weighed thirty to forty tons. Finally the upperworks were completed.

This manhandling would produce stresses in the bracing tube D-6 whose continuity had been interrupted by the hole for the hydrophone, and the effect of these stresses would be unpredictable. As we have described, the designer dealing with the hydrophones added the lining plate as reinforcement, but this became cracked in the very process of its attachment due to the poor quality of its metal, and this crack was liable to split even further. Design checks ensured that the bracing tube was strong enough in itself but much less attention was paid to local strength at the hydrophone fittings. One reason for this was probably a difference in how these tasks were perceived by the designers and builders. Checking the original strength of the virgin bracing was a main structural matter: dealing with the hydrophone device was a matter of outfitting, and thus secondary and peripheral to the structural engineering.

It has been explained that during manufacture and assembly there would be several loads acting on the bracing tubes. Similarly, in service,

5.8   Two Pentagone rigs under construction

they would be affected by various loads that included the weight of the structure, buoyancy pressures and anchor cable forces. The first two would be predictable for an intact rig and fairly easy to calculate, and the anchoring forces were monitored, controlled and limited by the cable winches. Certain other loads and effects could really only be guessed at, such as operating loads if the rig were to be used for drilling, impacts from vessels moored against the rig for supply or other working purposes, and the effect of the waves and the general movement or surge of the sea. The movement of the surface of the ocean would strain the bracing tubes in several ways. Waves would slam them directly, and also strike the various pontoons and columns at different instants and in different directions, throwing even more load onto the structure. One of the aims of the submerged pontoon design used for the *Alexander L. Kielland* was to keep down the wave impacts by putting most of the buoyancy well below the sea's surface, elevating the decks high above it, and reducing the lattice structure at wave level to a minimum. However, each wave would lift one or more of the buoyant pontoons and columns whilst others lay in wave troughs. Thus there was uneven loading, so the bracings were needed in order to hold the structure rigid. In addition, the water in the body of a wave does not advance as one mass; it varies in speed, so again there are uneven loads, continually changing in nature and size. Then, of course, when a wave tries to move the rig bodily the anchor cables resist so the cable forces vary in time with the waves too, giving another rhythmic effect. In this fashion waves produce the repeated loading that causes fatigue fracture and yet the design of the rig involved no explicit calculations as to the effect of repeated loads and the damage they might cause by cracking the structure. Rather, it was believed that the strength incorporated against general loading also gave security against fatigue. One reason for this view was the tendency to look to ship practice for guidelines on the special checks that should be made. Ships in fact provide a poor guide to rigs, as the kind of steel used in ships and the way ships are put together give much automatic protection against fatigue. However, the Norwegian inquiry commission found that if a fatigue calculation had been performed, using reasonable assumptions for the effect of wave loading, there would have been cause for concern because even if the rig had not been cracked in manufacture it would still have cracked in service and possibly have failed even sooner than it did. The commission went still further and expressed its view that many other things had been wrong all along, including deficiencies in other features of the design, dimensions and material quality of the hydrophone holder and its attachment to the bracing tube. Yet these aspects were all supposed to be covered by rules and regulations, so it is necessary to look next at these and how they were applied to rigs at that time.

5.4 Regulations

The design, construction, operation and inspection of rigs working under the Norwegian flag or in Norwegian waters came within a network of legislation devised by that government. This network was so complex that even a limited attempt at a full description is not possible here. Instead, explanations are given of a few aspects, and figure 5.9 reproduces a diagram from the commission's report.

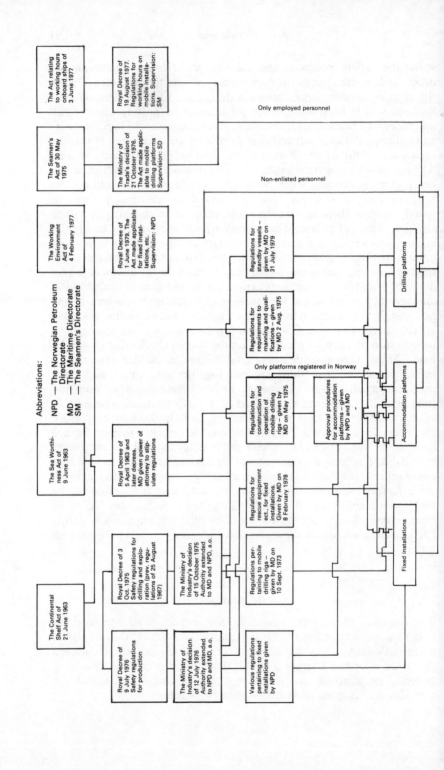

Abbreviations:

NPD — The Norwegian Petroleum Directorate
MD — The Maritime Directorate
SM — The Seamen's Directorate

The Act relating to working hours onboard ships of 3 June 1977

Royal Decree of 19 August 1977. Regulations for working hours on mobile installations. Supervision: SM

The Seamen's Act of 30 May 1975

The Ministry of Trade's decision of 21 October 1976. The Act made applicable to mobile drilling platforms Supervision: SD

Only employed personnel

Non-enlisted personnel

The Working Environment Act of 4 February 1977

Royal Decree of 1 June 1979. The Act made applicable for fixed installations, etc. Supervision: NPD

The Sea Worthiness Act of 9 June 1963

Royal Decree of 5 April 1963 and later decrees. MD given power of attorney to stipulate regulations

Regulations for standby vessels – given by MD on 31 July 1979

Regulations for requirements to manning and qualifications – given by MD 2 Aug. 1975

Only platforms registered in Norway

Regulations for construction and operation of mobile drilling rigs – given by MD on May 1975

Approval procedures for accommodation platforms – given by NPD and MD

Regulations for rescue equipment ect., for fixed installations. Given by MD on 8 February 1978

The Continental Shelf Act of 21 June 1963

Royal Decree of 3 Oct. 1975 Safety regulations for drilling and exploration (prev. regulations of 25 August 1967)

The Ministry of Industry's decision of 15 October 1975 Authority extended to MD and NPD, a.o.

Regulations pertaining to mobile drilling rigs – given by MD on 10 Sept. 1973

Royal Decree of 9 July 1976 Safety regulations for production

The Ministry of Industry's decision of 12 July 1976 Authority extended to NPD and MD, a.o.

Various regulations pertaining to fixed installations given by NPD

Drilling platforms

Accommodation platforms

Fixed installations

The legislation shown in figure 5.9 is aimed at three types of installations. Originally a clear distinction could be made between two of them, i.e. mobile floating rigs and platforms supported from the sea bed. The former at first resembled ships and so tended to have maritime rules applied to them. The latter were used for oil and gas gathering and resembled, if anything, gigantic seaside amusement piers, so new rules were needed for them. When accommodation rigs came along they cut across this simple categorisation. They were mobile for moving to where they were needed, but for many purposes of regulation were regarded as fixed because when in use they were always associated with one particular fixed platform at a time. However, to confuse matters further all the early accommodation rigs had been converted from drilling vessels and so had been examined under the regulations for these initially.

Acts of Parliament are at the root of the Norwegian legislative network concerning North Sea operations. For example, the Continental Shelf Act delegated authority to royal decrees that could deal with such matters as approval of oil exploration and exploitation, and extend to safety regulations too.

However, these decrees also allow a ministry to delegate its authority to further groups of institutions, and the Ministry of Industry had delegated authority to the Maritime Directorate in the case of exploration or drilling, and to the Norwegian Petroleum Directorate in respect of oil or gas production. Under the heading of control of mobile platforms the report of the commission of inquiry gave the following list of bodies to which authority had been delegated under continental shelf legislation.

1. The Maritime Directorate: design and strength, stability, furnishing, fire protection, emergency power sources, rescue equipment, nautical equipment, anchor buoys, alarm instructions, exercises and training, meteorological and environmental data, strength of the helicopter deck and fire fighting system, general work supervision, including control of lifts, cranes, loading and unloading equipment, pneumatic system, ladders, safety equipment, work procedures etc. The Maritime Directorate had also been ordered to co-ordinate the practical implementation of the control activity as well as to give the formal consent to use of the platform on the Norwegian continental shelf.
2. The Norwegian Petroleum Directorate takes care of everything concerning technical drilling equipment and the drilling process. The directorate further has the control of divers, diving equipment and diving operations. The directorate also controls the preparedness plans for accidents and emergencies.
3. The Aviation Administration: helicopter decks, including their location, design and equipment.

4. The Communications Directorate: the location of the radio room, radio and telephone equipment and other communication facilities.
5. The Directorate for Seamen: organised safety work and records of those on board.
6. The Health Directorate: sick rooms with equipment, first aid equipment, hygiene conditions, medical aides, doctors, qualifications of personnel as concerns first aid.
7. The Norwegian Waterfall and Electricity Administration: electrical facilities and their classification in regard to explosion danger, zone divisioning, establishment of zones and ventilation, electrical installations and equipment in dangerous areas.
8. The State's Institute for Radiation Hygiene: transportation, storage and use of radioactive equipment.
9. The State's Explosives Inspection: storage and use of explosives.

For fixed installations the delegated authorities are listed as:

1. The Telecommunications Directorate as concerns telecommunications systems;
2. The Aviation Administration as concerns conditions relating to aviation;
3. The Coastal Directorate as concerns planning and equipment for marking and identification, maritime radio positioning appliances as well as electrical emergency power systems for the systems under the direction of the Coastal Directorate;
4. The Maritime Directorate as concerns rescue equipment and rescue exercises. The authority also comprises the location of the rescue equipment onboard the facilities as well as the launching system for lifeboats. By decision of the Ministry of Local Government and Labour of 26 July 1979, the responsibility for the primary function of standby vessels was transferred from the Norwegian Petroleum Directorate to the Maritime Directorate. For this reason, the Maritime Directorate controls not only the seaworthiness of the standby vessels but also that the standby vessel has capacity and equipment to take onboard and cater for the number of persons for whom the standby vessel is intended. However, it is not within the scope of the Maritime Directorate to ensure that the standby vessels by themselves, or together with other approved vessels, have sufficient capacity to cater for the persons staying onboard the installation(s) which the standby vessel serve. This is an aspect which is under the Norwegian Petroleum Directorate's area of responsibility.
5. The Norwegian Petroleum Directorate is the institution to which has been delegated the most comprehensive authority under the safety regulations. Somewhat simplified, it may be said that the Norwegian

Petroleum Directorate's role in the control and approval procedure for fixed platforms corresponds to that of the Maritime Directorate for mobile platforms.

Other ministries concerned with rigs included the Ministry of Justice which dealt with emergency preparedness for situations which could lead to personal injury, serious illness or loss of life, and which necessitated immediate evacuation. The Ministry of Environment had been given responsibility for regulations on waste products, as well as equipment and procedures which may have caused pollution of the surroundings. Authority over this had been delegated to the State Pollution Authority. For fixed installations the Ministry of Social Affairs had responsibility for hygiene, medical control, supply of drinking water, ventilation, heating etc. The executive control authority for this lay with the Health Directorate.

Between them these directorates and other bodies appeared to cover most aspects of a rig operation but the manner in which they were covered is significant here. It does not emerge in the report of the inquiry commission, but the Norwegian O. Noreng reveals the context of his country's legislation in his book (see bibliography). According to Norwegian administrative tradition, business is supposed to conform to public policies and regulations on its own, without much supervision. In the implementation of policies the Norwegian government is not usually very active and as a rule is not much engaged in matters of detail at a day to day level. In this Noreng regards the Norwegian administration as remarkably non-bureaucratic. He goes on to comment that North Sea oil policies were formulated in an ambitious and sophisticated way, emphasising theoretical argument and extensive documentation on policy, but it was left to trust that the oil companies would willingly and loyally behave according to the policies. Normally this might suit a small and homogeneous society like Norway but that nation was unused to the ways of the multinational petroleum companies. Similarly the companies were unused to such governments. Also the rules and provisions had had to be established on the basis of scarce information for although mobile rigs had been operated before, they had been located in the shallower waters and better weather of the Gulf of Mexico and the Middle East. As in all administrations, a rule or procedure once made acquires a life of its own and becomes difficult to change. The final points from Noreng can be examined using the diagram in figure 5.9, noting however that some of the organisations mentioned in this text are not on the diagram at all.

Noreng regarded the Norwegian Petroleum Directorate and the Marine Directorate as part of a primary government structure in relation to oil safety. The remaining directorate and similar organisations form the secondary structure. The importance of this distinction lies in the likelihood that the large and powerful primary structure will, in a conflict, favour itself in preference to the secondary structure. The organisations in the secondary structure have what Noreng calls partial objectives, implying only partial processes of government. The actions of secondary structure organisations often tend to be responses to events that have already taken place, and they have little direct influence on events until a disaster like the capsizing of the *Alexander L. Kielland* highlights their work.

A company needed a licence to explore for oil or to collect it when it had been discovered, and the application for a licence had to be accompanied by details of the equipment and procedures envisaged. These were to be sent out to the various interested authorities, who then commented where they felt it necessary. To assist designers in preparing their schemes there were detailed regulations in existence covering many aspects of a rig, its work and its staff. Some appear in this account, but there were also some over-riding requirements. The drilling rig was to be designed in such a way that it would function properly under the weather and wind conditions that could be expected in the waters in which it would operate. The regulations went on to say that the structure should be strong enough to withstand the most unfavourable combination of effects produced by the environment and arising from operation of the rig. It was also to have sufficient stability to float upright in the water.

The owner or the builders had to ensure that all drawings relating to the work were submitted to the Maritime Directorate. From there the appropriate sections went to the Telecommunication Directorate and the Waterfalls and Electricity Administration. Other matters remained in the hands of the Maritime Directorate.

Although regulations concerning manning, qualifications of personnel, areas of individual responsibility, training and practice drills were all laid down, certain gaps existed at the time of the disaster and were pointed out by the inquiry. For example, in relation to safety training on fixed installations there were guidelines but no binding requirements. The guests on accommodation platforms were not required to have safety training but once the *Alexander L. Kielland* had been stricken they were in greater danger than the full-time crew for they were in surroundings that were unfamiliar to them.

The Maritime Directorate stipulated regulations for rescue equipment on fixed production installations and the accommodation facilities that were linked to them. The regulations covered the equipment itself, manning of lifeboat stations and lifeboats, and exercises and training, but escape routes to rescue stations, the protection of rescue stations and general specification of the rescue provision at each station came under the Petroleum Directorate. This body also had charge of approving the necessary plans for emergency preparedness and action in the case of an emergency. The Maritime Directorate had the duty of approving the seaworthiness, equipment and capacity of the standby vessels – whose number and location in a field were approved by the Petroleum Directorate as part of their approval of the emergency plans. Finally, it was a requirement in the safety regulations that lists be kept of all persons on board a rig or on their way to or from it.

Checking the seaworthiness of a new rig is a much bigger job than counting life-jackets, and cannot be done by a single inspection. Rather, there is the need for specialist and experienced personnel and expensive test equipment to be on hand in order to check that the materials and processes used in building the rig are good enough. Much the same applies to periodical inspection. Because there are some similarities between rigs and ships (though there are some important differences too) the Maritime Directorate accepted certificates from what are called classification societies. The best known of these is Lloyds of London but in the case of the *Alexander L. Kielland* the society employed was Det norske Veritas, of Norway. The directorate set the outline requirements for the hull, engines, steering systems, pumps, valves and pipes, etc., while the classification society undertook the investigation of each individual rig or ship.

5.5 **Design of the rig**

Rigs of the *Kielland* type are referred to as Pentagone semi-submersible, the name deriving from the five vertical columns of the rig and the five buoyancy pontoons. Some compartments of the pontoons and columns could be filled with water so as to change the draft of the rig and the height of the main platform above the sea in order to allow different jobs to be done. For transportation and periodical inspection in sheltered waters a shallow draft would be selected so as to reveal as much of the structure as possible. At the other extreme the pontoons would be fully submerged for drilling in order to reach the more stable waters below the surface and reduce the disturbance caused by the effect of surface waves in heavy seas.

The first rigs used in the North Sea benefited from little previous experience, and still less from firm knowledge of the factors affecting their behaviour. Accidents played a part in encouraging the framing of regulations as lessons were learned about the difficulties and dangers involved in handling a rig and about the likelihood and consequences of fracture of metals in the low temperature seas of the continental shelf. As in many other aspects of the oil industry, research on Pentagone rigs took place on both sides of the Atlantic. This included tests using models to show how much the rig would be thrown about by waves, and measurements were made of how stable the design was when tilted.

However, no test simulated the loss of an entire column as expensive simulations are only justified if they are based on conditions that can reasonably be expected. Anyway, how could a column come off if the bracing had been welded properly and carefully inspected, as the regulations appeared to demand?

5.6 Inspection

Naturally, there were requirements for each rig to be checked during manufacture and operation, and the Det norske Veritas organisation was engaged to survey the *Alexander L. Kielland* so that it could receive a 'classification for suitability'. This is the equivalent to a ship being surveyed by the British organisation Lloyds and declared A1 for service. The survey called for a complete visual inspection together with examination by X-ray photography, use of magnetic particles that cling to the edges of cracks, application of penetrant dyes to show up cracks, and transmission of ultrasound to detect concealed flaws. In particular the welds were to be checked. Only a few defects were found, and these were insignificant, so the rig was allowed to go into service containing a crack that could have been as long as 70 mm. Perhaps the crack did not form until after the final inspections. If this were the case it would show that an examination should have been made after latent defects had emerged.

Surveys in service were to be undertaken at least once a year, and every four years the rig was to be brought into calm sheltered water and unballasted to lift as much of the structure as possible out of the sea. A careful examination was then to have been made, including inspection of the underwater parts. The *Alexander L. Kielland* was due to have its four-yearly inspection in April 1980, when the rig was to be brought to shore for final preparation as a drilling platform. It was open to the operators to apply to have the four year survey postponed for one extra year, and this had been granted, so the new date for the major survey was June 1981; in fact the rig capsized more than a year before this. It was easier if the annual surveys could take place in sheltered waters, but they could if necessary be carried out while the rig was at work. Horizontal braces such as D-6 would be underwater then, as would half the length of the columns, though actually one of the *Kielland*'s annual surveys had been undertaken at a time when the rig was raised high out of the water in preparation for a move and still the crack was not discovered. One reason for this omission must be that these annual checks did not specifically demand underwater inspection, though it could be called for if it was thought to be necessary. Also the real purpose of the annual check was to look at the general condition of the rig by way of random sampling and examine the progress and effects of any cracks, corrosion or permanent deformation that had been reported during the past year. Therefore, the survey was directed at the more obvious signs of damage, such as impact by supply ships and dents caused by loads falling or swinging from cranes. Only the four-yearly surveys could be expected to reveal a crack of the kind that was to be fatal to the *Kielland* rig, but in fact after the disaster similar cracks were found on the rigs that had in fact undergone four-yearly surveys. Some of these rigs had been constructed and operated under the eyes of Det norske Veritas, but others had been with Lloyds. The reason that the cracks on the *Alexander L. Kielland* rig had not been found might have been that they were not looked for; this part of the brace, near its mid length, was not regarded as critical. It appears that the procedures laid down in the survey rules were inadequate in that they did not specify clearly the points that should be checked. In addition such rules as did exist were not followed properly. In defence it must be admitted that experience with rigs in the North Sea was still quite limited, but even so better use could have been made of such operational knowledge as was available if the various classification societies had pooled their experience; it was not a common practice to do this though.

5.7 **Strength, buoyancy and stability**

In a structure such as a rig there are several ways in which catastrophic failures can occur. Three of these possibilities are that the platform could break up, capsize, or sink; failure could entail one, two or all three of these, simultaneously or in succession. As regards the likelihood of failure, no two structures are precisely alike, and neither do they undergo the same experience in service. Also, there is always the unexpected mishap that cannot be fully guarded against, if only because its nature and severity are by definition unexpected. Thus, for example, a supply barge out of control might have struck a horizontal bracing tube such as D-6 and rendered it useless. The remaining bars would be too weak to stop column D behaving then as it did in the disaster unless the rig were floating in a calm sea – but this is the least likely time for the brace to suffer a mortal blow! If the loss of a brace had ever been in the designer's mind the idea must have been put aside. Such a loss would have to be preceded by abnormally poor seamanship on the part of experienced tug captains, and having decided that loss of this piece of structure was too unlikely to be catered for, there was then no need to compensate for possible loss of D-6 by providing extra bracing. Omission of this made it easier to work ships around the rig and reduced the amount of steel used, thus lightening the whole construction and giving less scope for waves to batter the rig. In that last sense, omitting a brace could be said to have made the rig safer.

In the regulations governing the design of a floating structure such as an oil rig or a ship the possibility is always admitted that some part of the hull might be holed so that water can enter and some buoyancy be lost. To prevent a single hole causing the loss of an entire vessel the interior of a ship or the lower parts of a rig are divided into watertight compartments so that a single hole will affect only one compartment, destroying only a small fraction of the entire vessel's buoyancy. If the junction between two compartments is struck it can cause the loss of both their contributions. The designer of a novel layout, and the authority framing regulations, will take into account the likelihood of losing different numbers of compartments. As the number that might be simultaneously lost increases, the chance of such damage diminishes very rapidly. A balance is struck, expressed in terms of a design requirement that a vessel remain afloat although a certain number of compartments are open to the

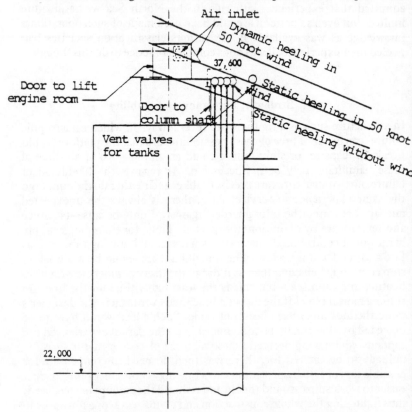

5.10   Water lines in calm water after filling of two compartments of column B, determined by calculation

sea. The *Alexander L. Kielland* was built to its correct specification for watertight compartments but still came to grief. In essence there was a failure to allow for the loss of a complete column and its pontoon, together with the buoyancy they provided. However, something that might have saved the rig had in fact been allowed for: it was supposed that, following a collision, two adjacent tanks in one leg of the rig had filled with water, after which the unlucky rig had been struck by a sudden gust of wind so that it heeled over violently before coming upright again. The resulting angle of heel would submerge the tops of the columns (figure 5.10) where there were doors for access to equipment such as ballasting valves and the propulsion motors installed in the columns and pontoons. To stop water entering through these doors they were specified as 'watertight', to be kept firmly closed and clamped at all times unless a crew member was actually passing through. Other fittings on the tops of the columns, namely air inlets and vent valves, were designed to be secure against entry of water. If the tops of the columns were immersed then one side of the lower deck would be too, so this was intended to be strong enough to withstand partial immersion. The doors here were specified only as 'weathertight' but would have withstood some immersion. Other openings in these lower decks should have been kept closed as far as possible (figure 5.11). The rig might have stayed afloat much longer if these rules had been obeyed and the doors kept closed.

5.8 **The capsize**

Deprived of the support of one pontoon and column the rig slumped to one side. The top of column E was immersed and water entered it through doors that had been left open, and through the ventilators. Soon column C filled too. The weathertightness and strength of the deck gave it buoyancy at first, but many apertures had been left open and it too began to fill (figure 5.12). The rig was slowly filling, and sinking lower in the water, but more serious was the continuing loss of buoyancy on the side where column D had been lost. As the rig tilted further over, heavy items such as the drilling tower high up on the rig had no buoyancy beneath them and eventually these weights took over and capsized the rig. Calculations had been made to check that the rig would float upright in many combinations of conditions, and if the damage to the platform had been restricted to that envisaged in the regulations, such as a barge puncturing a pontoon, the requirements of the design would have ensured that the platform did not sink or capsize. However, the loss of some buoyancy would have changed the way the members of the supporting structure were loaded, and in that new condition they might have lacked the strength to cope with further damage such as the same

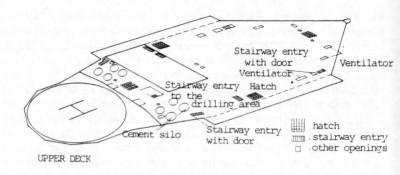

UPPER DECK

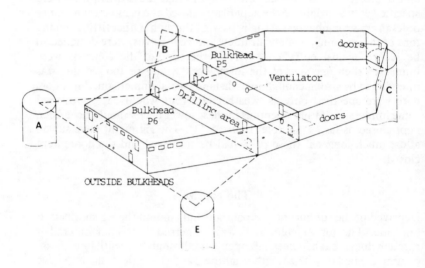

OUTSIDE BULKHEADS

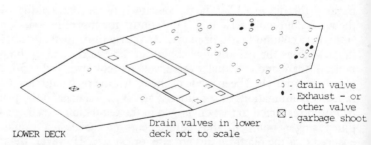

LOWER DECK

5.11   Openings in lower and upper decks, as well as outside bulkheads, in the deck house of *Alexander L. Kielland*

Intermediate deck and inner bulkhead with openings have not been shown

barge striking a bracing bar. Unlike a moving ship this could easily happen to a rig and so ensuring that a damaged rig would have enough buoyancy would serve little purpose if the rig then broke up. The inquiry commission even questioned whether the loss of some buoyancy in one of the five pontoons would so affect the balance of forces in the rig that normal loads such as the weight of drilling equipment would bring about collapse of the structure.

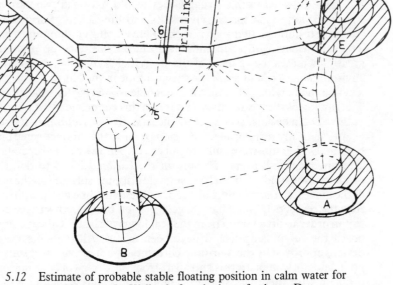

Deck volume under
still water level

Submerged area

5.12 Estimate of probable stable floating position in calm water for *Alexander L. Kielland* after the loss of column D

In their report on the *Alexander L. Kielland* the inquiry commission said that there had not been enough allowances made for the interactions between failures occurring together or in succession. Indeed, the loss of the *Alexander L. Kielland* involved to some degree all three ways in which a rig can fail: one fracture led to others, causing loss of buoyancy and partial sinking, allowing water to enter and culminating in the capsise.

5.9 Escape and survival

An alarm bell sounded briefly when the rig started to list to one side but it was hardly necessary as it was immediately clear that the rig was in serious trouble. For one thing the lights went out, for at a list of about 20° the main electrical generator switched off, and before the standby generator could come on the list had passed the limit for this equipment too. Even the batteries for emergency lighting failed because electrical connections were shortcircuited or broken by the tilting. However, the lack of light did not interfere with escape to a great extent as there was still enough daylight. What did interfere though was the sliding and falling of heavy objects such as chairs, tables and equipment in the main rooms, and the wardrobes and lockers in the sleeping quarters. These items were rarely fastened down.

Probably most of the men were able to escape from the enclosed spaces but while engaged in this struggle they would have had two particular survival aids to look for: survival suits and life-jackets. Survival suits resemble traditional flying gear, with all-enveloping clothing and a hood. The suit fastens with a zip and when put on and done up properly it greatly increases the chances of the wearer's survival in a cold and wet environment. Without a suit the survival time in the North Sea could be less than half an hour; in a suit it is possible to survive for much longer. The suit keeps the wearer afloat but it is in this connection that criticisms of them begin because they were not necessarily self-righting in the sense of automatically turning an unconscious man so that his face came out of the water. The suits were bulky to put on, the zip awkward to operate. As a result, nearly all users of a suit on the *Kielland* failed to don them properly. Some suits did not have suitable gripping surfaces on the palms of the gloves, so the handling of a rope or lifesaving line became difficult. Also the rescuers found it hard to get a grip on the smooth surface of the suit in order to lift a victim from the sea; loops for hauling the victims on board the rescue ship would have been useful. All the suits were of designs approved by the Maritime Directorate, but provision of suits was not mandatory on platforms and apart from the design of suits one other problem with them was storage. The two-dozen crew members of the *Alexander L. Kielland* had suits on board, but tended to keep them secure in their sleeping quarters as the suits were personal issue, bulky to carry around and awkward to stow in handy corners. Some of the guests on the *Kielland* had suits with them but others had left them at their work

	Number rescued	With life vest (jacket)	With survival suit	Via the sea to life rafts	Via the sea to supply ship	Via the sea to personnel basket Edda	Via lifeboat no. 3 to lifeboat no. 5	Via lifeboat no. 3 to personnel basket Edda	Via lifeboat no. 3 to life raft	Via lifeboat no. 7 to lifeboat no. 5	Via lifeboat no. 7 to personnel basket Edda	Via lifeboat no. 7 to life raft	Via lifeboat no. 7 to supply ship	Lifeboat no. 1	Lifeboat no. 5
Small cinema room	14	12		3	1		3							5	3
Temporary cinema room	17	11		4	1		7							8	1
Mess hall	14	8	1	2			2	2						4	1
Pantry	4	1													1
Cabins aft	10	6	1					1	1			1		6	1
Control room	2	2			1	1							1		
Engine room	2	1				1					1				
Sack room	1	0													1
Radio room	1	1													1
Corridor below mess hall	1	1													1
In the shower	1	0													
Cabins 3rd floor	1	1			1		1			1					1
Cabins 4th floor	7	6		1	1	1	1			2					
Cabins 5th floor	3	2			2		1								
Cabin unspecified floor	4	3	1				1								
Day room in acc. module	1	1			1										
Toilet 4th floor	1	1					1								
Provisions room aft	1	0													
Corridor by acc. module	1	1											1		
Coordinator's office	1	1												1	
Not interrogated	2						1							1	1
Total:	**89**	**59**	**4**	**12**	**6**	**3**	**18**	**3**	**2**	**1**	**1**	**1**	**2**	**26**	**14**

Table 5.1 *What happened to each individual survivor?*

stations on other platforms. According to table 5.1 (from the commission's report) only four of the survivors rescued were wearing survival suits.

The remaining item of individual survival gear was the life-jacket or life-vest, which resembled the buoyancy waistcoat familiar to air and sea travellers. There were more than twice as many life-jackets as there were people, but thirty of the eighty-nine survivors were not wearing one. It is not known how many of those who died failed to get a jacket. Like the survival suits, most of the jackets were in cabins but this still left about two hundred available on deck, although some of these were inaccessible because of the loss of column D and the adjacent structure.

Life-jackets are a traditional and convenient means of preserving life in a sea disaster but despite their long period of development they still have certain disadvantages. Some types are lacking in the same way as the survival suit, that is they do not automatically bring the wearer's face upward in the water. One other problem that was of particular importance when escaping from the rig was that when a wearer entered the sea from a height of over three metres the jacket rode up, lifted by water, and gave the wearer's neck a sharp blow. The effect became worse as the height increased so that a jump from over ten metres was very hazardous. A glance at the dimensions of a Pentagone rig like the *Alexander L. Kielland* shows that a jump from the deck would usually exceed ten metres.

Rafts

On the day the *Kielland* capsized it carried eight rafts that could be launched from davits, and twelve that were intended to be just thrown into the sea. In fact none of the rafts was properly launched or even thrown into the sea before the rig capsized, although most of the twenty are believed to have come loose and floated when the rig turned over, as thirteen were recovered after the accident. Both types could take twenty people each but only sixteen men were saved with the aid of rafts and these were probably two that had been thrown from the adjacent Edda 2/7C rig. All five men on one raft were to suffer severely from the cold until spotted by a supply boat at 20.00 hours. As the deck of the supply boat was too high for a direct jump the five took it in turns to leap towards a hanging ladder. Four of the men succeeded but one disappeared into the sea.

Lifeboats

There were seven covered lifeboats on board the rig, each nine metres long and able to take fifty persons (figure 5.13). Figure 5.14 shows the layout of the lifeboat provision in relation to other factors, but it must be remembered that column D had been lost entirely. The boats were stored

5.13 A typical lifeboat for a rig

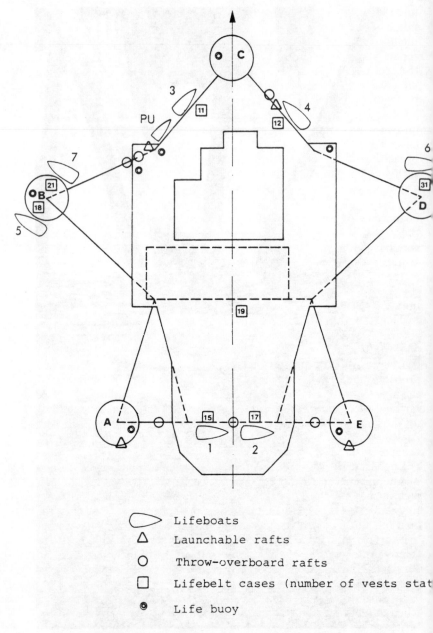

Lifeboats
Launchable rafts
Throw-overboard rafts
Lifebelt cases (number of vests stat
Life buoy

5.14 Alexander L. Kielland, extent and location of rescue equipment

under davits capable of launching lifeboats even if the rig heeled to one
side or other by 15°, or tilted fore or aft by 10°. The lifeboats were
intended to be entered whilst they lay on deck, then lowered on their
ropes. Not until the ropes that attached them to the rig had slackened as
the boat reached the sea and floated could they be unhooked. This was
intended to prevent one or both ends of a boat being released
prematurely and allowing the boat to fall, but we shall see later how these
good intentions fared. The boats were equipped with an engine, a radio
for two-way communication, and a radio beacon to enable the boat to be
located by rescue services. As regards their use in evacuating a rig the role
of each boat is examined in turn, and table 5.1 gives further details of how
each survivor escaped.

Twenty-six men entered boat no. 1. The stowage ropes were undone
and the engine started. By now the platform had heeled so far that the
boat needed to be lowered only a short distance to reach the sea, but once
there the hooks could not be released. They had to be undone
simultaneously and not while under load so in a heaving sea, with waves
six to eleven metres high, this was a problem. One man began chopping
at the front wire, trying to sever it, and finally the front hook did
somehow come free. The boat had been pounded against the rig and a
hole knocked in the boat's wheelhouse, so the rear hook could be released
by hand. Some two hours after the launching of boat no. 1 the survivors
aboard established radio contact with the Ekofisk accommodation
platform and the supply ship *Normand Skipper*. The emergency radio
beacon was also working but the radio itself worked only poorly; this was
probably due to bad earthing – no one on board knew of the fixed
earthing point one metre below the radio. Neither was the spool of
earthing wire thrown overboard as suggested in the radio instructions,
for the survivors were concerned lest the wire tangle round the propeller.
At 1.00 am two Norwegian helicopters arrived and took up the boat's
occupants.

Lifeboat no. 2 was partially submerged when the platform listed, and
no attempt was made to use it. Lifeboat no. 3 was lowered with at least
eight men. Only the aft hook could be released and the boat was swept
first under and then on top of the rig. Six or seven men escaped from the
boat and nearly all were later saved (the reason for uncertainty here is that
one survivor refused to disclose the exact manner in which he reached
safety). Lifeboat no. 4 was lowered but crushed, and there were no
survivors. Judging from the wreckage the ropes were probably never
released.

Lifeboat no. 5 was situated at column B, to which most men had fled
when the *Alexander L. Kielland* listed. Only fourteen men entered the
boat, as others were too fearful that it would be crushed during lowering
but in any case it could not have been lowered as to do so would have

dropped it onto a crossbrace of the platform. All that those aboard could do was to loosen the ropes, close the hatches and hope. When the platform capsized, the boat entered the water upside down, but fortunately the hooks released and the boat drifted away, though it was taking in water through submerged windows of the wheelhouse. Survivors in the water swam to this boat and the joint efforts of men inside and outside the boat righted it. Nineteen men were taken on board from the water, but not without problems as the hatches proved rather small for large people in bulky life-jackets. The engine was started, but smoke and oil came out so it was stopped again: perhaps being inverted had done it little good. The emergency radio beacon was switched on and at 7.30 pm the supply ship *Normand Skipper* found the boat, let down a net to it and twelve men clambered up. Meanwhile the lifeboat was being thrown against the ship and liable to be smashed so they stood off from each other. Only at 2.00 am was the radio persuaded to work; like the engine, water had probably damaged it when the boat was upside down. Helicopters finally rescued the remaining men between 2.00 am and 4.00 am.

Lifeboat no. 6 was on column D and so was lost when the column came off. Lifeboat no. 7 was near to column B and as such was accessible to the many men nearby. The tilting of the platform put the davit ropes under great strain and one of the hooks was twisted, but the boat was lowered, with the engine running. However, on reaching the water it became submerged and rose to the surface inverted. In the boat were some half a dozen men, only three or perhaps four of whom escaped to safety through the side hatches. One man had to leave his life-jacket behind in order to get out.

Edda 2/7C

Edda 2/7C was a production platform alongside which the *Alexander L. Kielland* had been positioned for nine months before the accident. In good weather the accommodation rig was moved to within 20–25 metres of the *Edda* 2/7C to enable a gangway to be strung between them, making it much easier for men to pass to and fro. On the day of the accident the worsening weather led to the gangway being hoisted on board the *Alexander L. Kielland*, which then winched itself away on its mooring ropes to a safer distance. The life saving equipment aboard the *Edda* was intended only for the emergency escape of its own personnel but, as the stricken rig was so close, good use was made of the equipment on this occasion. Six inflatable rafts were lowered and five men reached one of them from which they were picked up by a supply boat.

The *Edda* rig's personnel basket was provided to cater for emergencies in day-to-day operation of the rig and could be attached to the hook of one of the *Edda*'s two cranes. The basket was lowered four times and rescued seven men, but weather conditions and the distance between the rigs prevented further rescues by this method as the wind and tide took those men who were in or on the water ever further away from the *Edda*.

The peril was not over yet, even for those men who believed themselves safe on the *Edda*; the capsized *Kielland* could have swung into it and so all but a volunteer fourteen-man emergency crew were evacuated from the *Edda* by helicopter. Fortunately no such collision occurred; the two sections of the *Alexander L. Kielland* drifted harmlessly away, leaving the *Edda* untouched.

Helicopters

Three main groups of helicopters were available to help in a rescue such as this. The first consisted of helicopters stationed in the oil field. They were able to be on the scene quickly but at the time of the disaster had not been equipped with the special apparatus needed for the rescue duties they now faced. In addition their crews did not have the training and experience for rescue work so although a small helicopter stationed on the field reached the platform before it capsized, it was unable to effect any rescue. Landing on the stricken rig was out of the question even before it capsized, because of the poor weather and the tilt of the rig.

The second group comprised helicopters based on shore and used for transport. One such machine set out at 8.00 pm. It had been equipped with lifting gear for rescue but unfortunately the crew members had received no training in its use. In the event it lifted three men from a lifeboat by the use of a basket, thus avoiding the need to send down a rescue man.

Poor visibility, darkness and high winds made flying difficult for all the helicopters. Normally even the third group, land based rescue helicopters, could not fly unless visibility was better than 800 metres. A Royal Air Force Sea King helicopter lowered its rescue man to a rubber raft and nine men were lifted off but after a similar Norwegian helicopter had rescued thirteen men from a lifeboat it had to interrupt its activities because the lifting wire became stuck. Another Norwegian Sea King had lifted only two men from among the seventeen in a lifeboat when the lifting wire snagged on the hatch of the boat, the wire broke and the hook was lost. A replacement hook carried on the helicopter allowed the lifeboat to be cleared eventually. In all, helicopters played a part in the rescue of fifty-six men.

Standby and supply vessels

As part of the emergency preparedness plan there were ships known as standby vessels stationed on the North Sea fields; normally a ship was to be stationed within a radius of one nautical mile of each exploration or drilling rig. However the regulations governing the operation of a

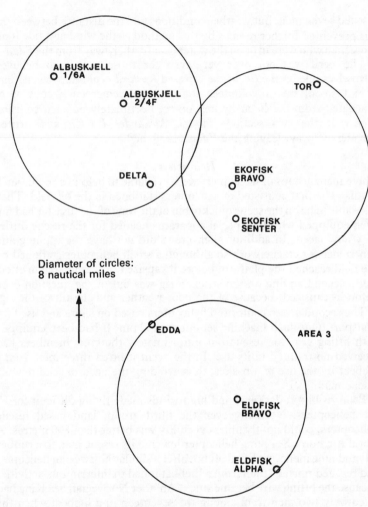

5.15   Grouping of rigs for standby vessel coverage

production or accommodation rig did not specify a distance, but merely stated that the vessel should be near enough to fulfil its duties.

One such duty was to rescue persons in the water, and on the basis that half an hour is the maximum time a person can survive in the North Sea, the vessel at the Ekofisk field was supposed to be positioned so that it would be able to reach any rig of that field in less than twenty-five minutes. To accomplish this the standby was organised as follows. Three circles were drawn up, eight nautical miles in diameter, to include all nine rig sites (figure 5.15). One standby vessel was to be located at the centre of each circle, so that any rig could be reached in twenty-five minutes, given good weather.

The locations for the standby ships were worked out by the operating company's transport department in conjunction with their safety department. The transport department would discuss the chartering and arrangement of a standby vessel with the shipping yard, and inform the traffic co-ordinator for the field when a relief was on its way out. The co-ordinator would then tell the captain where he should station his vessel and which rigs he was covering. The motor ship *Silver Pit* was assigned to a particular circle that included *Edda*, its accommodation neighbour the *Kielland* and the Eldfisk rigs *Alpha* and *Bravo*. The transport manager had told the shipping chandler that the *Silver Pit* was to be in area 3, midway between *Edda* 2/7C and Eldfisk *Alpha*, and the duty captain of the *Silver Pit* told the inquiry commission that normally the location for the standby vessel was given through the shipping company, the shipping chandler or the captain. Once on the field a change of position was to be given or authorised only by the safety officer on the platform covered; if there was more than one then the safety officers on those platforms would have to agree on any change.

For several months the *Silver Pit* had been stationed near the Eldfisk *Bravo* and the captain who took over the vessel early in March said he understood that it was covering only that rig and not the others in area 3. Hence it is no surprise that the *Silver Pit* was one mile southeast of the Eldfisk *Bravo*, six miles away from the *Edda*. In the event the vessel did well to arrive between 7.15 pm and 7.30 pm. It made radio contact with a lifeboat but failed to find it. Acting on orders it was sent to investigate a light towards Albuskjell but found nothing. No survivors were picked up or sighted, nor even any bodies; only wreckage, life-jackets and empty rafts.

The safety officer on *Edda* knew the name of the standby vessel for area 3, the *Silver Pit*, but most other people believed that the standby for the *Alexander L. Kielland* was the *Normand Skipper*. Actually this was only a supply boat which also did duty as an anchor handling boat for the *Kielland*, but in any case it was neither fitted out nor certificated for standby. Fortunately, the owners had equipped this and another of their ships with entry nets that could be hung from each side, and those on the *Normand Skipper* did sterling service on the night of the disaster as the ship picked up fourteen of the twenty-six survivors rescued by supply vessels.

Wireless communications

Apart from problems with the radio sets in the lifeboats there were few snags in wireless communications. At 6.33 pm the radio operator on the

Alexander L. Kielland broadcast a 'Mayday' emergency message. Directly after this the radio stations and Main Rescue Centre ashore were aware of the accident and were taking action. By 6.42 pm all ships and helicopters in the area had been instructed to go to the scene.

In total, some seventy-one civilian vessels and nine naval ships (from four countries) were involved in the rescue, as were nineteen helicopters, and one Norwegian and six British reconnaissance aircraft. Initially, the surface fleet concerned in the rescue was marshalled by the Ekofisk Centre ship co-ordinator, while the Ekofisk Hotel helicopter co-ordinator did the same for air traffic. Later a Dutch destroyer and a British Nimrod reconnaissance aircraft took over these duties. To avoid confusion on Ekofisk all communications from there to the Main Rescue Centre ashore went through the Phillips base at Tananger, via a satellite link. With hindsight the staff of the rescue centre felt this to have been too slow a procedure, one result of which was a lack of knowledge of the true extent of the disaster and an inability on their part to know how many resources to allocate.

Rogaland hospital

This hospital acted as the central receiver of casualties. Although well prepared in many respects, its emergency plan showed a need for revision after the disaster, as it had not allowed for an emergency of long duration, with the result that arrangements for relief and replacement of staff were inadequate. The alarm procedure needed improving and an information office would have been useful, together with more extensive plans for working away from the hospital. Despite a certain lack of preparedness in this last respect, a useful medical station had been set up at Sola Airport and an advance team sent out to the Ekofisk accommodation rig.

5.10 The comments of the commission

Because of the international features of North Sea work the inquiry commission arranged for an English translation of the summary of their report to be included in the Norwegian language version. Naturally the commission gave its opinion that the safety level for floating rigs could and should be improved. In addition to the specific points mentioned already in this account the commission recommended adoption of a general approach that would bring together the consideration of rig type, function, design, manufacture, operation, emergency handling etc. The possibility of interaction of hazards was stressed, and the need to make allowances for human actions and omissions.

In terms of the systems approach that later chapters of this book will stress, not only must the safety of individual parts of a scheme be considered, but the way a failure in one part may have unexpected effects on another needs taking into account. This applies to everything from rig bracing bars and columns on a rig to preparedness for quick response and longer term emergency coverage in hospitals ashore. Complications arise when rig safety measures such as weathertightness and access to escape routes conflict. Attention to regulations may grow lax with time and this relaxation of compliance can come at a time of danger when structures such as rigs have aged and changed their use. The responsibility for foresight here lies with the authorities because the firm that first commissions a rig is likely to resist paying for excess safety that will only be used, if at all, by a later operator.

The story of the *Alexander L. Kielland* reminds us that even with the best laid preparations the unexpected and the unconsidered will occur, and in the event of upsets to carefully laid plans it is the ability of people to improvise, and the provision of an opportunity for them to do so by the incorporation of margins and second lines of defence in the original scheme that can mitigate a major disaster.

6

Buses in South Yorkshire

This case study is concerned with the history of a policy of low bus fares in South Yorkshire, and the arguments for and against it. The account is based on published material listed in the bibliography; the local information was compiled by Barbara Morris of Sheffield City Polytechnic.

6.1 The issue

As Sheffield's evening newspaper *The Star* reported on 8 May 1979, low bus fares in South Yorkshire have caused fiercer argument than perhaps any other local issue. It is, however, not only a subject which generates a great deal of controversy amongst the local residents and businessmen, it has also, at various times, set the county council at odds with local city councils and Labour and Conservative governments. Each group is seeking to exercise control over the situation and seeking to justify this intervention by claiming that it is for the good of the community.

Public transport in an urban area is a complicated matter and the media can be accused of over-simplification in the way they have presented the story to the public. As Eric Barr put it in the South Yorkshire morning newspaper *The Morning Telegraph* on 22 October 1974– 'Push up fares and passengers stop travelling. Give hefty handouts to subsidise bus costs and the rates go up to pay for them'. The issue is basically whether South Yorkshire Metropolitan County Council should subsidise bus costs from the rates, even though this does result in what are probably the cheapest bus fares in the country and the highest number of passenger trips per head of population outside London, where the figures are, of course, inflated by commuters from outside the area and by tourists.

6.2 The public transport scene

Before looking in detail at the situation in South Yorkshire as a specific case it is necessary to draw a more general picture and explain some of the changes that have taken place in transport since 1950. The major and most obvious factor has been the growth in the numbers of lorries and cars on the roads. Personal travel doubled between 1953 and 1971 and goods transport increased by a half, nearly all in lorries. The increased numbers of cars and lorries on the roads have caused congestion which has delayed bus services and made routes more expensive to operate. There are other interactions too. In its analysis of the transport problems of the early 1970s the Independent Commission on Transport's report, 'Changing directions', depicted the dynamics of personal travel in the form shown in figure 6.1. Having been conceived in the mid-1970s rather than the early 1980s, the mechanism is shown as driven by rising incomes, but these interactive loops can be entered anywhere. Clearly the actual situation is even more complex than that depicted but the diagram suffices to show the basic links between bus and car, in town or country.

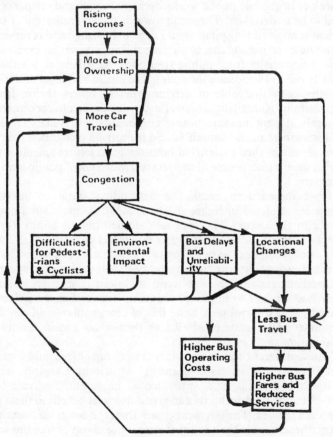

6.1 Cause and effect in passenger travel by road

Bus fares trebled between 1953 and 1971 but the overall expenditure of the average person (on everything) only doubled, and the cost of buying and running a car went up by only fifty per cent. In a survey of car users in London in 1970, 29 per cent said that London Transport services had deteriorated in the previous year, the most common complaint being bad time-keeping by buses. Traffic congestion is the most obvious cause of this but there are other influences such as staff shortages. Here there are further interactions, for the financial difficulties of operators led to low wages and job insecurity, making it harder to find staff. Traffic congestion made the job disagreeable and embittered the relations between staff and passengers. This drove passengers away and created more problems for the operators.

If public transport were to be sacrificed and the car allowed to reign supreme, large-scale public works by way of roads and car parks would need to be undertaken. The trend towards the centralisation of services such as schools and hospitals would need to be halted and reversed. This would be an enormous charge on the public purse, so that even car users benefit financially from public transport, regardless of whether they actually use it. In addition the young, the infirm and some of the elderly are physically incapable of driving whereas others shrink from the responsibility it entails or cannot afford a car. Yet again, car ownership in a household is not the same thing as a car being freely available at all times to all members of the household. So it must be recognised that where there are established patterns of housing, jobs, leisure amenities and so on, between which people need to travel, provision of public transport is necessary.

If we intended to break the descending spiral of interlocking influences depicted in figure 6.1 how could we maintain a good bus service in the towns? The approach studied here is South Yorkshire County Council's ideas for cheap or free travel on buses, with the costs subsidised from the rates or by central government. The hoped-for effect of reducing or abolishing fares would be to halt the increase in car usage and perhaps even reverse the trend. Reduced congestion would then allow bus services to improve, reducing still further the incentive to travel by car. If travel were to be free of charge this would enable staff economies to be made on the buses themselves and in the transport organisation's offices.

A quite different argument in favour of cheap or free public transport would reason that it was a means of redistributing wealth. If public transport is seen as being provided as an essential service for the have-nots, the local authority can give a financial benefit to these people by reducing fares. The payment comes from the better off, but they too can get benefit from their indirect support of cheap or free bus services merely by using the buses more often. So in addition to arguments based on transport engineering and social economics, cheap or free travel can be seen as a way of bringing people from different social classes together. These arguments have swayed the councillors of local authorities and are suitable (with the right presentation) for putting to an electorate. However, a careful examination of the detailed effects of cheap or free public transport shows that there are also some undesirable outcomes that can ensue, and that the effects might not be as great, or in the same direction as was intended.

For nearly all car travellers, the significant differences between car and bus are speed, walking distance, waiting time and predictability, so making bus travel free would not, of itself, make bus travel attractive. When fares are reduced, the first travellers to transfer from their cars to public transport would be those people in low income groups who at present see a car as the most economical form of transport. The remaining car users would be able to increase the speed of their journeys and as these higher income groups often value their time savings highly they would be even less likely to use the bus, and social mixing would not occur.

Lastly, if cheap or free fares bring an influx of extra passengers at peak hours this would put up costs because extra vehicles and staff would be needed. Already, bus companies complain that the severe imbalance between peak and off-peak means that staff must be offered higher rates to work split shifts, or be paid while on duty but idle between peaks. The peak hours for bus usage are also those of the worst road congestion so most passengers see their journeys at their worst. Moreover these long-suffering commuters are likely to be the most discriminating passengers of the day, and being wage earners are more than likely to be the main arbiters of car purchase.

6.3 Bus subsidies

Before the 1968 Transport Act was passed, buses were expected to be run on commercial lines, unsubsidised by the state. Some municipal systems received small indirect subsidies from the rates but other undertakings actually made a contribution to the rates; this leaves out of account of course the provision and upkeep of roads, which represents an enormous subsidy for buses when compared with tracked transport such as trains or trams. In 1965 the urban section of the bus industry almost broke even, with a capital debt of only £12 million upon which to pay interest. By 1970 there was a revenue deficit of £2 million on a turnover of £130 million and the capital debt had risen to £21 million, requiring a further £2 million to service it. With a total deficit of £4 million it was clear that the industry needed bailing out.

The 1968 Transport Act decreed that rural bus services in need of support could receive grants from local authorities, who would then be reimbursed by central government for half of this expenditure. This was not the case for urban services. A municipality could subsidise its own services from the rates but would receive no central grant. The Act did, however, provide for central grants to be paid on capital expenditure. This was done because local authorities already received payment for capital works on roads, and so might have invested in road improvements alone (mainly to the benefit of car users) rather than in bus equipment so a bus grant was a gesture in favour of public transport. The lack of subsidy for the operation of buses as distinct from the purchase of new ones was partly the usual slowness of reaction of bureaucracy to the fast gathering troubles of the buses; bus services were running down quietly; but it was also a relic of traditional thinking at the government's Treasury Office. There it was felt preferable to subsidise the once and for all purchase of a new bus rather than the cost of running it. Forecasts of capital expenditure can be made to appear accurate and reliable; a promise to pay costs could be an open ended commitment that if granted for one year would be difficult and unfair to withdraw for the next. In this, the executive level of central government also sought to protect local authorities from the vagaries of political ebb and flow.

The effect of the introduction of this capital subsidy was a rush to buy new buses, to the benefit of their builders, but even the most modern of buses is unable to attract many car users; the comfort and convenience of a car is not easily reproduced in a bus and people tend to compare the better journeys they have made by car with the worst they experienced on a bus. Also there were disappointments over the poor mechanical reliability of some new bus equipment which led to breakdowns and interrupted services. On the road, the new buses still had to face traffic congestion, so the operators sought to influence their local authorities to use the promised central grant reimbursement to assist bus operations by making bus-only lanes and bus priority measures on busy roads. Few succeeded, but later Acts of Parliament made their task easier by bringing transport, highways and planning together under the umbrella of local government. They were helped by the Local Government Act of 1972, in force with effect from the financial year 1975/6, which gave county councils the power to spend the money they raised from rates, and money supplied by central government for transport purposes, in whatever way seemed to them to be most helpful. Bringing together the planning, legal and financial arrangements made a comprehensive approach possible. Some of the efforts made by one county council, South Yorkshire, form the subject of the remainder of this study.

6.4 **South Yorkshire**

One of the new metropolitan counties created under the 1972 Local Government Act was called South Yorkshire. This new county covers an area of about 1,600 sq. km, and includes the areas previously administered by the county borough councils of Sheffield, Barnsley, Doncaster and Rotherham, part of the former West Riding of Yorkshire, and small areas which were formerly part of Nottinghamshire. The population was about 1.3 million at the time, with ninety per cent living in urban areas.

The region's development was based upon rich coal seams and iron ore deposits lying beneath the surface. During the industrial revolution the area developed rapidly; the use of coal and coke in steel manufacture spearheaded industrial development along the Don valley to the south, and to the north around Barnsley and along the Dearne valley. Communities began to develop around the new industries but they evolved independently and established individual characteristics. The area reflects its history: coal mining, metal manufacture and engineering industries are still the major employers. In recent years this dependence on a narrow and traditional industrial base became a major cause for concern so in recognition of the unemployment and economic problems of the county it was declared an Intermediate Area in 1972, attracting government incentives for industrialists to invest there. The situation has changed very little since then. Only Sheffield has a fairly wide range of job opportunities and even in that city there is a heavy dependence upon the steel industry.

In addition to the social and economic problems associated with major dependence on traditional heavy industry, the new county also had environmental problems arising from the same source. Air and water pollution was rife, despite the determined efforts of Sheffield in particular (which is now one of the cleanest cities in Europe in terms of the level of air pollution) and there was a legacy of derelict land, old decaying buildings, substandard housing and spoil tips left by the coal mining industry. However, the county is one of great contrasts. Despite the domination by heavy industry in the main urban centres, and the concentration of population in those areas, South Yorkshire also has much rich agricultural land and dramatic upland scenery. Over half of the area is rural, with the landscape varying from the high gritstone moors of the Pennines in the west to the flat lands east of Doncaster. As well as supporting a small but healthy tourist trade and a substantial agricultural industry, the rural areas provide major supplies of minerals such as limestone, sand and gravel.

6.5 **Transport legislation**

Because of the very individual and independent nature of the four major urban conurbations in what was later to become South Yorkshire, each had developed its own public road transport system and mass public road transport in the county can be traced back to these. Transport legislation in the 1930s tended to be restrictive and protective but not with the aim of co-ordinating transport. Only in London was a single authority responsible overall for transport in a large area. The 1947 Transport Act aimed at integration by nationalisation. The Act of 1953 effected partial denationalisation and restored competition as the aim, and a 1962 Act decentralised and spurred commercial attitudes in transport. In 1968 the Labour government's Transport Act required that all transport services should be related to their costs although some should be grant aided on social grounds. Historians of transport such as Barker and Savage point out that in that period transport suffered from too much surgery based on inadequate diagnosis. Organisation was seen as 'the problem', and better organisation was regarded as the road to a solution. Actually there was a lack of understanding of the way economic changes were reshaping the demand for transport and the relative costs of providing its essential elements.

The 1968 Transport Act introduced the long awaited concept of Passenger Transport Areas, within which Passenger Transport Authorities (PTAs) and Passenger Transport Executives (PTEs) would be established. Each authority was to be responsible for setting the general policy to be followed by the executive, which in turn was to be responsible for securing or promoting a passenger transport system. Under the terms of the Act the system was to be properly integrated and efficient, and meet the needs of the area, having due regard to town planning, traffic and parking policies, and to economy and safety in operation. The minister responsible for transport was to establish Passenger Transport Areas where he considered it appropriate, and at the time four such areas were designated. South Yorkshire was not amongst the first, which were Merseyside, West Midlands, Tyneside and South East Lancashire and North East Cheshire. Maybe more areas would have been set up but substantial reorganisation of local government was in the air. This crystallised as the 1972 Act which reorganised local government in England and Wales, introducing the new metropolitan and non-metropolitan counties. These arrangements have attracted criticism on many grounds but their role here is that the Act now made each metropolitan county a Passenger Transport Area, and the county councils became Passenger Transport Authorities under the terms of the Transport Act 1968. Integration of transport, highways, planning and so on was now a possibility. South Yorkshire became not only a metropolitan county but also a Passenger Transport Area. The South Yorkshire Passenger Transport Executive (SYPTE) was set up on 1 January 1974 and in April of that year SYPTE and the South Yorkshire County Council as the PTA assumed their new responsibilities.

Amongst its many tasks, including that of amalgamation of the former authorities, the newly elected council needed to formulate policy for the PTE. Following the traditions of the area, the council was Labour-dominated and one of the election pledges of the Labour candidates was to work towards a local bus system that provided free travel. This was despite the fact that surveys carried out as part of a land use transportation study going on at the time in Sheffield and Rotherham showed that free travel was well down the public's list of transport priorities.

6.6   Transport policy statements

Under the terms of the 1968 Transport Act the new PTA was required to publish a statement jointly prepared by the PTA and the PTE setting out the policies they intended to follow and the action they proposed to take to meet the requirements of the Act; this was done in November 1975. The Act also required the PTE to make public, with the approval of the county council, a plan describing its proposals for achieving full integration of passenger transport. The PTE published its development plan in November 1978. Each year, government made a block allocation of funds known as the Transport Supplementary Grant to each county council and in making this allocation account was taken of the progress the council had made towards formulating and implementing appropriate transport policies for its area. County councils were required to submit annual statements of their transport policies together with costed programmes for implementing them. These statements gave detailed plans for the forthcoming year and described the long-term strategy and five year expenditure programme. This annual statement is known as the Transport Policies and Programme (TPP) and it was devised for control of the implementation of long-term plans.

In summary, the policy of the South Yorkshire County Council and the PTE as described in these documents was as follows:

Overall goal

To provide a convenient and safe transport system, having regard to economic, environmental and social considerations and to the inter-dependence of transport planning and land use planning. As far as public transport was concerned there was a need to provide all members of the community with access to an adequate range of opportunities for work, shopping and leisure activities.

Short- and medium-term policies

To secure a fully integrated public passenger transport system for the county, to improve the standards of service available to the public, to reduce private vehicular traffic in the two centres and to improve the environment generally, and to continue to improve and rationalise the already existing concessionary fares for the elderly and the young.

PTE policies

The Passenger Transport Executive has a statutory duty to make sure that as far as is practicable revenue covers costs, and to make provision for the renewal of its assets. This duty, together with its main function of securing or promoting 'the provision of a properly integrated and efficient system of public passenger transport to meet the needs of the area with due regard to town planning and traffic and parking policies, and to economy and safety of operation' (as defined by the Transport Act 1968) underly the policies of the PTE.

Development Plan

In this plan the PTE said it believed that the aims of the county council would help to promote an efficient integrated public transport system. The plan went on to summarise the policies it was following in order to achieve its objectives. These were to:

(a) recognise the need for economy;
(b) ensure that if it were necessary to keep options open this would not prevent effective action;
(c) consider the possible introduction of reserved-right-of-way systems as well as the development of bus services and to encourage the development of new forms of public transport and research into improving existing forms;
(d) support the county council's policy of giving traffic priority to buses where this would help to make public transport more attractive;
(e) ensure that the PTE development plan and the county structure plan (see later) were not in conflict;
(f) draw on the results of the various transport studies (see later);
(g) try to acquire ownership of other bus undertakings in South Yorkshire since this was considered the only way in which the PTE could control services effectively;
(h) review existing bus services with a view to improvement, rationalisation and development;
(i) seek to improve and extend facilities for passengers waiting for or changing buses;
(j) provide the best possible standards of comfort, convenience and reliability for passengers;

(k) operate bus private hire and other activities so as to provide additional net revenue;

(l) use local negotiations to formulate staff agreements on pay and conditions of service so as to match manpower resources with operational requirements, subject to any government pay policy in force at the time.

As will be seen from this summary, although the policy statements made in the period 1975–8 were fairly comprehensive they made no reference to free travel or even a low bus fares policy– an omission which may seem strange given the subject of this case study. In fact, the policy documents referred merely to the county council's fares policy, itself described elsewhere in the joint policy statement as having the ultimate aim of the provision of free public transport for all. Whilst this declaration had a major impact on the contents of the policy statements, nowhere was any reference made to it in the formal definitions of policy. The reasons for this can only be surmised but it seems likely that the omission was deliberate and arose from one or both of two factors. The first is that although the documents did make reference to very long-term policies, they were nevertheless statements of short to medium-term policy so full statements of very long-term policy could be viewed as inappropriate. The second is the fact that whilst the county council (as PTA) and the PTE were formulating transport plans, the county council was also formulating policy for the new county, to be expressed as its structure plan. For this the council was required to engage in publicity, consultation and participation exercises. Transport was one of the issues dealt with in the structure plan and although the published draft contained a clear policy statement about cheap fares this was withdrawn after public comment on the draft and replaced by an explanation of the council's position of fares containment, but only in the text accompanying the final policy statement.

It should be recognised that fares policy was only a part of transport policy in South Yorkshire and that planning and providing transport was seen by the county council not as an objective in itself but as a means to other economic, social and environmental ends. Thus cheap fares were just one element in a complex interlocking network of policies and arrangements to provide transport, recreation, shopping, employment, housing and a vast range of other services, some of which were directly under the control of the county council and some of which it could only affect indirectly. To this extent it is perhaps unrealistic to attempt to look at cheap fares as an issue in isolation. Nevertheless, given the importance attached to it in the local area and the controversy it has generated both locally and nationally, the remainder of this study will concentrate upon the cheap fares issue in its own right, focusing on the problems involved in attempting to implement an election promise which although it was apparently given the blessing of the local electorate has provoked much opposition.

6.7 Public transport in South Yorkshire

The concept of Passenger Transport Executives was introduced in recognition of the fragmented ownership, control and planning of public passenger transport which often occurred in major urban areas where public transport and the need for it extended beyond existing local government boundaries, and where a variety of agencies were concerned with its provision. This was evident in South Yorkshire. The prime task of the SYPTE when it came into being in April 1974 was to weld together the public passenger transport services provided by the several different agencies using these transport links and to provide a properly integrated and efficient system. Under the terms of section 20 of the 1968 Transport Act the PTE had a duty to examine and keep under permanent review all local railway lines as part of this integrated system but its major responsibility was for bus operations. Each of the four major urban areas had developed its own public road transport system. In addition to these systems, many small private operators existed with their own policies and operating conditions. Municipal influence was widespread and important but, whilst there was some joint operation and a high degree of timetable co-ordination, each of the municipal enterprises also had its own policies in respect of fares, standards of service, wages and staff conditions.

When the PTE came into being, the county had an extensive network of bus services in both urban and rural areas. These were provided by the corporations of Sheffield, Rotherham and Doncaster, enterprises which were then vested in the PTE to form the basis of its direct bus operations, and by the Yorkshire Traction Company, a subsidiary of the National Bus Company (NBC) in Barnsley. A further seven NBC subsidiaries provided services into the area and sixteen independent operators had services operating either wholly or only partially within the county. The mileage run in the county was split amongst the three groups as follows:

Passenger Transport Executive	65 per cent
(the former municipal enterprises)	
NBC subsidiaries	29 per cent
Independent operators	6 per cent

Fares throughout the county varied considerably, from the independent operators who needed to make a profit, to the municipal enterprises where a measure of fares containment was already being practised and a variety of concessionary fare schemes existed. The municipal enterprises in Sheffield and Doncaster had not increased fares since 1971, whilst in Rotherham fares had been increased in 1973. In Doncaster and Rotherham the bus operations were making profits but in Sheffield the principle of rate support to subsidise losses had already been established by the city council's Labour group. A grant of £240,000 had been made from the rates to write off a loss made in 1971, and in 1972 a grant of similar size was made to support free fares for the elderly.

In December 1973 the new South Yorkshire County Council pledged financial support from the rates to peg municipal bus fares, and the sum of £2.5 million was earmarked for this purpose; in the event this sum had to be increased to £3.5 million to meet additional losses brought about by the oil crisis. In the same month Councillor Roy Thwaites, chairman of Sheffield Transport Committee and chairman designate of the Passenger Transport Authority, said that despite the fuel crisis and cutbacks in public spending, free bus travel in South Yorkshire was only as far away as the politicians wanted it to be.

This then was the situation when the PTE came into being; it was faced with the need to develop strategies and operating plans in order to achieve the objective of an integrated passenger transport system, but in setting about this, it had to deal with a number of other agencies. It had to work with the National Bus Company to agree the services to be provided, and if necessary to reorganise existing services; it also had to co-operate with British Rail. Apart from these agencies which were involved directly with local services the PTE also had to establish links and liaise with the operators providing services across the county boundaries – since transport pays little attention to political divisions – and with the agencies affecting these operations. Foremost amongst these were the West Yorkshire PTE and other direct operators, but the SYPTE also had to liaise with Derbyshire County Council, since the southernmost part of its direct operations included part of Derbyshire, and with the Peak Park Planning Board which was the planning authority for part of the western side of the county. It also had to submit its policies to central government through the county council. By far the greatest influence on its planning however was South Yorkshire County Council itself, which at that time was carrying out its own planning exercise.

The PTE's plans obviously had to be compatible with those of the county council and in order to achieve this the county council and the PTE set up a Joint Transportation and Planning Unit in which members of the permanent staff of the county authority and members of the PTE worked together, so that the PTE was involved in all aspects of council transportation planning. In addition, arrangements were made for the PTE to work with the elected members of the county council and, because of the need for local planning and day-to-day direct operations, with the four metropolitan district councils in Barnsley, Rotherham, Doncaster and Sheffield. The county council set up a Passenger Transport Committee and a Planning and Transportation Joint Sub-Committee on which elected council members served so the PTE had a close relationship with these bodies. Overall authority, however, was vested in the county council as Passenger Transport Authority and all plans had to be approved by this body as well as being acceptable to the council in its various other roles in the local government, such as planning and development authority.

6.8 Structure planning in South Yorkshire

As well as the problems associated with the changes in local government introduced by the Local Government Act (1972), the new council had to cope with a new planning mechanism. That which had been set up by the Town and Country Planning Act (1947) was considered to be slow, inflexible and insensitive to both social and economic influences and to the views of the general public. Thus, in 1965, a new national system was proposed which revolved around strategic structure plans. These were to be wide ranging in respect of economic, social and physical planning, rapid in that only the strategic elements would require government approval, flexible because the structural elements would be subject to continuous monitoring and review, and open since there would be greater opportunity for public participation. At a lower level there would be detailed local plans. The principle embodied in these proposals was adopted in the Town and Country Planning Act (1971), which introduced new planning procedures requiring the local planning authority to carry out (amongst other things) a survey of its area, examine the matters which might affect its development or the planning of its development and produce a written statement of its development policy. This structure plan should:

(a) interpret national and regional policies;
(b) establish aims, policies and general proposals;
(c) provide the framework for local plans;
(d) indicate action areas;
(e) provide guidance for development control;
(f) provide a basis for co-ordinating the decisions of a wide range of agencies;
(g) bring the main planning issues and decisions before the Minister of the Environment and the public.

The new two-tier structure of local government (county and district councils) and the changes resulting from South Yorkshire being designated a Passenger Transport Area meant that whilst the function of the structure plan was unchanged some adjustments were needed to cater for new responsibilities and there was some overlap of responsibility. This in turn meant that a number of participants other than the county council had to be involved in preparing the plan.

The time-scale chosen for the plan was a ten-year period up to 1986 and the planning process would be carried out in three phases as follows:

1. Phase 1: This phase was concerned with identifying the key issues to be dealt with in the plan and it had three stages:
   (a) *Determination of problems, satisfactions and opportunities in South Yorkshire* This involved working parties of planning staff who provided a professional view and an extensive programme of public participation and consultation to obtain the views of the electorate and other interested agencies.
   (b) *Definition of key issues from (a) above* This stage involved working parties from within the County Planning Department who defined and selected the key issues – clusters of problems needing policy decisions – for the structure plan. A 'Key issues document' was then approved by the county council as a basis for formal consultation with district councils and other agencies.
   (c) *Determination of the approach to be used in developing, recommending and selecting policies and proposals* This stage provided the basis for work in phase 2.
2. Phase 2: This phase encompassed the work needed to produce a draft structure plan, and it had four stages:
   (a) definition of policy options for each issue;
   (b) detailed development of feasible policies;
   (c) assembly of developed policies into alternative strategies;
   (d) selection of preferred strategy.
This phase was essentially a joint exercise between the permanent staff who had been involved in phase 1 and the elected councillors.
3. Phase 3: The final phase was concerned with reaction to the draft plan and, as in phase 1, consultation and participation were involved. The work took place in three stages:
   (a) *Consultation on the draft plan* This stage included statutory public participation which was achieved through public meetings, exhibitions, films, group discussions with selected members of the community, and consultation with the district councils, neighbouring planning authorities and other agencies affected by the plan. During this stage as well the draft was presented to members of the government departments in an attempt to resolve any major problems prior to formal submission to the final plan.
   (b) *Amendment to the draft plan* Following the consultation on the draft the council made any amendments they thought necessary.

(c) *Determination of priorities* The final stage in the planning process was the establishment by the council and its agencies of priorities for action in the early years of the plan.

6.9 Transport planning

Prior to the start of the structure planning process and during its early stages a considerable amount of data on transport matters in South Yorkshire was collected by three land use transportation studies centred on Barnsley, Doncaster and Sheffield/Rotherham. This was used in developing the structure plan as well as the measures described above. In addition a computer-based model of transport characteristics of the county – the South Yorkshire County Transport Analysis System (SYCTAS) – was designed to help analyse the data.

During Phase 1 the data collected indicated that as far as public transport was concerned the frequency and coverage of services was generally satisfactory but that the following problems could be identified:

1. Traffic congestion on the approaches to Sheffield and Doncaster affected bus speeds and reliability;
2. There was an anticipated increase in peak hour demand for public transport to the centres of Sheffield and Doncaster;
3. Within the urban areas there was some difficulty in making journeys by public transport in orbital directions;
4. Levels of service varied throughout the county with services in some rural areas being somewhat deficient;
5. Public opinion appeared to be highly sensitive to fare levels;
6. Public transport operating costs were expected to increase in real terms;
7. The location of rail lines limited the scope for making greater use of rail for local passenger transport.

The widespread environmental problems associated with traffic passing through residential and shopping areas also had an impact upon the planning of public transport.

From an analysis of these problems and an examination of existing policies, together with the need to comply with the Transport Act (1968), transport was defined as a key issue for the structure plan. The question to be answered was defined thus: 'What level, pattern and type of transport provision will best serve future population distribution and employment in South Yorkshire?'

During the second phase, eight policy options were developed for this issue. These were as follows:

1. Option 1 entailed free travel by public transport within South

Yorkshire with operating costs being met entirely from public funds. There was little scope envisaged for investment.

2. Option 2 involved a continuation of 1975 levels of revenue support and concessionary fare payments which could be accommodated within 1975 levels of transport finance whilst leaving some finance available for investment.
3. Option 3 reduced the general revenue support from 1975 levels but extended concessionary fare arrangements. Some investment in highway and public transport improvements would have been possible.
4. Option 4 was similar to option 3 in that it was based on selective subsidies but here existing concessions would be maintained and subsidies extended to support non-profit making routes which were needed. Investment similar to option 3 was possible.
5. In option 5 existing concessionary fares would be retained, but no other subsidies would be provided. An electrified local rail service would be developed and bus services modified to match it.
6. Option 6 included more modest investment in local rail services and an improved and extended bus service. It would also allow urban and inter-urban road investment as well as retaining fare concessions.
7. Option 7 would have closed the local passenger rail network and introduced additional limited stop buses as well as a light rapid transit system in Sheffield. Existing concessionary fares would be retained.
8. Option 8 was similar to option 7 but instead of fare concessions, additional highway investment would be undertaken. This option was rejected by the county council because it excluded concessions to needy sections of the population.

After the process of developing these policy options, and preparing and selecting a preferred strategy, a fares policy was defined as part of a comprehensive series of transport policies. This was that 'in the period up to 1986 bus fares will not be increased, and subject to an agreement being made under section 20 of the Transport Act 1968, some local rail services will be subsidised'. This policy was in keeping with the council's overall strategy which was influenced by the problems existing in South Yorkshire (described earlier), an anticipated shortage of resources to tackle them in the period up to 1987, and its declared aim to help the areas and groups in greatest need. Transport was seen as a means of meeting other objectives and whilst issues of congestion and accessibility and the role public transport could play in alleviating them were important, of equal importance was the impact of transport proposals on issues such as employment prospects in the county. These issues led the council to a preference for public transport and to a low fares policy as a means of aiding the 'have-nots'.

During the course of the development of the detailed proposals it had
become clear that it was not possible to give a commitment to free travel
by 1986 and so the policy adopted was based on a different level of
subsidy. Evaluation of the various proposals led to the policy defined
above. More specifically, the reasons for its adoption were as follows:

1. If past trends were allowed to continue, with fares increasing, a
   decrease in the use of public transport could be expected, along with
   an increase in the use of private cars. The council believed that cheap
   fares would encourage people to use public transport and, whilst not
   halting the increase in the use of private cars, would slow it down.
2. If the predicted decline in the growth of private car use came about,
   the side effects would be beneficial. Congestion would be less severe,
   speeding up journeys by both public and private transport and
   making services more reliable, thus tackling some of the problems
   identified earlier. It would also postpone the need for improvements
   to some of the area's roads, and would mean that proposed
   restrictions to peak period car usage (so that buses could flow more
   freely) would be less severe than would have been the case.
   Additionally, reducing the rate of traffic growth would enable plans
   for road closures to be implemented without creating long queues or
   diverting heavy amounts of traffic to other roads.
3. Such a policy would mean that public transport costs would be
   recouped mainly from ratepayers and taxpayers – since a high
   proportion of local authority revenue expenditure is financed by
   government grant – and this would lead to a redistribution of income
   to the benefit of public transport users, who tend to be in lower
   income groups. Evidence from a number of sources shows that
   expenditure on public transport decreases as income rises, both in
   cash value and as a percentage of disposable income. Thus revenue
   support would benefit the lower paid more than the higher income
   groups. Additionally, although an increase in rates to pay for the
   support would have an impact on everyone, the expansion of rate
   rebate schemes would offset this to a large extent for the lower income
   groups. Calculations from the 1972 Land Use Transportation Study
   showed that even if the support were financed totally from the rates,
   the lowest income group would gain benefits two and a half times
   greater than their contribution, whilst in the highest-but-one income
   group the contribution would be three times greater than the benefit.
4. As well as the direct financial benefits from fare subsidies, other
   advantages would follow. Lower fares would improve the mobility of
   people in the lower income groups, enabling them to make more and
   longer journeys. This would not only improve access to various
   amenities such as shops, libraries, hospitals, etc., but it could also

benefit the long-term unemployed by enabling them to look for jobs further away from home.

The anticipated cost of subsidising bus revenue over the ten year period to 1986 was put at £173 million at 1975 prices. This was based on an estimated ten per cent average inflation of public transport costs (general cost inflation at the time was eight per cent) and the assumption that there would be a growth in patronage of buses and improvements in the level of service. In the event, the level of inflation was grossly underestimated.

The council believed the policy was extremely beneficial for South Yorkshire residents. However, it was contrary to government policy at the time, for in 1976 the government favoured a decline in the revenue support for buses as part of their restrictions on public expenditure over the next few years, although it was not opposed in principle to fare subsidies. Also, in 1976 the government argued in a transport policy consultative document that generalised or undiscriminating subsidies were economically inefficient and socially wasteful, and that although it was often claimed that subsidising fares relieved congestion in the cities there was no evidence that it had any great impact. However, subsidies for particular groups – those on low incomes who do not have access to a car, people living in rural areas where lack of public transport could impair community life, and special minorities such as the young, the old and the disabled who depend heavily on public transport – would be justified on social grounds. It was also somewhat at odds with TUC statements on transport which in 1975 had said that a minimum level of subsidised flat rate fares, and at best a free fare system, should be introduced in central urban areas but that the subsidy should be financed by a payroll tax on employers in central areas so that the total burden would not fall on the general rates.

During the third phase of the planning process the transport policies in general, and the fares policy in particular, received a great deal of criticism. Over one thousand responses to the draft plan were received from a wide variety of sources ranging from individuals to government departments and of these 281 were concerned with transport, the next highest number, 188, being concerned with employment. Over one half of the comments on transport were directed towards the cheap fares policy. When analysed, these comments were reduced to forty-five types, of which fourteen were against the policy, three were completely for it and the remainder contained reservations of various kinds. As a result of this, the policy statement was deleted from the draft but the council's position on fares containment remained unchanged, and it was written into the text accompanying the final version of the structure plan.

6.10 **Benefits of the policy**

In its public statements about its operation of its passenger transport policy South Yorkshire claims several successes. Bus fares have been maintained at January 1975 levels and the fare for an average journey of two and a half miles in late 1982 was 7p in South Yorkshire, compared to between 27p and 45p for other metropolitan areas. Passenger journeys have risen from 324 million in 1974/5 to 344 million in 1981/2. Since 1976 passenger journeys made in SYPTE buses have increased by 7.1 per cent whereas the average for other metropolitan PTEs shows a 22.4 per cent decline. Bus mileage in 1981/2 totalled 50.9 million, a 6.7 per cent increase since 1974 compared with a reduction of 14.5 per cent since 1974 in other PTE areas.

It seems reasonable to conclude that in operating terms the council's policy was justified. The decline in bus patronage has been halted and the cheap fares have not led to inefficiency, at least in comparison with other similar enterprises. This has not been achieved, however, without the expenditure of rather more than was anticipated and it has been accompanied by continuing opposition, some of it from sources which surprised the councillors considerably.

6.11 **Reactions to the policy**

As has already been mentioned, in 1973 the new South Yorkshire County Council pledged support from the rates of £2.5 million to peg municipal bus fares (not those of the NBC subsidiaries) but in the event this had to be increased to £3.5 million to meet additional losses brought about by a fuel crisis. This was only the beginning of unexpected and steadily increasing burdens on the rates. A major surprise was in store for the Labour county council though, when in 1974 their policy met opposition from a government of their own party. This opposition, which was maintained by later governments, both Labour and Conservative, led eventually to even larger increases in the transport subsidy provided from the rates.

Local public transport is financed to a large extent by government grant, part of which, the so-called bus grant, goes some way towards paying for new buses. The other part is the transport supplementary grant and part of this was being used to keep bus fares down when in December 1974 the government not only told councils that bus fare increases should keep pace with rising costs, but also that all public bus undertakings should plan to finance their operations entirely from fares revenue by 1980, with the exception of some rural services. In early 1975 an even stronger line was taken by government when councils were instructed to stop subsidising fares from the rates. The government agreed to continue to pay the bus grant but decided that the transport supplementary grant would be reduced progressively. There is little doubt that this came as a shock to South Yorkshire County Council. The only way it would be able to continue with its policy under these circumstances would be to increase the payment from the rates, and since the government had no power to prevent a rates increase such a policy inevitably meant rate bills going up.

Reluctantly, squeezed by inflation and the apparent lack of government support, South Yorkshire's fares were increased in January 1975 but the council remained committed to the cheap fares policy. An £11 million subsidy was paid to the PTE and in addition £940,000 was paid to subsidiaries of the NBC to keep fares down. A further grant of £260,000 was made to the NBC when it asked for fares to be increased to enable it to make loan repayments being demanded by government.

The action was attacked by the local political opposition. The local Liberal Party said that whilst the free fares pledge had been laudable at the time it was made it was no longer appropriate in the existing economic climate and should be abandoned. The Conservative Party said that it was criminal to raise a 5p rate (the cost of the subsidy) to prop up an ailing fares policy. Support for the opposition was forthcoming in March 1975 when the Sheffield/Rotherham Land Use Transportation Study recommended increases in bus fares of fifty per cent in real terms, so as to avoid large rate subsidies. Based on extensive public attitude surveys, the study team believed that passengers would rather have a convenient and reliable service than a great deal of money spent on subsidies and said that the majority of bus services should pay for themselves. Despite this, the council refused to budge from its policy, and in March 1975 introduced county-wide cheap bus fares for children, at about one fifth of the adult fare. Specific opposition to this action came from one of the local independent operators, who said that hordes of children would roam South Yorkshire and that vandalism would increase – though this did not prove to be the case.

Further calls for the abandonment of the policy came from the political opposition when the county council's spending figures were published in September 1975. Total county council expenditure at the time was £20 million, of which the transport subsidy took the incredible total of £11 million, made up as follows:

Loss on bus services	4.7
Subsidies to NBC	1.2
Subsidies to BR	0.3
Concessionary fares	4.9

Individuals seemed rather less concerned: a newspaper survey carried out in the following month received only 151 replies. Of these, sixty-nine were in favour of increasing fares by fifty per cent, eighteen wanted service cuts to prevent a rates increase; nineteen wanted a combination of actions, most of which favoured increased fares and reduced services and forty-five were in favour of increasing the rates to keep fares at their current level. Nevertheless, the council reaffirmed its policy of continuing to subsidise its own routes and those of the NBC in contravention of the government directive.

Early the following year the Transport Minister, Mr William Rodgers, asked South Yorkshire County Council to increase its fares. The government's reasons were many. There was a need to cut public expenditure generally, and this was particularly important given the government's commitment on public expenditure to the International Monetary Fund. The government did not wish to be perceived as discriminating in favour of one authority against the others and felt that there was a danger of other councils following South Yorkshire's example and bringing about a collapse of its transport financing policy, which was based on the need for public authority transport undertakings to be as financially viable as the municipal enterprises had once been.

South Yorkshire, however, refused his request. Sir Ron Ironmonger, council leader at the time, summed up the response to Mr Rodgers by saying that it would be nonsense to talk of increasing fares.

We said it would mean an end to cheap fares and substantial redundancies in the work force. We also told him we were committed to full employment, not sacking people. We said we considered this, and cheap fares, as part of our contribution to the social contract. Everybody at the Ministry said how marvellous we were, but nobody changed their minds.

Response to this defiance was varied. The Department of the Environment was initially noncommittal, saying it would wait and see what the total council spending was rather than comment on one sector of it. NALGO and the local branch of the 'Transport 2000' environmental pressure group supported it, but the Sheffield ratepayers action group decided to take legal advice on the Labour group's decision and launched a fighting fund to oppose it. In December the government finally made its response known in no uncertain terms by cutting the transport and roads grant from £6.5 million to £5.5 million. It was insisted that this was not a 'rap over the knuckles' but a means of helping rural areas to improve their services if grants to heavily populated areas like South Yorkshire were cut. This was followed in January by public support from the Transport and General Workers Union, but the City of Sheffield Chamber of Commerce attacked it, saying that almost all Sheffield companies would oppose subsidies from the rates, and some Doncaster ratepayers said they were considering withholding rates payments in protest.

In July 1976 the Transport Minister again asked the council to increase local fares and they again refused. This was followed by the first public attack on the fares policy by a government minister, who said that South Yorkshire County Council was a rebel, paying an astronomical amount to keep fares down; he made it clear that the government would not help to pay for the policy. The alternatives were to abandon it or to ask for a huge rates increase.

The policy was pursued in the face of strong criticism, but there was some support, both nationally and locally. In September, for example, thirty-two Labour MPs congratulated South Yorkshire County Council in a Commons motion which said the policy would encourage more people to use public transport. However, in October the government threatened to cut transport support. An ultimatum from Mr Rodgers said that cuts in grants would be made, no grants at all would be paid to rebel councils, and tighter borrowing restrictions would be imposed unless cuts in transport programmes were made. Other councils who were refusing to increase bus fares, such as West Midlands County Council, gave in but South Yorkshire decided to accept the cuts in grants and use higher rates to maintain its policy. It refused to cut the transport programme and as a result it received a grant of £291,000, a massive reduction compared with the previous year's £5 million. The minister stipulated that government would not provide a penny of support for cheap fares.

Similar policies were pursued by the Conservative government when it came to power but despite this, and the final exclusion of a specific cheap fares policy from the structure plan, the council has continued to maintain cheap fares. However, theirs is an extremely expensive policy for the anticipated cost to the rate payer in 1982–3 was £65 million out of a net county council rates bill of £96 million. This cost was made up as follows:

General fares subsidy	37 million
Concessionary fares	25 million
Support for local rail services	2 million

The county council rate accounts for about 31 per cent of the total rates in the area which in 1982 were 251.5p in the pound. A domestic ratepayer in a house with the South Yorkshire average rateable value of £130 will be paying £35 for the South Yorkshire transport system. The county council stated in its publicity material on transport that the subsidy on each bus journey in 1982/3 is estimated at 19.9p, the highest paid by the six metropolitan counties.

There is still continuing opposition to the policy, and in 1982 the government was contemplating legislation which would severely curtail the council's powers to continue the policy. The legislation would be intended to remove uncertainties about subsidies, by laying down a clear and consistent legal framework for the payment of subsidies. It would also, in the government's view, ensure better value for money since authorities will be encouraged to seek greater efficiency by renewing and, if necessary, reforming management structures and operations of their undertakings with a particular view to identifying whether smaller and more accountable units within the whole would bring greater efficiency. Also the legislation would be intended to encourage the development of further opportunities for the private sector to provide urban passenger transport and ancillary services by requiring the PTEs to review which services and facilities, such as catering and maintenance facilities, should be put out to competitive tender so that they would be provided most economically. In its paper 'Public transport subsidy in cities', which sets out the foregoing ideas, the government explained that present proposals were being brought forward to tackle the problems of passenger transport subsidies in London and the metropolitan counties. However, the government also warned that it is examining whether a more fundamental reorganisation of transport responsibilities is required.

7

Short studies

7.1 Introduction

The five main case studies in this book have been set out in considerable detail. In contrast, this chapter presents a number of shorter studies, and although each one merits a full study in its own right, detail is given on only a few aspects of each story. To enable the reader to delve deeper into each failure the bibliography gives sources of further information. Where possible, for each of the large scale disasters there are references made to books which will enable further analysis to be carried out, without recourse to the official reports of formal inquiries, which may be hard to obtain.

7.2 The airship R 101

At 6.36 pm on 4 October 1930 the largest airship in the world, the British R 101, left Cardington, near Bedford, to set out on her maiden voyage, to India via Ismailia in Egypt. Seven and a half hours later she came to earth near Beauvais in France, only 345 km from her place of departure. In the seconds following the impact with the ground she became a blazing wreck, in which all but six of the fifty-four people aboard perished. Among the dead were her captain and officers, and all six passengers. The victims included the British Secretary of State for Air, the Director of Civil Aviation, the Director of Airship Development and two Assistant Directors, one of whom was the designer of the R 101. The crash marked the end of British development of airships, at least for many years, for R 100, cousin to R 101, never flew again and was broken up for scrap.

Before 1914 the airship had achieved a superiority over the aeroplane for passenger transport. Pressure of war began a reversal of this but in the early 1920s only the airship held out the prospect of maintaining a regular and speedy service by air between the countries of the British empire. Between 1922 and 1926, pressure to push forward airship development built up. As a result, a three-year programme costing £1.35 million was started. In 1926 the representatives at an imperial conference were told that the airship programme would be developed in a spirit of scientific caution, with safety paramount. Two airships were to be built, one by the Air Ministry and called the R 101, the other by a subsidiary of Vickers Ltd., the Airship Guarantee Company, would be called the R 100. This arrangement was intended to encourage competition in design and ensure that the complete failure of one airship would not terminate the whole programme. In the event, these time-scales, cost estimates and good intentions were not realised.

The R 100 was designed by Barnes Wallis, later to become well known as designer of the Vickers Wellington bomber and the dam-busting bomb. His machine satisfied the specification in respect of lifting capacity, strength, speed, accommodation and weight, but one other clause in the specification, that the power plant 'be operated on a fuel which could safely be carried and used in sub-tropical conditions' was said not to have been satisfied, because the R 100 used petrol engines. The designers of the R 101, an Air Ministry team, incorporated many features that were new to airships. The structure was bolted together from mass-produced steel units, and oil engines were used for propulsion instead of the more usual petrol engines. After the first few test flights the lifting capacity was found to be inadequate so modifications were made to lighten the airship. Also the gas-bags inside were allowed to expand to their fullest extent, and a whole new section inserted into the centre part of the craft. The length of R 101 was now 237 metres (777 feet).

The R 101 left for India after only 127 hours of testing, during which the longest flight was one of thirty-one hours duration. All the trials had been carried out in good weather, and even more surprisingly, only one trial flight, of sixteen hours duration, had been completed after the new bay had been inserted. The airship had not even flown at full power. The precise reason for the descent at Beauvais can only be surmised, using suppositions based on previous difficulties which had been experienced. To give one example, the fabric skin of the airship had given way on previous occasions. Maybe a split opened up while the craft was over France, exposing the flimsy skin of the gas bags containing the lifting medium, hydrogen, to the wind and rain. Certainly the weather was worse than any the R 101 had flown in before. This might not have been the only cause of loss of lift. When the gas-bags were fully expanded they came into contact with protrusions on the steel structure of the airship. Soft pads had been interposed at many places to try to prevent chafing that could lead to leakage of hydrogen.

The R 101 would not have set out on its journey to India so soon had not the authorities felt compelled to allow it to do so, and unless they had convinced themselves that it was safe. The Secretary of State for Air wished to demonstrate to a conference later that month that the airship could help to unite the countries of the British empire, and in framing their reaction to this the people who could have stopped the flight going ahead faced a dilemma. The publicity provided by a successful flight would justify their faith in the airship– as R 100 had done by a successful flight to Canada. On the other hand, the dangers which might be encountered on a flight to the Middle East and India, if it was made without due preparation, could also be the end of airship development. After long delays in the building programme, the success of the R 100 and the feeling that they were under pressure to make a success of R 101, those responsible for allowing the flight perhaps took the wrong decision. With hindsight, the airship could not be developed then as a regular means of passenger transport; the best that can be said is that the loss of the R 101 and the lives of her victims prevented further waste.

7.3 The de Havilland Comet 1 airliner

The prototype of this aircraft first flew on 27 July 1949, and on 2 May 1952 it began the world's first jet airliner service, giving Britain world leadership in fast passenger travel. However, of the few Comet I aircraft built, four crashed. Problems with take-off caused one accident at Rome; these were solved by modifying the flying surfaces. Then, at Calcutta, another Comet crashed during a storm. The cause could not be properly traced as the wreckage was not made available to the British authorities. In 1954, while flying over Elba, Comet G-ALYP went into the sea, the wreckage being too widely dispersed for easy salvage. The wreckage that could be retrieved gave no clue as to the cause of the accident. Some fifty modifications were made to the Comet fleet and the aircraft continued in service, but the authorities had to admit that although the modifications covered everything that their imagination had suggested as a likely cause for the disaster, no definite reasons for the accident had been established. Within three months of the Elba incident another Comet, G-ALYY, disappeared into the sea at Naples. Certificates permitting the Comets to fly were withdrawn. If the Comet had been a national success and source of pride, it was now a failure.

By dint of great efforts on the part of marine salvage experts, working in conjunction with the Royal Navy, more of the wreckage of G-ALYP was recovered. At the same time another Comet, G-ALYU was subjected to full scale testing of the strength of its fuselage. The test ended in explosion of the pressure cabin, initiated from a small crack. Examination of the wreckage from Elba revealed a similar cause: the mystery was solved.

At the inquiry into the disasters it emerged that the metal around the cabin windows was subjected to a much higher load than expected by the designers. Tests by de Havilland had not shown this up. Their tests for pressure cabin strength in this respect had been made on two separate halves of a complete cabin. When separated and modified for ease of testing the halves exhibited greater strength than they would have as part of the finished aircraft. Furthermore some of the early tests served to strengthen the structure of the test samples so that later tests were even further misleading as simulations.

The official inquiry stated as one of its conclusions that 'the accident was not due to the wrongful act or default or to the negligence of any party or of any person in the employment of any party'. Nevertheless, questions must be posed about the way that affairs were handled. Was it correct to allow flights by Comet aircraft to continue although the causes of the Elba accident were still not known? Surely a paper published in the *Royal Aeronautical Society Journal* for 1949 had drawn attention to the likelihood of metal being strengthened as regards some forms of testing, when subjected to tests in other ways beforehand? Did the earlier accident at Calcutta have the same cause as the later ones? Testing a new design takes time and money; how can someone decide what expenditure is reasonable?

7.4 The Stockport aircrash

On 4 June 1967 a Canadair Argonaut aircraft was returning with seventy-nine passengers and five crew from Majorca. As it prepared to make an approach to land at Manchester airport it suffered two successive losses of engine power, and crashed. Of those aboard the plane, seventy-two died. The immediate cause of the accident was the loss of power of two engines on one side of the aircraft. The resulting asymmetry made it too difficult for the pilot to hold the aircraft straight and to maintain height.

The first loss of power was due to fuel starvation. By means of an arrangement of pumps and valves controlled from the flight deck, fuel could be piped from any of the aircraft's eight tanks to any other tank. This also enabled any one of the four engines to be supplied from any tank, and fuel could be transferred across the aircraft in order to balance it. During the final flight one of the fuel transfer valves had inadvertently been left slightly open so that, unbeknown to the pilot, one main tank was being emptied of fuel. On the final approach the fuel supply for each engine is taken from the tank nearest to it. One such tank had emptied, so the engine now connected to it stopped.

The reason for the loss of power from the second engine, which occurred shortly after the first, is not known. Two possible explanations are that there was another inadvertent transfer of fuel, or that the crew identified incorrectly which engine had failed originally, and switched off the second by mistake. If this had happened, and they had realised their error, they might have had time to put things right. These aircraft carried no specific indicator for engine failure and it must be remembered that the crew would be severely taxed in those few minutes. The pilot would have been fully occupied in handling the main controls, while the workload of navigation, communications, lookout and handling other controls exceeded the capability of the second pilot.

At the inquiry that followed the crash it emerged that evidence was available to both the crew and the ground staff that inadvertent fuel transfer had occurred on previous flights with this type of aircraft. The records that are kept of fuel consumption from the different tanks during flight would have shown it up. Actually, pilots had on various occasions drawn the attention of ground engineers to peculiarities in fuel consumption. But when the engineers went to check the valves they reported that they could find nothing wrong. This would most likely have been because the valves were placed low down on the flight deck, with the result that the engineer working while the aircraft was stationary on the ground could easily reach down to the valve and set it properly. He could concentrate on the task in a way that the pilot could not do on a noisy and busy flight deck where there were many other matters to attend to. Careful examination of fuel valves showed that mechanical wear in the mechanism made it too easy to leave the valve slightly open. It is sad that other operators of this type of aircraft had learned of the problem of the valves but had failed to inform the authorities.

7.5 **The DC-10 aircrash near Paris**

On 3 March 1974 a DC-10 aircraft belonging to Turkish Airlines crashed shortly after taking off from Paris, killing all 346 occupants. An insecurely fastened door that served a hold below the passenger cabin had blown open, allowing the hold to become depressurised. The pressure of the air in the cabin tore out part of the cabin floor and pushed it down into the hold. From there, together with the seats that had been fastened to it, and the passengers in those seats, it was forced out of the aircraft. Vital controls for the aircraft ran through this part of the structure and with these controls jammed, severed or damaged the aircraft dived out of control to hit the ground at high speed.

The outwards opening door of the hold had been designed so as to be secured by latches which were held by locking pins whose positions were shown by flight-deck warning lights. During a pressurisation test of an early DC-10 on the ground, improper latching had allowed a forward door for cargo to blow open, causing decompression of the fuselage, and floor damage. To deal with this, production aircraft had a small vent flap set in the doors so that unless all the doors were latched and locked properly the vent flap would remain open, preventing pressurisation and alerting the crew to the problem. Additionally, the door handle, which was some 25 centimetres long, would project and thus act as a warning signal if the door was not secure. However, the handle did not operate the door mechanism by a direct action, but through a lever and rod arrangement and if the latching and locking mechanism was not aligned properly, forceful operation of the handle could buckle the levers that it operated. Thus the handle and vent flap would be in the closed position even though the door was not locked. Additionally, warning lights were provided so as to indicate to the crew the state of the latching and locking mechanism. However, the switches for these indicators had been tampered with so as to render them useless as warning devices; they signalled 'safe' when all was not.

Amongst the US aviation authorities and the manufacturers of the relevant parts of the aircraft there were officials who had been aware of the danger of a door coming open, and a similar though not disastrous incident in June 1972 had not led to effective action being taken. The sub-contractor who had made the fuselages had assessed the danger but remained content to report it and to leave the responsibility for compliance in the hands of the main manufacturer. In vital documentation containing details of how to make the door safer, voluntary action by airline operators was relied on rather than mandatory directives. It is said that handling the issuing of this documentation in this fashion was the result of a growing practice indulged in by the manufacturer and the authorities, who made 'gentlemen's agreements' between themselves.

Improvements to the aircraft, involving better locking arrangements, stronger cabin floor and vents in the floor, have added the equivalent of the weight of ten passengers to the DC-10.

7.6 The explosion at Flixborough

Shortly before 5.00 pm on Saturday, 1 June 1974, the Flixborough works of Nypro (UK) Ltd. near Scunthorpe were virtually demolished by a massive explosion. Of the workers on the site, twenty-eight people were killed and thirty-six injured, while in the surrounding area, fifty-three people were recorded as casualties. Off-site, some two thousand buildings suffered damage.

Between 1964 and 1967, various items of plant were erected on the site in order to carry out the manufacture of caprolactam. Production of this chemical, used in making a type of nylon, began in 1967 and from then until the disaster Flixborough was the only plant in the UK engaged in this work. Part of the operation involved the use of six large vessels which were connected in series by piping. In these vessels the substance cyclohexane was processed under the action of heat and pressure. At the end of March 1974 one vessel developed a leak through a crack and was removed. The resulting gap was spanned by a pipe, twenty inches (half a metre) in diameter. Because of the relative heights of the two vessels that it connected together, the pipe required two bends in its length. The ends of the pipe were joined to the respective vessels by flexible bellows. However, there was a failure to recognise the engineering problems inherent in what seemed such a simple matter. No proper design study was made, no proper consideration was given to the need for the pipe to be supported from the ground, no reference was made to the written guidance issued by the manufacturers of the bellows, or to British Standards. The assembly was such that it was liable to rupture at pressures below that at which the safety valve would operate, and before operating temperature was reached. Finally, no safety testing was carried out.

On the fateful day, difficulties were experienced with starting up the plant and in the process of dealing with these the temperature and pressure of the contents were briefly allowed to exceed the operating level. Later that day, the temporary assembly of pipe and bellows gave way, releasing large quantities of cyclohexane. As it expanded and mixed with the air the cyclohexane exploded.

At the court of inquiry which followed the disaster, the following points emerged. No one at the works had been concerned about finding the cause of the original crack that had led to the installation of the temporary pipe. Furthermore, no checks had been made of the remaining five vessels in order to see whether they were likely to begin to crack and leak. The works engineer had left the company, and whilst steps were being taken to replace him a services engineer, mainly experienced in electrical work, took over the role. On the engineering side, there was no professionally qualified mechanical engineer who might have recognised the weakness of the temporary pipe and its bellows.

At one end of the scale, the explosion at Flixborough drove home lessons for all engineers and metallurgists about the behaviour of materials and structures. At the other end of the scale, the incident called into question the way that chemical plant and similar hazardous processes were growing in size and yet some were sited much nearer a centre of population than was the Flixborough works. The nearby villages suffered badly from damage but the nearest town was six miles away. On site, the accident occurred on a Saturday afternoon when nearly all of the hundreds of employees normally there during the week were away. Flixborough was a warning.

7.7 The collapse of Rolls-Royce

On 4 February 1971, at the company's own request, a receiver and manager was appointed to take over the affairs of a firm whose name had been a symbol of British integrity, excellence and reliability: Rolls-Royce.

Since the formation of the firm in the first decade of this century the name Rolls-Royce had figured in the history of this country. High quality motor cars were the company's first products and they rapidly established the reputation of the firm, which took over one of its biggest rivals, Bentley, in 1931. But Rolls-Royce were not only known for the cars they produced; it was in the field of aviation that Rolls-Royce made its greatest contribution. The Eagle engine did duty in the first world war and two of these engines took Alcock and Brown's Vickers Vimy on the first non-stop Atlantic flight on 15 June 1919. The engine known as the 'R' type powered a Supermarine seaplane that won the Schneider trophy outright for Britain in 1931 and this engine was later developed further, gaining air, land and water speed records. Subsequently, the company's Merlin engines served as the power plants for Spitfire and Hurricane fighters in the Battle of Britain, and for the versatile Mosquito aircraft, the renowned Lancaster bomber and the American Mustang fighter.

After the war the company decided to remain in the aero-engine industry, developing and producing jet engines. The list of aircraft powered by the company's products reads like a roll call of British aviation – Viscount, Vanguard, Comet, Canberra, Lightning, Hunter, VC10, Valiant, Victor, Trident, BAC 1-11, Nimrod, Phantom.

In October 1966, Rolls-Royce acquired Bristol Siddeley Engines, a company comprising the former aero-engine interests of the Bristol Aeroplane Company, Armstrong Siddeley, de Havilland and Blackburn. Work was underway at Bristol Siddeley on the Pegasus engine for the Harrier and the Olympus for Concorde. The acquisition meant that there was only one major manufacturer of aero-engines in the United Kingdom, but that manufacturer, Rolls-Royce, was about to embark on the venture that would lead to its bankruptcy.

In the early 1960s the firm began work on a large engine to power what have become known as the wide-bodied jets. This led to the signing of a contract in 1968 with the American Lockheed Aircraft Corporation for the design, manufacture and supply of an engine known as the RB 211. The placing of the order was greeted with great enthusiasm in this country – it was one of the largest single export orders ever obtained by a British company. Rolls-Royce was still determined to stay mainly in aero-engine manufacture rather than using its talents in other engineering fields where the skill of its management and workforce would undoubtedly be assets. The company had been unsuccessful in a bid to produce the engines for the first jumbo jet, the Boeing 747, and in 1967 it was predicted by the company that their share of sales in the aero engine market would decline from £58.9 million in 1969 to £3.5 million in 1975. Therefore, it was fortunate that Lockheed were already discussing the RB 211 engine for their 1011 Tristar aircraft. Unfortunately though, this attempt to break into the American market brought Rolls-Royce into direct competition with US manufacturers who were able to enjoy the advantages of a large domestic market and massive support from the US government in the form of military contracts. Rolls-Royce spared no effort to gain a contract for the RB 211, sending over teams of up to twenty engineers, led by the managing director of the Derby Engine Division, which became responsible for work on the project.

The engine had to be twice as powerful as any the company had put into service hitherto. Many of the internal parts needed to run at higher temperatures than earlier versions; the engine had to incorporate new features of design that required specially invented materials. These jumps in development were very large when compared with the previous engines and the amount of direct experience with the particular design of engine was surprisingly limited. Test engines had run for only a short time, and even the lower-powered model of the engine, the RB 211-06 had not yet run at all. Indeed the engine that was finally promised, the RB 211-22, had 18 per cent more thrust than the 06 model, but was to be within the same overall dimensions. This was only achieved by running the engine at even higher temperatures. Unfortunately, research on the type had not kept pace with the promises that were made because neither the firm nor the UK government was willing to find the finances. In contrast, the US manufacturers had been able to keep up their programmes of research and development, and so were ahead of Rolls-Royce in some vital respects such as the technology of materials that are to survive at high temperatures in an aero-engine.

Lack of technical know-how was only one of the contributory factors in the demise of Rolls-Royce. The investigators appointed under the Companies Act to inquire into the firm made several comments about the firm's management, and these will be explained later in this account. Before that, certain particular features taken from the same report of the case deserve mention.

Firstly, an engine that preceded the RB 211, the Spey, had had its development completed within its original cost estimates, and this gave a false sense of security to those at Rolls-Royce who negotiated the contract or were party to its terms and to the decision to accept it. In fact the Spey engine benefited greatly from the work on two preceding engines, the Conway and Medway, and Rolls-Royce's success then at estimating the cost and time-scale for a new engine was due to a policy of gradual technical development rather than large steps. In the case of the RB 211 this rule was broken.

Secondly, in July 1967 the division's Director of Engineering died unexpectedly. He was a brilliant engineer and had provided dynamic leadership which could not be replaced. Thirdly, the engineering department had just been reorganised. Before this all the designers had been responsible, through various levels of seniority, to the Chief Design Engineer; together they had been responsible for the design of all the engines. Development engineering had the same arrangement. The new scheme was project-orientated. Project groups were set up, each headed by a Chief Project Engineer who was usually an experienced development engineer. The more experienced designers found themselves outside the project groups, advising them all; these designers found this frustrating as it removed from them the opportunity to maintain continuity within their own speciality.

Finally, the engineering department was heavily committed to work on several other engines, and there was general understaffing and shortage of experienced men in the stress office, where many careful calculations had to be carried out in order to determine strength of engine components when they were subjected to high temperatures.

In the face of strong competition from the American firms, General Electric and Pratt and Whitney, who both had engines on offer that were in a more advanced state of development, the Rolls-Royce negotiators secured what was, in the view of the Companies Act investigators, probably the best contract that they could. We have already seen that the engine finally agreed upon was to be more powerful than the one over which negotiations had begun originally, but despite this it was also to be cheaper, and early orders for the engine were to receive a financial discount too.

At the outset of negotiations it had been the view of Rolls-Royce, Lockheed and the other firms in the industry that the market could support only one manufacturer of airframes and one of aero-engines. In order to keep out competitors it was at first agreed that a minimum of three airlines had to become customers for the first aircraft so that other airlines would then find that they had to stay with Lockheed and Rolls-Royce. However, this agreement was changed later; it was agreed that the contract could go ahead if only two airlines came in. As a result, almost as soon as the contract had been signed, the American aircraft manufacturer McDonnell Douglas teamed up with General Electric, thus effectively splitting the potential market in two.

It had already been decided with the British government that they would meet seventy per cent of the costs of the early stages of the project (known as the 'launch costs'), subject to a maximum of £47.1 million. In return for this investment the government were to receive a share of the profits as soon as these rose above certain agreed levels. However it was made clear that no further financial support would be forthcoming. As the contract was for a fixed price, Rolls-Royce would have to carry the risk of cost and wage inflation, so to try to protect themselves Rolls-Royce tried to reach similar deals with their own suppliers.

The original programme for the RB 211-06 engine on which negotiations had commenced would have committed the firm to expenditure amounting to some 30 per cent of the existing net worth of the company, excluding intangible assets. The RB 211-22 programme increased this commitment to 60 per cent. Cost escalation is commonplace in aerospace projects, and it should have been in the minds of the Rolls-Royce board of directors that despite the success of the engineers and accountants in predicting the cost of the Spey engine development, the RB 211 estimate could be out by a factor of two or three, and that such an error could bankrupt the firm. The extent to which Rolls-Royce saw itself as inviolate, with the government bailing it out in the national interest if there was trouble, can only be a matter of speculation. Certainly, from a defence point of view Rolls-Royce had to remain in business and maybe the firm saw the already existing promises of government support, and the latter's interest in the wording of the contract, as signs that the government already had in mind the need to help out further. Another view is that the board did not, at the time, identify sufficiently well the risks the company faced. Both of these alternative explanations find some support in the report of the investigation.

The contract had been signed in March 1968, and by the autumn of 1970 it was clear that Rolls-Royce had insufficient funds to enable the task to be completed. Between these dates, several events contributed to the failure. A costly design change was made at Lockheed's request but Rolls-Royce made no charge for it because, it is said, they had doubts about the suitability of the original design in this respect anyway. Negotiations were in progress with Lockheed to increase the engine thrust still further; Rolls-Royce were not contractually bound to this but felt morally obliged to do so. Progress on the engine design was slower than had been expected but production dates demanded that designers release drawings to the workshops knowing that the design might well prove unsatisfactory. Other designs were passed to the manufacturing areas before tests had been carried out. The result was that many manufactured parts had to be scrapped and remade when the need for modifications became clear.

The design changes put up the research and development costs, and also affected the estimates of the cost of the engine when in full production, which by September 1970 had already exceeded the selling price. In the autumn of 1970 some £60 million of additional finance was obtained, £42 million from the government and the remainder from banks, but as more forecasts were made it became clear that there was no hope of producing an engine to meet Lockheed's requirements in the time available. In extending the development time the company would run out of cash. There would also be claims for financial damages for delayed delivery, and massive losses when engines and parts were manufactured and sold. Lockheed did not have the resources to help, and it appears that even the government was advised that if it provided a bridging loan it might be said to be a party to the carrying on of a business in contravention of the Companies Act. All of these setbacks led to one decision. A receiver had to be appointed.

It has already been suggested here that people in charge at Rolls-Royce must soon have come to realise that the RB 211-22 would cost more to supply than Rolls-Royce had available either from their own funds or by using the limited funding from government, but it is suggested that they expected the latter to bail them out in the national interest. However, after the collapse, the government protected that interest in a way that might well have come as a surprise to Rolls-Royce, for the firm was divided up. Rather than propping up the whole of the company the government allowed it to crash, picked up the pieces it needed for defence and civil aviation, and sold off what remained. Thus Rolls-Royce (1971) Limited was formed to acquire the assets of the gas turbine engine divisions, while the motor car and oil engine sides of the firm were offered to the public sector.

Several reasons for the failure of Rolls-Royce, and contributory factors in its collapse, have been mentioned previously. The official investigation under the Companies Act by the inspectors appointed by the Department of Trade and Industry pointed out other aspects of the story that must be considered relevant.

The higher management of Rolls-Royce comprised a main board of the whole firm and, at the next level down, divisional boards such as that for the Derby Engine Division where the work on the RB engines was handled. The official investigators were of the opinion that the information in the papers seen by the main board, on the basis of which decisions were made, was voluminous but largely narrative in nature. Where statistics were presented there was a lack of standard forms of presentation, and neither was the presentation consistent as regards content. There were failures to highlight the most important matters for consideration, and one significant instance of this is the so-called 'Metcalfe Report'. This was prepared by the first programme director for the RB 211 in mid-1969. The report described the state of the estimates for development of the engine, even at that early date, as 'clearly intolerable'. The report also predicted a heavy financial loss on the project. The papers of the main board devoted only a few lines to the matter: 'There are still serious mechanical and performance problems with the RB 211 but in our judgement the task remains difficult but achievable'. No mention was made in the minutes, and many members of the main board claimed never to have seen the report or been made aware of its significance at the time.

The board of the Derby Engine division was judged by the investigators appointed under the Companies Act as unable to carry out effective management. It was too large, twenty-two members, and all but one of these were engineers. Members tended to regard it as a vehicle for discussion rather than a body which took decisions leading to action. The RB 211 project took the managing director of the division out of the country for long periods, and caused him ill health. No one was there to replace him, both on account of his recognised ability and the fact that the deputies had their own tasks to perform.

It is said that Rolls-Royce tended to be a company whose management was dominated by engineers. The investigators felt that those members of the main board who were not engineers relied on those who were, and they in turn had their approach coloured by the conviction that the Lockheed job should go ahead. In the words of the investigator's report, 'given apparent confidence of success on the part of the engineers it is perhaps understandable that the potential consequences of failure were not discussed. Certainly there are no minutes recording any such discussion'.

The investigators concluded their report by drawing attention to some of the advantages Rolls-Royce enjoyed. The main board included directors whom any company would have been pleased to have. The company had skilled and experienced engineers, and could call on outside help of the highest quality. Its banks and the government had confidence in it, its competitors respected it and its reputation was second to none. Yet one engine product caused it to collapse because the size and cost of the engineering task was seriously underestimated. Once the contract had been signed, excellent work was done on the engine but no form of financial or managerial control could meet the requirements of cost, time, novelty, manpower, leadership and so on.

When embarking on a venture that would commit enormous resources, as objective a view as possible must be taken by those responsible. But the decision to proceed had to be made in the context that without a share of the market in aero-engines for large civil aircraft the future of the firm would be only a shadow of its past. To fail in this was unthinkable.

8

Systems and understanding

This chapter sets out to show what is meant by 'system' and 'understanding' in the context of this book. However, in later chapters our studies will be concerned with the use of these ideas in connection with 'failure', a concept outlined in chapter 1, so failure will be illustrated first, using one of the case histories. Thus an analysis of the history of the *Alexander L. Kielland* accommodation rig would produce the following points on failure.

The rig, which had been intended to perform satisfactorily in the North Sea over a period of time, broke up and capsized in a sudden and catastrophic manner. Although it did not actually sink, this was of no benefit to those in the water, for none of them used it as a refuge. The disaster was front page news for several days and led to the setting up of a major inquiry. Prior to the incident, agencies acting under powers given to them by the Norwegian government had declared the rig safe but after the disaster this judgement was found to be wrong. Over the years there had already been revisions of the standards for rigs, but this disaster highlighted a need to change the rules again.

The capsize of the rig led to its evacuation, and we can trace the story back from these events. Behind the loss of column D was the steadily increasing length of the crack in bracing bar D-6 and the failure to detect the crack during manufacture or annual inspection. Failure arose in the carrying out of the welding of the hydrophone fittings and in the setting of standards for the welding. Failure had occurred earlier still, in the design of the fittings and in the attitude to their significance as possible sites for fractures in the bracing bar. The capsize and evacuation gave rise to many further failures: notably the loss of life, but also financial loss. These failures posed threats of interruption to the flow of oil and gas from the North Sea.

Failures have multiple causes, some very distant. The loss of life of a particular man from the rig who died trying to board a supply vessel can be traced back through a chain or network of events to the original desire on the part of Norway to exploit the North Sea oil and gas fields. This is itself connected to events in the Middle East, America, Great Britain and other oil producing regions of the world. The giant international oil companies are involved; they had the means and the will to gather oil and gas. The wider economic setting of Norway and other nations is significant too. So in these and other ways the story of the *Alexander L. Kielland* goes beyond the description of the rig itself. Like the final failures, the story comprises a multitude of small events set among some larger ones, and a complicated and interconnected history that is at times confusing. How, then, can we make sense of this situation, and of others like it? One of the main contentions of this book is that a systems approach provides a way of coping with the complexities of a story like that of the *Kielland* rig.

The systems approach employs the idea that the observer or analyst should assemble descriptions of systems, each based upon a main activity in the situation under study, or upon the smaller contributory activities that make up the whole. The main assemblies are called systems; these may be subdivided into subsystems, and when subdivision into smaller and smaller pieces ceases to be fruitful these final subdivisions are called components. Components also occur outside the system, in the surroundings: components that interact with the system make up what is called the environment. These basic ideas will be explained and illustrated in this and later chapters.

In order to study a situation it will be necessary to build up a picture of the systems that seem to be appropriate. This may not be an easy task: the situation can contain a mass of information, and there are pitfalls that can lead the investigator astray. To guide the assembly of systems the following stage by stage approach has been devised. It is summarised at the end of this chapter.

The first stage is an awareness of activities in the situation. For the *Alexander L. Kielland* the central activity was accommodation of personnel from other rigs. Within that were other activities such as transport of personnel, the provisioning of the rig, preliminary procedures of designing and building, regulatory exercises such as inspections, and many other activities. There were the various day-to-day movements of ships working with the rig and a small amount of activity concerned with readiness for search and rescue in the event of an incident. The activities that required a system for their achievement even included that of 'standby', which is another way of saying they were merely waiting for something to happen.

The second stage requires a commitment on the part of the observer to stay with and continue the study of a particular set of activities (not a system yet). This commitment may be that he or she is employed in some capacity within the activity or has been called in to investigate a failure. The nature of the commitment will influence what is regarded as failure, and the mental picture of the systems that produce it.

The third stage in the process is to see whether some of the features of systems are present. To make this possible the essential features of a system must be referred to. A short four-part definition of what a system comprises is given below:

A system is an assembly of components, connected together in an organised way.

The components are affected by being in the system and the behaviour of the system is changed if they leave it.

This organised assembly of components does something.

This assembly has been identified as of particular interest.

For the moment we are only looking to see whether there are sufficient attributes of systems present. Are there a number of components connected together in a way that could, in any respect, be called organised? Take an activity from the *Alexander L. Kielland* story, for example, the launching of lifeboats from the stricken rig. The layman might say that the launching was characterised by a lack of 'system', but what does the systems approach reveal? There were a number of components and subsystems: the boats themselves, the launching apparatus, the allocation of men to particular boats, the regulations governing the provision of boats and their contents, training in lifeboat drill and so on. Were they connected together in an organised way before the accident? In the minds of the authorities the answer would surely be yes. But was this so for the men on board the rig, be they crew or 'guests'? What did they know beforehand about the launching of boats and the freeing of them from the lowering ropes? When it was put to the test the system, such as it was, failed to achieve the expectations held out for it. It could be said in respect of the launchings, attempted launchings and handling of the boats and their equipment that many aspects had to be handled on a purely *ad hoc* basis, and that the system for survival and rescue that should have operated broke down. Radio operating instructions were not used in some cases and engines became damaged by immersion and inversion, which was hardly unlikely in a rough sea. In the event it hardly mattered to the overall arrangements whether a particular item was present or not, as it was often found to have been unused or unusable anyway. Such components were not well adapted for inclusion in a survival system for the North Sea. Taken together, these observations imply a lack of 'system'. This third stage has led us to see systems in some places at certain times, distinct lacks of systems at other places and times. Using the same standard we could compare aspects of the *Alexander L. Kielland* story with corresponding aspects in other rescue stories.

This method for the description of the systems has as its fourth stage the separation of one system from another, and naming. This leads to the emergence of systems and the definition of components in them. The need to place a boundary round each system demands that we be as unequivocal as possible about system contents, but in fact, we may be able to go only a little way in this direction. There may be a great deal of agreement about what constitutes 'the anchoring system of the rig', but there was great uncertainty about 'the standby vessel system'. The results of questioning would vary with factors such as the individual, his or her own viewpoint and role, the time, place and occasion, etc. Boundary and environment are among the most important of the systems ideas, so it is useful to explain them a little further before moving on. The boundary of a system is the demarcation between what is in the system and what is not. What is in the system will be those things that constitute an assembly having organised connectedness; their dependence on each other is strong enough to be seen as an internal coherence; their character would be changed by leaving the assembly, and their leaving would alter the assembly as well. The assembly of items is of interest and importance to a (named) observer and together the components do something, or more likely several things. Outside the system, beyond the boundary, is everything that is not in the system, but there is an important subset of this, the environment of the system. The environment can be regarded as being immediately outside the system as regards our mental picture and comprises those things that are not part of the system but do affect the behaviour of the system, or are affected by it. For 'the rescue system' that operated after the capsizing of the *Kielland* rig the weather was in its environment, important in its effect but clearly uncontrolled by the system, as were the cold sea and the onset of darkness. Another part of the environment was the Rogaland hospital because it yielded inputs to the system and received some of the outputs from the system. But components in the environment need not be of a physical nature. The Norwegian regulations applicable to rigs were in the environment, as were the skills of various rescuers. Whether a particular supply or standby vessel was part of the system or part of the environment is a typical example of the questions that a system approach should prompt. The variety of possible answers to such questions may thus throw doubt on the preparations for such an emergency. The other Norwegian hospitals would have been outside the environment of the rescue system until drawn in, perhaps to make standby preparations in case they were needed. Systems can grow by more and more of the world coming into their environment and then into the system itself. At each stage of growth the newcomers must be absorbed and integrated and in some cases this build-up can overload what is already there.

In the fourth stage, the system under consideration is named, as in the above examples. The next or fifth stage, which is called selection, might appear to be another naming process but it is really a statement of the kind of system that has been picked out; it is different from and more than the mere name. Thus the system named 'the accommodation system' would be imagined to have a manager, the accommodation manager. If you asked the employees what they did, they would not say they accommodated. Rather, their answers would be on the lines of provision for an agreed set of off-duty requirements of oil field workers (though not in those words). It is a life support system for leisure hours, a servicing system recharging and maintaining the well-being of the work force. It perhaps followed from this that the system had the nature of emphasising a promise of security rather than danger, calm rather than tension and so although in some of its physical features the rig resembled a drilling platform its ambience was one of a temporary home and safety rather than work and hazard. Therefore the workers' attitudes to safety drills and the need to keep their survival suits handy would be lax as compared with the attitudes of men at busy work stations amidst the noise and bustle of a working rig. That the staff were operating what was, in effect, a sheltering system should have been made clear to the permanent crew on the *Alexander L. Kielland*. They should have been called upon to play a greater role in the escape and rescue, in accordance with the expectations of the guests, who would have been unskilled at escape from that rig. That is part of the distinction between guest or visitor and host. Indeed 'host system' is a good name or description of the permanent part of 'the accommodation system'.

The other system named and detailed in this chapter has been 'the search and rescue system'. What kind of a system was this? It was 'a recovery system'. Amongst its activities were the delivery of ships, helicopters and so on, and the collection of the survivors. Some aspects of the rescue passed successfully through the delivery phase only to falter at collection. In the environment of this system for recovery are other systems, one for each potential survivor or group of survivors. They showed great variety, any property that can be assumed to have been in one could well have been absent in another. Examples of this are the inability of some of the survivors to handle ropes and ladders due to numbing of the fingers. The lifeboats had engines and radios but it cannot be assumed that they were in good order or that seemingly carefully devised routines were followed.

This method for system description has a sixth and final stage, the description itself. The prior stages serve to lead us towards this but even on the way there they yield insight, as we have seen. At this sixth stage full description requires the detailing of the system, its subsystems, their components and those in the environment. Attention is paid to the inputs and outputs that make up the interchanges between systems and environment and the state of the system is described in terms of key quantities and qualities. In this example the variables would include for instance the number of guests on a rig and the number of life-jackets at each assembly point.

The carrying out of the final description phase can be an enormous task unless it is limited by imposition of a particular aim. In a later chapter constraints will be introduced as ways of channelling the use of the systems approach and directing it towards the understanding of failure by the use of particular kinds of system.

In the meantime, and to conclude this chapter, a discussion is needed of what we mean by understanding, and how it relates to the ideas of systems.

Understanding, as referred to here, starts with a failure that is regarded as significant by an observer. The failure is seen as a disappointing shortfall in output performance, emanating from a system or systems. Failures arise from a host of contributory factors, each an aspect of system behaviour. The activity of understanding the failure requires the elimination of these factors, tracing them back, assessing the importance of each as a contributor, all the while seeking explanations for features in terms of others. Understanding is comprehension of the case; it is the achievement of a mental grasp of the information that is already to hand, followed by a search for fresh information. The whole picture comes together with the intention in our minds of making the story more intelligible, first to ourselves and hopefully also to others. Understanding deals in reasons, grounds, motives and consequences. It tries to make sense out of complexity, and seeks to put consideration of the whole on a par with or above the separate study of individual parts.

The links that can be forged between understanding and systems need not be laboured. The idea of system puts emphasis on the connections between components and seeing a degree of organisation. It stresses the role of each component in contributing to the behaviour of the system. If a component were not present in the system, the behaviour of the system would be different, the definition of system reminds us. It also says that every system does something, and more particularly, every subsystem does something too; each contributes to the failure and therefore we must understand a great deal about it and how it fits into the whole. Lastly from the definition, a system needs an observer with an interest, and this interest will influence the viewpoint of the observer, and even what he or she chooses to include in his or her 'system'. Similarly, 'understanding' will be personal to whoever undertakes it. As in the case of perceiving a system, there may well be much agreement on what comprises an understanding of a situation, but there can also be a large measure of disagreement.

Understanding is an output from a process that here is based on use of the systems approach. The process advances by searches for systems and subsystems set in environment, and it then looks for signs of control and management directed towards the achievement of objectives. A degree of understanding has been achieved when enough of the situation has been assembled in systems terms to the extent that some contributory factors can be cited for the output that is classed as a failure. However, that is likely to be only the beginning, for the overall search is recursive in that a second examination can look for the causes of the causes, so to speak, and so on.

Clearly, a limit to this is reached when the information ceases to be available or the search ends at a particular individual whose actions even he or she cannot understand or remember, and thus the trail disappears.

A question which must always be asked during an analysis is how we know it is both valid and correct. One answer is that we can never be completely sure because this understanding is subjective and disputable: different people may identify different sets of contributory factors. Nonetheless, one thing we must be able to say is that we have used the evidence in a way that we feel is honest, we have not knowingly falsified it or omitted inconvenient parts of it. We will have made thorough searches for new evidence, which if found will have been taken up and used. We cannot know that we are right because there is no such ideal, but in these ways we can build up our confidence and that of others that we recognise a set of standards and try to meet them.

Summary of the first steps in a systems approach

Stage 1   Awareness
Being aware of some activity; it is described, but not in systems terms.

Stage 2   Commitment
Having reasons for staying with the study, e.g., to describe, understand, repair or maybe redesign. Answering the question, 'Why am I doing this?'

Stage 3   Detection
Trying the four-part definition of system to see systems attributes.

Stage 4   Separation
Separating some systems of interest; putting trial boundaries on them; giving titles of systems, for example, 'a rescue system'.

Stage 5   Selection
Selecting and stating the kind of system that the system is, for example 'conflict resolution system', 'managed refuge system'.

Stage 6   Description
Describing in systems terms the components, subsystems and environments, their states and the connections between them and so on.

9

Systems and failures

In earlier chapters we have looked at what we mean by the word failure and how a systems approach can be useful as a way of looking at a particular situation together with the context in which it occurs. Now we shall go on to examine the value of a systems approach in the study of failure.

In everyday life people often tend to think of failures as isolated events that happen more or less by chance and suddenly appear from nowhere. If they think about the background to a failure at all they usually see the failure as the final event at the end of a short, linear chain of events that had a definite beginning followed by a short straight path to the inevitable outcome – disaster. Once the chain of events was set in motion nothing could divert it from its path. Taking a notorious example of a real life disaster and viewing it in this way we would describe the sinking of the White Star liner *Titanic* in 1912 by saying that there was an iceberg in the path of the ship, the ship hit the iceberg, the *Titanic* sank and the lives of 1,513 of the 2,224 people aboard were lost. But it is pointless to describe failures in this simplistic way. They are neither 'acts of God', nor do they appear from a clear blue sky. Rather they occur in a particular context, as rain appears after storm clouds have gathered.

The *Titanic* was on its maiden voyage at a time before the International Ice Patrol (which warns ships of ice in the North Atlantic shipping lanes) had been set up, and was steaming at twenty-two knots, a speed that was adjudged after the collision to be too fast for the existing conditions. The liner had been considered to be 'unsinkable' because four of the sixteen watertight compartments into which its double-bottomed hull was divided could be flooded without endangering its buoyancy but the iceberg ripped a three hundred feet gash in the right side of the ship and in so doing ruptured not four, but five, of the watertight compartments. The Leyland liner *Californian* was less than twenty miles away from the *Titanic* at the time of the collision but did not hear any cries for help from the stricken vessel because her radio operator was not on duty. Furthermore, the *Titanic* had only 1,178 lifeboat spaces for the 2,224 people aboard. All of these factors form a part of the context of the *Titanic* failure.

The context of a failure can be seen in terms of one system, or several systems from which the failure is perceived to have emerged. No study of failure can allow a sufficient level of understanding to be achieved unless we adopt some such device as looking at whole stories in systems terms, and, indeed, unless we also look at the environment with which the systems interact, examine the subsystems involved and so on through the catalogue of systems concepts like those discussed in the previous chapter. We have already talked about some subsystems in the brief description of the *Titanic* failure. Amongst these were the communication subsystem between ships, the subsystem for passenger survival and the design subsystem.

To take a further example of the use of system concepts let us think about the boundary of the *Titanic* system. Where a system boundary is fixed will depend upon why we are studying the system and its failure. In relation to the *Titanic* example, we may be interested in the technical aspects of the design system in terms of considering why an 'unsinkable' ship sank, or we may be interested in the social implications of the disaster. Why, for example, was the proportion of survivors so much greater amongst the first class passengers than any others? Some of these elements and subsystems would be within the boundary in both examples but there would obviously be many differences.

One of the major drawbacks of studies of failure, which at present usually take the form of accident and other inquiries, is that, because the spur for them to happen only comes after the event, they serve mainly as *post mortems*. The opportunity to encourage the widespread application of the findings as preventive medicine to similar situations is often missed and most inquiries are set up to study a named disaster even though the same kinds of fundamental failures occur over and over again. Just how many double-decker buses have to be sliced in half before something is done seriously to alert drivers to the presence of low bridges? In contrast to the valuable learning role that they could take on, inquiries have often been carried out in a spirit of 'justice being seen to be done'; and because they take a long time to complete, recommendations that have emerged from them have been too late.

When inquiries are far removed in time and/or place from the events that brought them about, their findings are seldom used to the full. Part of the reason for this is that change is often only brought about as a response to pressures from the public and that declines steadily with time as new disasters replace last year's tragedies. An example of this is the thalidomide story. As time has gone by the response has changed from 'we cannot let this happen again', to 'we must compensate the victims', to 'the victims have now grown up – doesn't time fly', and yet the echoes of the original failure still reverberate. Drugs still appear on the market after passing through supposedly rigorous testing procedures and then have to be withdrawn due to the discovery of harmful side effects.

The major justification for spending time, money and effort in studying failure is that the lessons learnt from the studies can be applied in order to guard against failure in the future. Investigation should be an investment in the future as well as a look back at the past. Failures need to be understood, and it is the argument of this book that understanding is best achieved by exploring the systemic background of the failures. In a complex system, failures are never due to a single cause, so by taking this kind of view of the failure and its setting, that is, by seeking systems in the situation, the layers of causes of the failure become clearer and more ordered in the mind. The patterns that enable us to trace causes from events arise from our detection of the interconnectedness that lies within what, on the face of it, may have seemed a dauntingly complex, confused and often apparently chaotic mess. Use of a systems approach at the very least provides a general way of making sure that the whole of a failure and its setting is examined in a rigorous way by focusing attention on the causes of the failure rather than on its symptoms.

Once the patterns have become clearer the way is often opened up for coherent but, even more importantly, generalisable explanations of what happened and why failures emerged. The next step will then be to use this new understanding to predict potential failures so that instead of failures being studied solely on an *ad hoc* basis their wider value can be realised, as lessons from what has happened are used to shape what will happen in the future. Properly applied, the study of failures can help us to fulfil our objectives in our everyday lives. Failures are not just the catastrophes and disasters that hit the headlines, they are also the missed opportunities and relatively minor disappointments that occur and are then overshadowed by more current problems. The lessons from large-scale projects that fail to achieve the targets that were set for them such as the failure of the Humber Bridge to generate enough revenue to pay for its construction can be of value when considering, say, the purchase of a £1,000 microcomputer that is then not used sufficiently to justify even that relatively small-scale investment.

Perhaps one of the most useful ways of describing failure using systems terminology is as the production of undesirable outputs of the system. Like other systems 'insights', this description has greater depth and significance than may at first be apparent. There are two major ways to measure the performance of a system by using the system's outputs. One way is to compare the inputs to the system with its outputs and thus to measure its efficiency; the other is to compare the outputs with the objectives of the system and thus to measure its effectiveness. As well as providing information about performance, these measures should also be used in efforts to control the behaviour of the system. The systems concept of control will be examined in detail in chapter 11 but basically certain outputs of the system that are judged to be important are looked at and, if possible, measured in some way. The results that are obtained are then compared with what can be termed the desired outputs and as a result of this comparison attempts are made to change the inputs or the processes going on within the system in order to reduce any discrepancies that may have been found. An example of this could be the comparison of actual weekly production figures from a factory with the production targets. Any shortfall might be accounted for by examining the inputs to the production process, its efficiency or a combination of the two, providing of course, that the targets were realistic in the first place.

An extremely important point that must be emphasised is that in the case of complex systems, which almost all of the systems we are likely to examine will be, it is not possible and probably not even desirable, to monitor all of the outputs, and indeed sometimes it may not be practicable even to define or predict the presence of all of them, so normally only some of the outputs are looked at when the control procedure outlined above is used. One of the values of a systems approach is that it can identify which outputs it is most important to monitor. It may be a relatively easy task to quantify actual and desired levels for the major outputs that the system was designed to produce but many of what might be termed 'accidental' outputs can be of major significance for failure. Consider, for example, one important output of socio-technical systems that is sometimes not even considered until 'things go wrong' and is always difficult to quantify – worker satisfaction. It could be argued that one valid and reliable measure of worker satisfaction is the level of industrial disputes. What, however, if the level of satisfaction remains just above that needed to trigger industrial action?

If the level of satisfaction in a manufacturing plant remained steady over a long period of time but just above the level which would trigger industrial disruption, it may have had the effect of reducing production performance, but to a limited extent, so that the cause of the reduction was never determined. Indeed, the reduced levels may have become the norm as time has gone by. In such a situation, only a slight reduction in worker satisfaction may be sufficient to tip the balance of the industrial relations scale to a dispute. Many may then perceive the dispute as a failure in industrial relations that suddenly appeared from nowhere; perhaps there was a disagreement over whose job it was to move a filing cabinet, but the causes really could be traced back much further. The dispute or failure would be a normal or at least an expected output of the system. To put it simply, it would represent but a small change in the level of the worker satisfaction output. The change, though small, appeared critical because it changed the apparent state of the output from 'success' to 'failure'.

Suppose we make a straightforward comparison between the

objectives and the actual outputs in order to examine the effectiveness of the system in terms of the extent to which the objectives have been met rather than to intervene in the behaviour of the system. We may achieve what for many people may be the 'acid test of failure'. Has the system met the objectives that were set for it? It must be noted here that the objectives can be set either from within the system or imposed upon it from the outside depending upon the nature of the system. In the case of the *Alexander L. Kielland* rig a major objective was to provide a safe, secure 'floating hotel' for oil men. This objective, one that would have been obvious, was not met. The possibility of a fractured strut leading to a capsize was not obvious to the designers. They had not considered that such damage was likely or that it could lead to such dramatic results and so did not cater for the eventuality of a capsize. The capsize was not consistent with the meeting of the overall objective but also an unexpected, and certainly undesired, output of the system. Expressed in another way, the provision of safe, secure accommodation was an output that suddenly ceased to be present.

The systems approach disciplines the analyst to look at all of the outputs of the whole system, both desirable and undesirable, and at the same time to search for the reasons why outputs that should be present are absent. This avoids falling into the trap of concentrating solely upon those outputs that the system was, on the face of it, or in the eyes of its designers, intended to produce.

The trap can be even more seductive when changes are taking place over a considerable period of time. Changes can manifest themselves in a variety of ways and may be such that they go unnoticed for some time. In addition to the actual outputs themselves changing, it is also possible for the ways in which they are perceived, and the way judgements of them are made, to change too. Changes in the climate of opinion generally can also bring about large differences in the way in which the outputs of systems are viewed.

Consider the rise in the level of support given to those who wish to conserve nature and to protect the surroundings in which we live from pollution. Partially as a result of this support, changes have been made, such as the imposition of far greater controls on the emissions from chimneys and more rigorous and effective policing of the regulations than ever before. These changes have meant that more resources have had to be allocated to the control of the unwanted outputs of production processes and in certain instances products have had to be taken off the market because it was not practical to manufacture them without contravention of the regulations or without causing conflict between the manufacturer and surrounding residents or pressure groups. An example of one such product that has disappeared from the market as far as amateur gardeners are concerned is lime sulphur, which was the only effective treatment against the most serious threat to blackcurrants, the blackcurrant gall mite. This pest is associated with a disease of blackcurrant bushes, reversion virus, which cannot be cured or controlled and renders the bush fit only for the bonfire. The loss of lime sulphur to the market place may be regarded as a failure by those who made it, those who sold it, those who used it and those who ate the resulting blackcurrants. To those who live near the plant where it was made it is probably regarded as a resounding success (unless, of course, they grow blackcurrants and the gall mites find them – then they may be in something of a dilemma!).

Another significant temporal change can be the rise or fall in the demand for a particular product or service. A system may have been designed to cope with an estimated rate of demand that took into account particular predictions for future growth or decline. Those predictions may have since been proved to be much too high or low and in some cases even the starting level may have been wildly inaccurate. If the rate of usage increased beyond the estimate, the system may appear to have produced a failure whereas really it only failed to meet new targets or standards, not those that it was designed to achieve. The failure of the surfaces of many of the sections of our motorways to withstand the wear and tear caused by the volume of traffic passing over them may be viewed as an example of this.

The volume of traffic, and in particular the number of heavy vehicles using the motorways, is actually far greater than was ever envisaged when they were being built. For example, the stretch of the M1 between junctions four and five carries eighty thousand vehicles a day, of which about a quarter are heavy goods vehicles. But the M1 was designed for a maximum flow of fourteen thousand vehicles a day. Thus, the goals being set for the system have been changed over the years. In effect the system itself has been changed from a road system designed to carry x vehicles to a road system expected to carry $(x + y)$ vehicles. As a network to carry $(x + y)$ vehicles this road system has appeared to fail. The road surface has worn out and has had (or will have) to be replaced, and serious traffic congestion occurs whilst the repair work is carried out. Such is the scale of the apparent failure that it was estimated in 1980 that the cost of major repairs to motorways could easily rise to £100 million per year. In addition, the Department of Transport reckons that the value of time lost by drivers during motorway repairs is equal to forty per cent of the cost of the repairs. Some of this cost must eventually find its way on to the prices of goods in the shops, for it all adds to distribution costs. Perhaps the system might well have been able to achieve the original goals it was designed to meet, and only failed to achieve the goals imposed upon it at a later date, well after the design stage. The considerable modifications that have to be made to motorway bridges and viaducts and the increasingly greater costs of maintaining and resurfacing the carriageways are, in fact, the prices that have to be paid for changing the system's goals.

There is another, more cheering, side to this coin. A system that has failed to achieve its original goals may become successful when measured against newly defined criteria. The Humber Bridge, whose story to date was set out in the previous chapter, may yet exemplify this. As a toll bridge link, able to generate enough revenue to pay back its construction costs to the government and to other creditors it has manifestly failed. If those debts were to be written off by the government the bridge could perhaps achieve some measure of success as a tourist attraction and as such be able to generate enough income from tolls to pay the operating and maintenance costs associated with it, whilst at the same time bringing new trade to help to restore some prosperity to the economically depressed Humberside area.

To return to an earlier point, one of the greatest values of using a systems framework to study failure is that it encourages a broad examination of both the failure itself and the context in which it occurred. Consideration of the systemic background of a particular failure will lead to a much greater understanding of all the influences and flows of both materials and information that existed in the situation. Of particular importance are the links between subsystems and between the system and its environment, but even more than this, the consideration of the whole system and its environment should prevent the narrow blinkered approach which has previously been a characteristic of many failure studies. Engineers have tended to look for technical problems, ergonomists have searched for human error or for mismatches between man and machine and, indeed, each expert has tried to seek justification for his own pet theory as to 'why things went wrong'. We began by emphasising that failure was, to some extent, in the eye of the beholder but we must not assume that subjectively based value judgements are necessarily prejudiced. The systems approach to failure is not only a multi-disciplined one but also one that demands an open mind.

This subjective element and the willingness with which the analyst must take on board new ideas and new ways of looking at situations forges a strong link between the systems approach in general and the way in which we have defined failure. Failure is an observation about something, *not* the thing itself. Similarly, central to the idea of a system is the concept that the system is an assembly of parts which a person has identified as being of special interest. That 'special interest' defines the system, its boundaries and environment and also its perceived characteristics. In order to arrive at the special insight into a failure situation that a systems approach can bring, it is necessary to accept that a system may, in fact, only exist in the eye of the beholder. Some systems, such as the air traffic control system at an airport or the British telephone system, may, on the face of it, appear to have a definite identity but, even so, their boundaries change with time and so even if the observer and the reason for study remained the same, the system might have changed when looked at on later occasions.

In 1981, for example, the British telephone system underwent a change of ownership. Prior to that it was a nationally-owned network operated by the Post Office but in October of that year British Telecom formally replaced the Post Office as the system's 'owners'. In addition to this change, the organisation lost its monopoly in relation to the supply and maintenance of some equipment and some telecommunications services. The British telephone system is no longer synonomous with British Telecom; other organisations are now playing a part in the system, whose boundaries have shifted and become more mobile. The casual observer may feel that 'the system' with its telephones at work and at home, out of order telephone kiosks and irritating sales campaigns featuring the cartoon character Buzby has not changed; British Telecom may still perhaps regard themselves as 'the British telephone system' but this view would not be appropriate if, say, a major competitor was looking at the system in order to investigate the market potential for a new type of mobile telephone. This perceived shift in the nature of the system may explain how well the system is able to respond to failures. It may be that one single unified organisation could provide a less piecemeal response or, on the other hand, its bureaucratic nature may slow down its response when compared with the cut and thrust approach of a profit orientated private business.

Surely if the view is accepted that failure can only be defined and judged subjectively then in studying it an approach must be used that makes allowances for this subjective nature. The systems approach not only does so, it positively demands it in a way that government commissions and courts of inquiry cannot, founded as they are in a belief in the concept of absolute truth. One word that the inquiries and the systems approach both place heavy emphasis on is *whole*. However, the whole is viewed differently in the two cases. A court of inquiry is limited by its terms of reference, and within these by the interpretation placed upon them by the participants. Rules of admissable evidence are applied and whilst the use of legal process can bring about the production of information that would otherwise be unobtainable, the overtones of blame and punishment will inhibit exploration of certain avenues of inquiry. In contrast, the systems approach is free to adopt styles of investigation that are particularly relevant to the problem situation. Whatever approach was used the study would be unsatisfactory if it stopped at a particular person's wilful or neglectful act and did not explore the background further. The systems approach will be affected by the viewpoints of the investigators in just the same way as an official inquiry could be, but in the former the role of the investigator must always be recognised as a key factor, for it is inherent in the definition of a system.

Thus, if one were to imagine a systems approach being used in an official inquiry it should be clear that the approach would be stifled; this is not the best way to learn from failures.

10

Systems comparisons for understanding

In earlier chapters of this book we have described some case histories and explained what we mean by the terms failures, systems and understanding, and the relationships between them. A failure was a shortfall in the quantity or quality of the output from a system: it would be a cause of anxiety. Understanding would be sought by the investigation of causes, contributory factors, effects, side effects and indeed, all pertinent issues in a case history of a failure. The systems approach would be paramount among the methods for developing an understanding. Although there may be disagreement about whether a failure has emerged in a given situation, no absolute and agreed understanding of systems behaviour, and even dispute over systems themselves, nonetheless there is a need to understand systems failures, and the approach suggested in this book will rely on comparison, and in particular the comparison of systems.

In order to use the notion of system in understanding a situation, we shall first of all, as it were, place that idea beside us where we are working. Next, we go to the case history and search for evidence of the features that are characteristic of 'system'. This evidence is assembled so as to contribute to revealing the extent of system in what we are studying. The search is directed at answering the question: are there systems here? But the point of the exercise is not only to find systems, it is to generate and achieve understanding along the way. Reinterpreting and rearranging the evidence will be a part of this process, as too will be the search for further evidence in order to find out whether a particular link in a system can really be claimed to have existed and how strong it was. The subjectivity of the investigator will influence the result, but this is an integral part of the approach. Indeed, one benefit of it is that it can make a virtue of the taking of several viewpoints by which to form judgements. When we examine different areas and adopt different viewpoints, some attempts will yield systems, others will not. There might be a missing link, a lack of connectedness, that serves to contribute to a failure; component might be missing at the crucial time. There might have been lack of interest on the part of the people involved or inattention to some necessary aspect of behaviour. We hope that in fact we will find poorly designed or badly organised and incomplete systems when analysing a case history, because these discoveries will be useful in our search for understanding. The next part of this chapter will be devoted to an example of the comparison but before that an outline is given of how the process might aid understanding, and the way understanding is itself used.

A prime consideration, a convincing pay-off for some people, might be the way that comparison for understanding aids the selection, design and implementation of change. Specifically, of course, the change would be directed at improving the situation so as to guard against future failure. However, comparison for understanding possesses more immediate advantages. The first is that the search for system, as distinct from a random perusal, encourages us to find out more about the situation under study and to direct our efforts more efficiently and effectively. The thrill of the puzzle or the chase acts as a spur to greater effort, and indeed more co-ordinated effort. The search could yield more data, or unsuspected connections between previously isolated raw data. The study of arrangement and operation of connections will be the primary key to better understanding.

Another virtue of this kind of comparison is that it provides convenient stages to mark progress in the investigation. The process for system description in chapter 8 does this by providing stages that can serve as milestones in the investigation. In chapter 11, further concepts for use in comparison are added to the basic ideas of system. It would be possible to divide up the work of investigation between several people or groups, each taking a different concept or a different central activity in the case history. Thus, in the TMI-2 case, the study of the activities that went on in the power plant itself might be separated from what went on in the surrounding counties. The necessary connections between each study group must be maintained or periodically brought up to date to reflect the connections between say what happened inside the plant and outside it, and between the results of comparisons made using different concepts.

If the comparisons can be divided into sections, and handled stage by stage without losing the overall picture, the stages can be used in communicating an account of the systems study, such as in a written report. Emphasis on the various stages will enable one incident to be related to another, not just in terms of superficial similarity but at a deeper level of analysis giving sounder generalisations. For the TMI-2 and the *Alexander L. Kielland* accidents taken together there could well emerge lessons about present-day attitudes to safety when high-technology activities have become everyday matters for the personnel and the public authorities alike.

The idea of system has been used for explaining comparison, and to provide a lead into the more formal ideas of system. But before looking at that a few examples will illustrate how the comparison process is carried out. Firstly, we shall take the period when the TMI-2 reactor first began to go wrong, and look at the arrangements for feedwater treatment and supply.

For instance, consider as a failure the interruption of various supplies of air or water in the reactor or its control circuits. On their own, taken one by one, the mishaps need not have come to be regarded as significant. Superimposed, and combined with other features and failures, they contributed to the overall failure of the entire plant so that it became unable to produce electricity. The release of water into a control circuit that should have only contained air betokens a connection for water passage that contributed to the failure. The system that should have monitored minor malfunctions as they happened, and prevented a repetition, should have picked up the previous times this trouble had arisen in the air circuit. These monitoring arrangements did not include the effective passing of information from site to site, and the importance of maintaining feedwater supply (a need recognised more fully at the sister plant TMI-1) did not influence those responsible for the plant TMI-2.

The comparison could be taken further; firstly, in terms of the definition of a system, the halted pumps changed the pumping system more than somewhat, so that circulation in the secondary circuit ceased. The effects of this lead us to examine a larger system, the secondary and primary circuits together. As the account pointed out, loss of a small component in the secondary feedwater circuit triggered failure in both circuits. Then other valves, wrongly closed, formed part of a system organised for disaster. It is hardly necessary to state that the feedwater circuits did not continue to operate or 'do something' in the manner intended. Finally in this example, the lack of interest shown in water circuit operation is clear.

The examples set out in the previous paragraphs used the simple four-part definition of a system directly, applying the four key tests of the system: organised connectedness, essentiality, interest and behaviour. In chapter 8 these appeared as part of a recommended procedure for describing systems. For the next example this description is used to assist the system comparison. It begins with the selection of an activity, for example the TMI-2 operators' monitoring of the relief valve on top of the primary circuit pressuriser (figure 2.15). A description of that monitoring is given, but not in system terms, in chapter 2. We shall next check that we have a purpose or purposes in mind for the study. For two and a half hours the operators and those who came to assist them believed the valve to be closed, yet it was in fact open, forming part of the path by which water was lost from the reactor and thus allowing the core to uncover and break up. The equipment for monitoring was badly designed in that it permitted misinterpretation and the operators failed to compensate for the malfunction of the equipment. Hence an examination of this aspect of the TMI-2 accident will prompt suggestions for changes in the monitoring arrangements as regards the operators and the equipment. Drawing attention to this group of malfunctions may highlight similar areas of potential failure.

Before carrying the description further the four part definition is applied, to discover whether there are systems at all. Taking the connectivity feature of systems first, there is connectedness in and around the monitoring: electrical circuits were activated, readings were taken, signals were interpreted, albeit wrongly. However the linking was also deficient in some places, such as the indicators of valve condition. Use of the state of the solenoid current as an indicator of valve position amounts to a lack of organisation of the necessary connection between escape of coolant and operator knowledge of that event. The solenoid could move independently of the valve and therefore the coolant flow system could become independent of the valve monitoring system. Further disorganisation can be found here, with the operators failing to deduce from temperature readings that hot coolant was still passing out of the valve, past the pipe temperature sensors and into the drain tank, where the blowing of another pressure relief valve went undetected. Much more could be said on the fragmentation of systems around this activity of monitoring flow out of the pressuriser but enough has been said to indicate how the first two parts of the system idea tell us something about the failure.

The remainder of the system definition concerns interest and behaviour. The operators failed to pick up the clues that pointed to the errors in the monitoring, their interest tended to be concentrated on supposed water level in the pressuriser, not flow into and out of it. In their defence, the behaviour of the monitoring equipment that morning was not one they had been trained to cope with, although a similar situation had arisen and been overcome at the Davis-Besse plant of Babcock and Wilcox.

The next stage of system description goes on to require notional separation of the systems of interest, putting trial boundaries on them and naming them. Now what should have been a 'monitoring system' was fragmented into a number of systems which provided indications of system state around the circuits but lacked connection. These connections could have been achieved by combining the signals from several indicators so as to signal 'flow in' and 'flow out'. The connection could have been by layout of the indicators on a control panel. The connection could have been made in the operator's mind, as a result of education and training. Notice that these comments are not put forward as solutions; mechanical redesign of the valve or its entire abolition might be preferred when the implications of various solutions are considered. Rather, these are examples of particular connections that were absent, and that were not compensated for at the relevant time. As regards naming the fragmented parts, this would be a list of the spots on the pipework from which indications were transmitted so as to be seen, not seen, or ignored.

The next stage, which is a particularly valuable one in this analysis, demands that we state what we feel to be the kind of system that we are dealing with. This part of the description has much to do with the purpose of the system, who runs it, for whom and in what context. The crucial fact emerging here is that what we are investigating can hardly be called a system at all, certainly not one that could be a water-loss alerting system for the duty operators, functioning independently of their ability to read several indicators and so create in their mind a picture of what is going on. The unusual behaviour of the plant that day constituted a system that no one had perceived before. It took a long time to see it.

The final stage of system description would be to go back in order to explore and explain details of the somewhat isolated happenings that should have comprised a proper system for monitoring. To do that, more detail would be needed than is presented in the case history described in this book. Instead, the next chapter introduces further concepts that are part of the system approach. They can be regarded as the description stage of the generalised notion of system, and provide the opportunity for further comparisons directed towards understanding systems failures.

11
Further paradigms for comparison

11.1 The background

The preceding two chapters of this book introduced a particular way of undertaking an approach to the understanding of a situation that has produced failures. The approach was based upon a search for systems in the situation or case history under examination. The aim of picking out the parts that make up systems served as a guide to seeking after fresh information on the background to failure, and to reassembling existing knowledge. To continue the approach, the investigator would have in mind a standard of what an effective system would comprise. Comparison of this standard with what had been assembled from the case history could lead in two directions. First, items that were needed for the 'standard' system, but were missing in what could be assembled from the case history, could indicate an inadequate understanding of the case, or suggest contributory causes of the failure. Moreover, these discrepancies would be couched in terms of systems concepts, and this would make it easier to draw general conclusions for a particular case study or group of studies. The other direction that comparison could take would be if the parts of the case study were found to fit together so as to form a system that was predisposed to failure. Few examples of this were given, as it is not until the later part of the present chapter that systems which have failure as a regular output are contemplated.

Earlier chapters have used only one standard for comparison. In this chapter several more will be introduced, and a name is needed in order to refer to them as a group. They could be called 'models', but that term might give rise to confusion with the 'modelling' of systems, on a computer for instance, in order to investigate how they work. Instead, the word 'paradigm' has been chosen for the standard forms of system used here in the comparisons. 'Paradigm' means a pattern, example or exemplar, and conveys the idea that it stands as a classic of its kind, an archetype. It is an ideal which is unattainable in perfect form, but which serves us well as a standard for comparison. The first that we examine here concerns communication.

11.2 **Communication of information**

One day in 1873, two goods trains stood at Menheniot station on the Cornwall railway, awaiting instructions from the porter-signalman to proceed. He was in the station telegraph office and the guard of the 'down' train waited on the platform outside. The guard for the 'up' train was not in sight. In due course the porter-signalman received 'line clear' for the down train over the telegraph, and putting his head round the office door shouted 'right away, Dick'. To his horror, the 'up' train pulled out. It was a heavy train pulled by two engines; the porter-signalman knew it was on a head-on path to a collision with a third goods train already on its way to Menheniot but he was unable to attract the attention of the guard. In the collision, one locomotive was completely destroyed and the other two very seriously damaged. The engine crew were badly injured, one being killed. The unfortunate porter-signalman did not know that the guards of both the goods trains at Menheniot were named Dick.

When information is to be communicated, a system needs to be set up. Naturally it is part of a larger system and therefore can be regarded as a contributing subsystem. Inside are parts that must be joined together properly, and indeed communication is just one form of connection. The parts can be identified as the sender and the message, the channel for communication, and the recipients and what they receive. A simple checklist such as in table 11.1 can be drawn up to draw attention to the critical features of communication, and the items for such a checklist are explained in the following paragraphs.

Table 11.1   *Requirements in communication*

Sender	Message	Channel	Recipient
sensitive	accurate	swift	literate
aware	direct	secure	attentive
selective	reliable	capacious	perceptive
sympathetic	up-to-date	economical	
	timely	low noise	
	adequate		
	economical		
	addressed correctly		
active	sent	open	present

The content of the message must be accurate, direct and reliable. It must also be up-to-date and timely. It must be adequate but economical lest verbosity obscure the point. It must be addressed correctly (in the Menheniot case it was not) and lastly it must be sent. The classic failure here is the competition entry that would have won – if the letter had been posted. The channel employed, be it the written word, telephone or radio, the spoken word or merely a glance, must be swift, secure from loss and tampering, of high capacity to cope with occasional extra load, economical, and low in 'noise' (noise comprises disturbances that are not part of the intentional signal). As an example, in preparing for dealing with a possible disaster the emergency agencies must meet beforehand to establish formal means of communication, for above all the channel must be open. In a physical sense, emergency telephones must not have had their wires stolen for the sake of the valuable copper they contain. (This had happened prior to the Aberfan disaster of 1966.)

It might be thought that the recipient need be only a passive participant in the subsystem. Actually he or she needs not only to be literate in the language used for communication, and attentive to what comes in, the listener also needs to be selective in disregarding 'noise' on top of the main signal, and sympathetic and perceptive so as to reconstruct what may not be entirely clear. On the other hand the news must not be unduly embellished. Finally, the recipient for a communication needs to be present at the 'listening post'. On 8 January 1979 a fire broke out on a tanker moored to a cargo discharge jetty in Bantry Bay, Eire. Initiation of emergency procedures depended on the constant presence of a 'dispatcher' in the control room ashore, but the subsequent inquiry concluded that he was not at his post when the fire began. The tanker was destroyed together with much of the jetty; fifty men from the tanker crew and jetty staff were killed.

Both the sender and the recipient of communications need to think of each other, each allowing for the nature of the other and the circumstances in which the other person is working. There are problems in the detection and perception of signals, and there will be variations of performance due to different degrees of stress and different kinds of motivation. This mutual awareness also extends to each recognising what might already be in the memory of the other; this can enable a message to be shortened or it may demand its lengthening; it affects the idea that each party has of what was meant. If the carrying of the message takes a good deal of time, this must be allowed for in phrasing it and in interpreting it. Much of the information needs to go into store for future use; while in the store it must be accessible, so its content must be summarised and its location detailed in some kind of index. When the information comes out of store it must still be of good quality. This includes physical quality: for example, the first and last pages of a telephone directory might be the obvious places for lists of emergency numbers, but these pages are the first to be disfigured, damaged or entirely lost.

Communication plays a part in all the failures that we examine here, or in other equivalent failures. Actually this should be no surprise, as most of the systems which we are dealing with are, or are intended to be, made up into systems by the very existence of communication of one form or another. This includes every kind of communication, from the passage of actual goods, through different kinds of formal and informal messages, to vague influences that only arise from one party's casual impression of the other party or mutual awareness of the other's power.

In the story of the *Alexander L. Kielland*, as in all the case histories here, there are communication defects. In framing its policies and legislation the Norwegian government expected from the oil producing companies a higher level of self-policing than the companies experienced in other operations worldwide. There is no evidence that this idea was communicated between the parties and made clear. Then there was perhaps misunderstanding, some might even say advantage taken, regarding the framing and issue of the regulations as one communication, and as a second communication the assurances in return that they had been followed. And at the other end of the story, Rogaland hospital looked back and found in respect of communication that their alarm procedures needed improving and that an information office would have been useful, presumably to deal with the flood of enquiries from anxious relatives.

11.3 **Control**

The systems that we are dealing with all do something; they behave by taking inputs from the environment, handling them and sending outputs back to the environment. The diagram of figure 11.1 expresses this. It is very simple but will develop as we proceed.

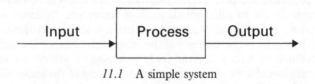

11.1   A simple system

Take as an example the fitting out of the *Alexander L. Kielland* for sea and, in particular, that part of this activity that was concerned with the provision of life-jackets on the rig. Inputs to this small process will include the life-jackets themselves, the equipment employed for packing them in place, and the instructions issued by the rig's manufacturer or the ship chandler carrying out the work. The outputs are the set of life-jackets in position, and a note from the installer that the work has been completed. But this is not the end of our examination of the process. The final arrangement was made the subject of inspection before the rig went to sea. The number and placing of the jackets was examined, or monitored, by inspectors, who compared what they saw with the standards laid down by the authorities. If they had found a discrepancy this would have been reported back to the installer and part of the installation would have been redone. In such an important matter a second inspection might have been made and would certainly be a possibility.

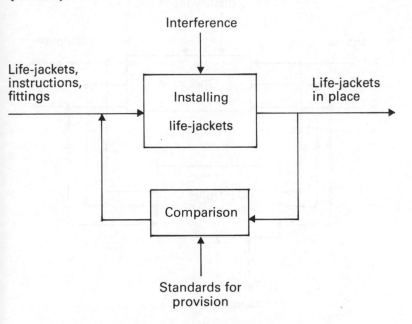

11.2 Control of life-jacket fitting-out

We can elaborate the simple diagram as it would be applied to the installation process, to produce figure 11.2, noting how a return loop passes from the point at which the output is inspected, back to the input. On the way, the information gleaned from inspection is monitored by comparing the monitor's report with externally set standards. One further point needs explaining. If the process of converting the given input to an output is effective, how can the monitoring show anything but satisfaction? Well, enough life-jackets might not have been supplied, the instructions might have been wrong, there might have been other equipment, permanent or temporary, in the way of placing the life-jackets where they were to go. The first two possibilities are expressed in terms of inputs, but the third, although strictly speaking also an input, is best shown as noise or disturbance to the process. The diagram that has been built up here depicts what we shall call control, and constitutes the control model or control paradigm. Its generalised form is shown in figure 11.3.

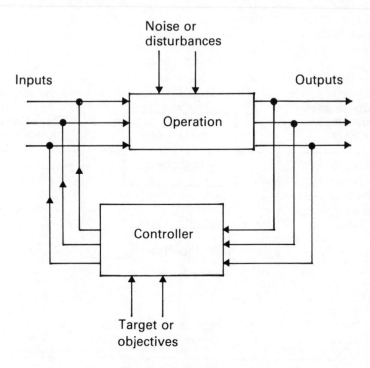

11.3   Control

The activity of equipping the rig with the right numbers of life-jackets, in their correct places, is not one that we regard as a contributor to failure, either in the sense that something was missing or that the system was intended to produce something that we now see as a failure. This system is only a contributor to failure in the sense that everything connected with safety, survival and rescue in the story plays its part, well or badly.

On the basis of the evidence available, use of the control paradigm on the life-jacket provision system for the *Alexander L. Kielland* does not reveal any mismatch. Before going on to give an example in which a mismatch is revealed we note an instance nearer to the origins of the idea of a system specifically intended to effect control. That origin is engineering control and it occurred on the *Alexander L. Kielland* many times over. The following example is typical.

To control the position of a rig like *Alexander L. Kielland* for the purposes of drilling, use is made of several pieces of equipment. The main ones are the sea-bed transmitters, hydrophones, winches, anchors and cables. The operator in the control room of the rig sets the anchor cable winches in motion by switches that send signals to the winch motors. If the signal says 'go' then the motors run and the rig moves. The output is a certain position, and this could be observed by a diver and reported back. However, if the hydrophones and sea bed transmitters are working, they send back what they hear to the control cabin, as a signal comprising a pattern of responses. Now, for each desired position of the rig the pattern corresponding to that position can be calculated and stored in a computer on board. The pattern for a desired new position can be taken out of store and kept to hand so that the pattern signalled from the set of hydrophones can be compared with the stored pattern. If there is a difference, then the winch motors are kept running; when there is no difference, the motors stop. The comparison and motor switching could be done manually or automatically. These components can be put on a diagram (figure 11.4) that corresponds to the classic control system diagram already referred to (figure 11.3).

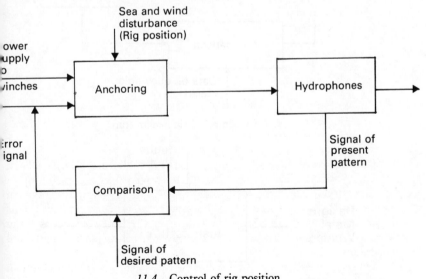

11.4 Control of rig position

The diagram of the paradigm for this kind of control contains six named items and six connections between them. In devising and running a system intended to bring about such control, all of the items and the connections between them must be provided and kept in good order. For understanding failure the paradigm provides opportunities for comparison, and in the next example the comparison will yield a mismatch.

For this example we take the process of welding the parts of the rig together. The control paradigm diagram provides an outline which we can annotate in relation to control. Figure 11.5 is the result. In practice, control of this process in the case of the *Alexander L. Kielland* tended more to resemble figure 11.6. That part of the control system that comprises monitoring, comparison with standards and altering the input was not present, or it was ineffective. If, in the absence of these parts of

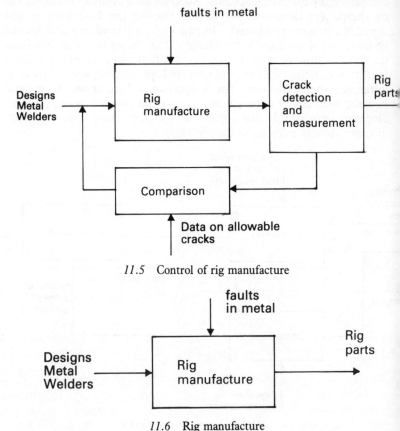

11.5   Control of rig manufacture

11.6   Rig manufacture

the system, it could be called a control system at all, it would be called open loop, meaning that the output is determined by the original state of the inputs and the disturbances. No further changes are made in order to compensate for later alterations in the input, or the arrival of further disturbances. An archer can only use open loop control for each arrow, his aim for an arrow is once and for all. In contrast, a guided missile will use closed loop control, in which a loop is formed by the signal link that feeds information collected from sensors back to the controls of the missile. Hence the use of the description 'feedback control'.

Together with the basic ideas of system and communication, control is the most important and frequently used of the paradigms. It is also worth pointing out that they are connected with each other. Communication and control will be effected by systems or subsystems; the connections between the parts of the control paradigm are communications. In contrast, the remaining paradigms stand apart more.

11.4 Systems safety paradigms

The willingness of systems investigators to adopt and adapt concepts from other disciplines has already been encountered in these paradigms. The human sciences and control engineering having so far furnished patterns for use, now a group is taken directly from a new discipline strongly related to failures, safety engineering. The aim in this area of professional activity is to investigate systems and thereby seek a certain level of safety. To do this, safety engineers employ several ways of looking at the system they are dealing with and we shall use some of these ways as paradigms.

The fault tree

Used as a technique, the construction of a diagram of the type that is called a fault tree begins with picking out a failure; this is called the 'top event'. Thus the top event might be the passage of radioactive material through one of the defensive barriers in a nuclear power plant such as TMI-2, the jamming of a lifeboat hook on a rig or the need to increase fares on South Yorkshire's buses. The study of failure by means of a fault tree next demands a careful examination of the system that might yield the failure. A study is made that looks at deeper and deeper levels of the contributory events that could lead to a failure output from the situation. The events, at the various levels, are related to each other in the fashion of logic, and drawn out for development and study in a tree design resembling the root system of a living plant. Special symbols are used, as shown in figure 11.7.

Resultant Event

Event resulting from the fault events and logic gates beneath.

Inhibit gate

The event above needs this event in addition to fault events and logic gates beneath

AND gate

An output event occurs if and only if all the input events occur

OR gate

An output event occurs if any one or more of the input events occur

Incomplete event

An event whose causes have not been developed This may be lack of information or lack of interest

Basic fault event

A failure of an elementary component, for which on occurence is likely to be available.

Transfer gate

The remainder of this part of the tree is drawn elsewhere.

11.7 Fault tree symbols

To give a simple example illustrating this idea, consider an everyday failure, a collision at a road intersection controlled by traffic lights. The top event is the collision, and we will take for consideration a right-angle collision in which one vehicle is passing over the intersection in one direction and the second is simply crossing its path. One vehicle (or its driver) had the traffic lights in its favour and the top event is thus conditional upon the 'innocent' vehicle being there, but it is actually caused by the 'rogue' vehicle, whose presence at the critical spot can be due to a variety of causes, a few of which are selected for this illustration. The road could be icy, the vehicle's brakes could have failed, the traffic signals could have been faulty, the driver could have been foolish or inattentive. Now any or all of these could occur together, but for the purpose of the illustration, any one of these alternatives can serve the purpose of putting the rogue vehicle in the wrong place at the wrong moment. Next the contributors to these middle level events are examined. The driver could be inattentive for several reasons again, such as tiredness or distraction of attention.

The possibility of brake failure introduces further branches of the tree. Motor vehicles are required to be fitted with at least two so-called 'independent' sets of braking equipment, so for the accident to occur there needs to be failure of both sets of brake equipment. There is thus a difference in the logic by which these failures contribute to the top event compared to the previous contributors. Figure 11.8 shows a partial fault tree for what has just been described.

In drawing up the diagram several aims are kept in mind. All pathways to the top event are sought out and included; the correct logical gates are employed, and the tree followed down to a 'basic' event. Ideally, for each basic event we have numerical data on the probability of that event occurring, such as the incidence rate of ice at the road intersection. If data are not available, the fault may need to be simply regarded as basic, by default, as it cannot be analysed further. In another case the fault can be declared basic if it is so rare as to contribute virtually nothing to the study. In our example a runaway and driverless vehicle would be one of these, if the road sloped away in both directions from the junction. Part of the diagram of a fault tree can be terminated by a triangular symbol when for lack of space the tree is continued elsewhere.

In the formal engineering of safety systems, such as the controls for a power station, the fault tree approach is found to have considerable benefits. In particular, it enables complex mechanical, electrical and electronic systems to be examined and explained in a way that no description in simple prose could do; the analysis is built up step by step in analytical or deductive fashion and the need to choose which symbols to use demands careful analysis of the background to failure. The encouragement to explore alternative origins of higher events leads to the

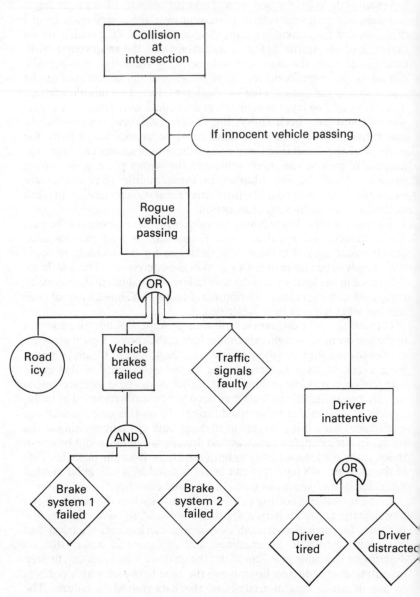

11.8 Fault tree for collision at intersection

discovery of combinations of events that were previously unconsidered. More generally the construction of the tree demands understanding of a system which itself might have been contributed to by many people and never seen as a whole before. The tree provides a focus for discussion on engineered safeguards, design changes and trade-off studies.

Some of these advantages also make the fault tree costly in time and effort, while some people experience difficulty in visualising anything but the most definite of concrete systems of engineering parts; this discourages them from using the technique when degrees or shades of failure are involved, as in our earlier example if we explored further the extent of icing and the different types of ice found on a road. Perhaps the temperature is right for ice to form, but sufficient road salt remains from an earlier application to prevent icing. Where the fault tree clearly comes to grief is over matters of human involvement. Just what is meant by driver tiredness? It is not possible to quantify tiredness. The events must have only two states, e.g., on/off, and these must be unequivocal. The events must be ones which only require a study of other events below them, not reference to those above. However despite all these possible drawbacks the fault tree is useful if only because of the questions it poses about contributions to the top event and, if used creatively, it can be helpful in guarding against failures.

As a paradigm for use in the method of comparison presented in this book the fault tree can be used in the following way. The top event is a significant failure from a system in the situation that is described in the story. The events that actually led up to this, together with those others which could have done so, are assembled in place on a fault tree using the appropriate logic gates. Put simply, this is the fault tree that would ideally have been in someone's mind before the incident. It would perhaps have demanded more foresight than it was reasonable to expect, but none of the cases involved factors which were unknown to physical, mechanical or human science, or contained combinations of influences that could not have been checked out beforehand. It is reasonable then to regard this fault tree as the paradigm for that top event, although it is not useful to blame people for not assembling it.

Next, a second fault tree can be assembled which shows what can be surmised of the fault tree events and their combination before the occurrence of the top event failure. It will correspond to a tree drawn today as a result of discussions between interested parties for a failure that, unbeknown to them, will happen tomorrow. For the case study this tree does not represent hindsight, but rather the precautions deemed important in the immediate past.

As an example, figure 11.9 depicts a fault tree paradigm drawn up for a top event 'loss of the rig' and based on information in the case study of the *Alexander L. Kielland*. Only a few of the multitude of possibilities are

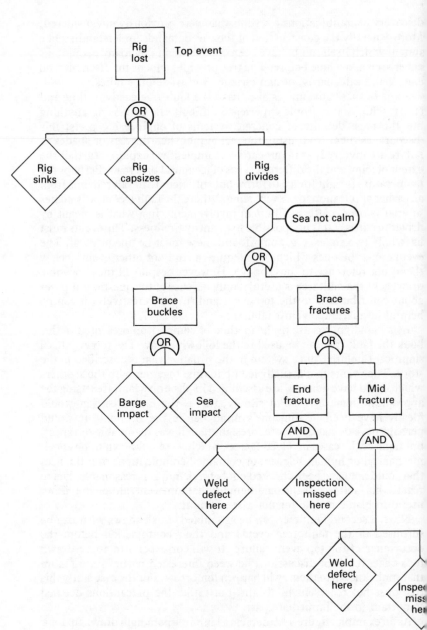

11.9 Alexander L. Kielland fault tree

examined, and these are mainly those for which information is available. Comparison with the account earlier in this book will reveal which members of the tree were omitted or mistaken in the preparation of the rig design.

Common mode failure

In the fault tree the basic events are assumed to occur independently, and only become combined in the sense of joint contributions to an upper event through an AND gate, or as alternatives through an OR gate. However there are situations in which basic events occur together or in rapid succession with some connection between them. The first of these is called common mode failure. It happens when vital components of a system possess some common feature that causes them to breakdown together rather than separately over a longer period of time. There are several ways in which this could happen. The influence of heat in part of a wiring duct will affect all the electrical channels passing through it; defective material or a badly conducted manufacturing process might affect a wide range of subsystems which each have one component the same. Casual maintenance can have a common effect on the equipment that drives a valve, the indicator of its state, and the safety locks. On the *Alexander L. Kielland* the tilt of the rig knocked out the main generator, the emergency generator and the supply from emergency batteries. In addition, it plunged the cabins and passageways into darkness. The same cause threw the chairs, tables and equipment of the main rooms into the paths of the men who were trying to escape. As another example, release hooks on the lifeboats gave trouble in more than one case. Perhaps occasional jamming of a hook is to be expected but so many gave trouble that they must be regarded as exhibiting a common mode of failure.

An important feature that can make common mode failure hard to guard against is that the original connection between the particular items that failed almost in unison may not be obvious at first sight. The fundamental defect that brought about the common mode failure of two or more items may have arisen in the design phase of the preparation of the equipment or the system. It may be due to unsuspected interdependence between electrical and mechanical subsystems or components in a system where safety was sought by building in redundancy or spare capacity. For example, redundancy of equipment or provision of standby subsystems may well have been achieved by using a variety of pieces of equipment, but each purchased nonetheless from a single manufacturer. In this way the equipment can contain common parts having identical design or fabrication errors that are particular to a single batch made at a certain time. This state of affairs may arise if an alternative material is used or a manufacturing technique is slightly defective for a short period. These are just a few of the ways in which common mode failure can come about.

To use the paradigm, the account of a case history would be examined to see whether items there show commonality in their breakdown; the use of the paradigm culminates in seeking a match between it and what is found in the account.

Cascade failure

In common mode failure the components concerned were affected by a common internal or externally applied factor, but one component did not necessarily interact with another. In cascade failure there is an interaction, sometimes referred to as the 'domino' effect. To explain this, if domino pieces are stood on end in a row, quite close together, and one domino is pushed so that it knocks over its neighbour, that one will in turn knock over the next, and so on in a chain reaction. Examples occur in all the case studies but a particular classic is found in the *Alexander L. Kielland* story, where the fracture of brace D-6 started a chain of failures. For a reminder of the paradigm, the domino idea provides a pictorial representation (figure 11.10). As in the case of common mode failure we use the paradigm by searching in the case history for local incidents that fit together to make a cascade to match the paradigm, and understanding is advanced by a match, not a mismatch.

11.10   Cascade failures can occur if one failure brings
about another, and so on

11.5 **Additional paradigms**

Some half dozen paradigms have been presented in this book so far. There seems no reason why there should not be many more that could be found. One likely candidate is the approach that has been called 'catastrophe theory'. The idea behind this is that whilst the changes that take place in a system can proceed in a steady fashion, there can also be sudden changes that actually constitute a jump from one condition to another, without a steady transition. The strike at Normansfield hospital is one such 'catastrophe'. The display of unrest increased steadily but then jumped to a new and higher level, the strike. In the case of bus subsidies the concern of government increased steadily but found expression as legislative changes that are sudden and dramatic alterations in the expression of that concern.

Other paradigms might be drawn from the areas of forecasting and planning. One technique used there is called 'critical path analysis' and includes the picking out from a series of processes those parts which, if they encounter any delay, will delay a whole project. The progress of the Humber Bridge could be examined to see whether in the event the appropriate critical path was considered in setting up the project.

Enough has been said to illustrate the existence of paradigms beyond those already suggested. The next chapter is devoted to a special group of paradigms that arise here because all the systems with which we are concerned have a human involvement.

12

Human factors paradigms

We have already looked at a range of paradigms that can be useful to us in our systems approach to failure but though many of those paradigms were concerned with the human aspects of systems they are not able to provide a sufficiently detailed framework to enable an adequate study to be made of the part man can play in a system, and hence in the production of failure. The role of man in systems failures is such a central one that it cannot be allowed to remain peripheral to our studies. To overcome this we shall add to the list of paradigms that have been discussed so far, some that stem from a body of knowledge that is commonly known as human factors.

In its widest sense, human factors is concerned with human characteristics, expectations and behaviour, and the ideas within it are used in order to try to enable man to carry out his work (or indeed any of the activities he might engage in) with maximum efficiency and effectiveness. Equally importantly it also seeks to ensure that his requirements for such things as health, safety and job satisfaction are met. Therefore, human factors is not just concerned with the man himself but with the job aids, tools and machines he uses, his surroundings and the people with whom he interacts. It should already be obvious that the subject is a very wide one but it is important to appreciate that its content is changing constantly by being updated and extended as the results of further research and development work reveal more about human behaviour and about the relationship between men and machines.

Human factors can play a dual role in the study of failure. It provides paradigms for comparison in its own right just as, for example, the control model and the systems safety paradigms and fault trees did, but at the same time some of the areas with which it is concerned can be thought of as part and parcel of some of the paradigms that we have looked at already in chapter 11. As an example of the latter form of use, let us consider the control model. If we try to assemble the components of that model and pick out the links between them we may find that the mechanism to provide feedback existed within the system under study but that the loop could not operate effectively because the monitoring function had been designed badly. This would have been the case if a pointer on a dial could not have been set clearly from certain positions or if an alarm bell could not have been heard because the background noise was too loud at the time. An example of this occurred during the Three Mile Island nuclear power plant accident when particular audible warnings sounded that would have alerted the operators to the real trouble; but because all the audible warnings sounded alike the reasons for the emergency could not be identified readily. Examples such as this illustrate one of the basic premises of human factors: operators must be provided with well designed equipment and surroundings if they are to be able to function effectively.

Human factors apply most clearly to failures in human activity systems and socio-technical systems. The former are systems in which at least some of the components are people and their activities. Socio-technical systems are human activity systems which comprise not only social subsystems but also technological subsystems and these interact with each other. The technological subsystems are based upon the tasks that are carried out within the system and include equipment, tools, facilities and operating techniques whereas the social subsystems are the relationships between the people within the system. The transport system in South Yorkshire can be regarded as a socio-technical system: the bus itself is a technological system and the operating and maintenance staff, together with the passengers, form social systems.

If an individual is not able to fulfil their role within such systems sufficiently well, then failures are inevitable. Indeed, one school of thought seeks to ascribe the cause of all failure to human origins. Even if this view is not accepted fully it is still extremely important to consider the part people play in a system and in particular the extent to which human needs are met and the extent to which people provide what is required of them. Conflict can often arise between these two sets of needs and then give rise to inefficient operation of the system. For example, research into the types of tasks where people keep watch or maintain vigilance has shown that the ability to detect signals is impaired by loss of sleep. Loss of sleep, however, is often associated with shift work, but the majority of process industries, defence establishments and similar systems where watchkeeping tasks are carried out have to function on a twenty-four hours a day, seven days per week basis, so a shift pattern of working has to be used. The operators must try to overcome the resulting loss of sleep problem without resorting to drugs, because many of the drugs that might have appeared to be useful have, in fact, been shown to reduce the levels of signal detection too. Therefore, where it is necessary to provide round the clock cover, the human factors of the situation must be studied very carefully and a number of variables must be taken into account. Possible approaches to tackling this could include the replacement of the human operator by an automatic device, an examination of different shift patterns in order to discover those which lead to minimum loss of sleep or the insertion of artificial signals which would tend to increase the operator's alertness. Alertness has been shown to rise as signal rate increases, sometimes enhancing the observer's level of performance.

Because human factors is such a vast subject and constantly expanding, it will only be possible to scratch the surface of it here. Our particular objective now, of course, is to look at the part it might have to play in the study of systems failures. In order to do this we will consider man as both a resource that is 'used' by the system and as a 'thinking human being' with all the needs, rights, goals, viewpoints and other attributes that distinguish a man from a robot.

It is possible to identify four different levels of human behaviour in a system.

Level 1: The individual – basic psycho-physiological functioning. At their most basic level, people could be used as a source of mechanical power. We are rarely used in this way nowadays largely because we are inefficient machines when compared with other machines and engines.

Level 2: The individual – control of tasks. In the role of controller a person is required to sense something, perceive what that something means, process that information by thinking and deciding and then take some action. In this area our efficiency, speed and accuracy are profoundly affected by the design of any machine components with which we work and by the environment in which we operate.

Level 3: The group – interpersonal behaviour. People usually work as part of a formal or informal group that influences the way in which they react to their work, helps to mould their opinions and goals and is, in turn, influenced by their relationship to it.

Level 4: The group – the behaviour of complete organisations. Superimposed upon the group and the norms of behaviour associated with group membership is the control and influence exerted by the wider system or organisation to which the groups belong. A very real source of conflict can be the difference between the goals of a group and the goals of the organisation, which are usually set by those at the top of the organisational tree. An organisation is very much an open system and as such it will interact with its environment. This too can be a source of conflict.

Consideration of these four levels should allow you to appreciate more clearly the scope of human factors. We shall now look at specific paradigms chosen from the very long list of those that could be applied at the different levels. Our purpose will be to compare what is or will be happening within the system producing failure with what would exist if human factors knowledge had been correctly and fully applied.

12.1 **Human factors paradigm 1**

Allocation of function

One problem that almost always arises when designing a system or subsystem is that of allocating functions between men and machines. In principle, the obvious way to do this is on the basis of the relative advantages of using a man or a machine to carry out a particular task, but such a straightforward solution to the problem is not always possible. Some functions cannot be delegated to a machine because the technology is not sufficiently advanced. An example of this occurs in the industrial inspection of the surface finish of the balls in ball bearings. No laser scanner or other fully automatic method has yet been designed that is able to distinguish between surface blemishes that affect the appearance only and those that are indicative of the presence of faults that would affect the performance of the finished bearing. Sometimes other functions cannot be delegated to a machine because the basic man–machine relationship of the machine serving man might be impeded. People must retain the functions of goal setting and goal switching, and sometimes of strategy switching, such as is the case when a pilot must decide whether an aircraft landing should be switched to another airport.

Nevertheless, despite these and other difficulties it has been possible for a general list to be drawn up that indicates the relative advantages of people and machines. The first such list was drawn up by Fitts in 1951 and later versions of it are still called 'Fitts lists'. Although the list is best described as a guide, it can be used as a paradigm. Comparison between the list and the actual allocation of functions within a system should indicate areas where obvious mismatches exist between the nature of the task and the characteristics of the man or the machine that has been allocated to it. A form of the list that was developed by Singleton in 1966 is presented here. It is interesting to consider how a list compiled in the 1980s might differ.

An example of the use of 'Fitts lists' can be provided by considering overload reliability in relation to a tracking task. The difference between us and machines is described in this list by the American term 'graceful degradation'. This means that the performance of the machine will drop suddenly whereas people will struggle on as work loads increase and merely perform progressively worse. In a radar tracking task the work load can be measured in terms of the number of aircraft per unit of air space. At low levels of load a machine is able to track an aircraft more

Table 12.1 *Fitts List*

Property	Machine	Human
Speed	Much superior	Lag one second
Power	Consistent at any level	2 horse-power for about ten seconds
	Large constant standard forces and power available	0.5 horse-power for a few minutes
		0.2 horse-power for continuous work over a day
Consistency	Ideal for – routine repetition precision	Not reliable – should be monitored
		Subject to learning and fatigue
Complex activities	Multi-channel	Single channel
		Low information throughput
Memory	Best for literal reproduction and short term storage	Large store multiple access Better for principles and strategies
Reasoning	Good deductive	Good inductive
	Tedious to reprogramme	Easy to reprogramme
Computation	Fast, accurate	Slow
	Poor at error correction	Subject to error
		Good at error correction
Input	Some outside human senses, e.g. radioactivity	Wide range (10^{12}) and variety of stimuli dealt with by one unit, e.g. eye deals with relative location, movement and colour
	Insensitive to extraneous stimuli	Affected by heat, cold, noise and vibration
	Poor pattern detection	Good pattern detection
		Can detect very low signals
		Can detect signal in high noise levels
Overload reliability	Sudden breakdown	Graceful degradation
Intelligence	None	Can deal with unpredicted and unpredictable
	Incapable of goal switching or strategy switching without direction	Can anticipate
		Can adapt
Manipulative abilities	Specific	Great versatility and mobility

efficiently but at a certain density of aircraft there comes a point at which the machine cannot discriminate the target aircraft from the others and its performance then falls to a totally unacceptable level. The performance of a human operator does not fall in this catastrophic way. The task will become more and more difficult but there will be no definite cut off point in terms of his or her ability to discriminate the target from the other aircraft. Thus, although such a task should, in theory, be allocated to a machine, at high load levels it can best be carried out by manual tracking.

12.2 Human factors paradigm 2

Visual display design

When describing humans at level 2, that is as controllers of tasks, it was stated that we were required to sense something and perceive what it meant. One way in which we are often required to do this is by obtaining information from a visual display. This was the case at the Three Mile Island nuclear power station where the control room staff were required to monitor the 'state' of parts of the plant using information gained from a variety of dials and indicator lights.

In order to ensure that a visual display is capable of being used in the way that the designer intended, guidelines based upon the characteristics of our visual sense and upon the operating constraints should be used. Visual displays can take a variety of forms such as a television screen, radar, written or printed materials, dials, gauges and so on, and general guidelines are already available for some of these. For others, recommendations may have to be assembled using the best information that is available at the time. Consider, for instance, a display that is primarily comprised of dials and indicators of the on/off, present/absent type as was in use at the Three Mile Island plant.

A good visual display will present information in a form that can be readily understood and lead to correct decisions and appropriate actions, or, to put it another way, facilitate the steps of the controlling process that come after the perception of what the display means. In order to allow this, the display must obviously be designed as part of a system, not as an isolated component. The general guidelines that should govern the design of a display of dials and indicators are given below. In the Three Mile Island control room most of these guidelines were transgressed at least once.

1. Viewing distance: the distance at which the display is to be used is important in determining the size of its details, their spacing and arrangement and sometimes their illumination and colour. If the indicators and dials are to be used in conjunction with controls the combination should be designed so that the display can be read at no more than an arm's length.
2. Illumination: the source of the illumination (inbuilt or external), its

colour and its brightness should influence the type, size and colour of the display.

3. Angle of view: visual displays are best read when they are in (perpendicular to) the direct line of sight. Obviously not all the components of a large display can be viewed perpendicularly so it is important to take steps to avoid excessive parallax effects.

4. The total effect of the display: when a group of dials, or other indicators, are grouped together information must be presented consistently on the various displays (for example all increases should obviously be presented by clockwise motion of the needle). It must also be easy to find a particular display from amongst those on a console.

5. Compatibility with associated controls: when displays are to be used in conjunction with controls the type and direction of control action the operator has to make must influence the type and direction of movement within the display. If a clockwise movement of the control represents an increase then a clockwise movement of a pointer on the display must represent an increase too.

6. Environmental conditions: when displays are to be used in adverse environmental conditions they must be designed to compensate for those conditions. In an aircraft, for example high acceleration forces and lack of oxygen may affect the crew's perceptual capabilities.

7. The operator population: displays must be designed for the kinds of people who will use them, be they young, old, illiterate, colour blind or whatever.

Each of these guidelines could be expanded considerably using data that have been collected as a result of much experimental work. For example, it has been found that the minimum distance between the major graduation marks on the scale of a dial should not be less than 0.5 inch, whatever the illumination or distance at which the dial is to be viewed.

As has already been pointed out, these guidelines were not followed in that Three Mile Island nuclear plant. Some of the dials were well out of the line of sight and in one case a maintenance tag was even allowed to cover part of a display. This provides an example of the extent to which human factors must not only be considered at the design stage but must remain important throughout the life of the equipment.

12.3 Human factors paradigm 3

The physical environment

(Note: the word environment is being used here to mean temperature, lighting, noise and so on, and not in its systems usage which is those elements outside the system boundary that affect the behaviour of the system or are affected by it.)

The physical environment in which people work can affect their behaviour. Environmental factors such as temperature, humidity, the presence of noxious gases, noise, vibration, acceleration and so on can decrease man's effectiveness and limit the maximum level of performance that he can achieve. Where tasks have to be carried out in adverse conditions allowances must be made for the environment and steps taken to limit their effect by providing protective clothing, acclimatisation training and other measures.

As an example of this paradigm, let us consider tasks that have to be carried out in hot environments such as those found where furnaces are in operation as in steel or glass works. Under normal conditions the human body is able to adapt to changes in temperature, humidity and air movement by regulating the sweat glands and the rate of flow of the blood in the skin so as to maintain a core body temperature of about 37°C. However, if the ambient air temperature rises too far above 27°C then the regulatory mechanism is unable to cope and as a result there is a slight drop in mental and physical performance.

At or above 32°C the drop becomes more noticeable, particularly when complex tasks are being carried out. The critical effective temperature at which a drop in performance can be expected varies for different types of tasks as illustrated in table 12.2.

Table 12.2   *The effect of high temperatures on performance*

Type of task	Max. temp in °C at which performance remains unaffected	Temp in °C at which a drop in performance can be found
Morse code reception	30.8	33.3
Problem solving	30.6	30.8
Mental multiplication	26.7	30.6
Lathe operation	26.7	30.6

If adverse environmental conditions are likely to exist it is necessary first of all to determine the nature of those conditions, usually by measurement techniques. These results should then be compared with data of the type shown in table 12.2 to discover whether performance is likely to be reduced. If it is, then either changes must be made to the conditions to bring them within the band that will not affect performance, or allowances must be made for the reduced levels of performance that are going to be found.

Research into the effects of exposure to cold conditions on human performance has not resulted in such clear cut findings as those for hot conditions. A survey of the research into the effects of cold that was carried out by Ellis (1982) revealed that, 'although mild cold stress does not affect the execution of some tasks it does have a deleterious effect on the performance of certain cognitive skills'. In order to try to clarify the position, Ellis carried out some research of his own but he too found that the effect of cold conditions varied considerably according to the type of task being carried out. In two different experiments, subjects performed a number of tasks before, during and following exposure to an ambient temperature of $-12°C \pm 3°C$, for a period of one hour. The tasks involved serial choice reaction time, where the subjects were required to classify a series of digits between one and eight as either odd or even, by pressing one of two large buttons; these then caused the next digit to be presented, and so on until five hundred digits had appeared. It was found that large increases in error occurred as mean skin temperature fell. These increases in error appeared to be largely independent of any falls in rectal temperatures though. Other more discrete tasks, such as a simple reaction-time test and a colour-naming test, showed no significant performance changes in the cold conditions and performance on a verbal reasoning test was slightly improved.

12.4 Human factors paradigm 4

Motivation of the individual

Our needs at work are determined by a number of factors. We will respond to other people, situations and issues according to our perception of them. The same events or issues will be perceived differently by different individuals. Our perception of and reaction to the product or service we are manufacturing or providing may affect our attitudes and feeling of job satisfaction. If two jobs are equally mundane and repetitive, but one is sited at the start of the production process and the other at the end, the latter will be perceived to be more satisfying because the worker can identify his efforts with the output of the factory much more closely.

An individual's level of aspiration is also important because people feel successful if they meet or exceed their own goals. The implication of this is that individuals with low levels of aspiration are more easy to satisfy but, of course, a lack of ambition and drive can bring as many or even more problems than a lack of satisfaction. The level of aspiration is linked closely to several further factors from amongst which we shall study just three: male–female stereotyping, cultural background and education.

There was once a widespread belief, largely unfounded, that women worked in order to earn 'pin money', because they enjoyed their workmates' company, or to fill in time until they married. They were expected to be less concerned than men that a job should help them to realise their full potential. The social climate has changed so much in recent years that this is no longer the case. Studies have shown, however, that women continue to attach more importance to shorter working hours, pleasant physical surroundings and convenient travel to and from work than men do, which may simply be a reflection of the extent to which women, rather than men, still have to take on the role of home-maker.

The standards, behaviour and attitude norms of the society, community and family in which an individual lives will influence considerably his or her perception of personal needs. The culture in some countries, such as Nigeria, is such that employees strongly prefer directive supervision where they are told exactly what to do and when to do it, and view a non-directive approach, where they are invited to participate in decision making, as a sign of weakness. In other cultures, industrial democracy is regarded as a right. Differences such as these have to be recognised by construction firms who operate projects world wide.

The average educational standard of the overall population has risen steadily and this in itself has changed the level of aspiration of many people. However, whereas many have benefited from the increase in educational opportunities, particularly in terms of the large increases in places at universities and 'second chances' to gain degrees such as those offered by the Open University or by part-time courses at colleges and universities, the days when an unqualified person could join a company and work their way to the top are now almost over and so, in this respect, some doors have closed.

A final factor that cannot be ignored is the effect that the overall economic situation has on people's needs and the way in which they express them. When economic activity is depressed and living standards are falling, dissatisfaction is less likely to lead to open conflict or industrial action. In times of high inflation the major sources of conflict in industry and commerce are likely to be economic. When the economy is buoyant, non-economic goals may be more to the fore though it must be accepted that conflict over non-monetary matters may sometimes manifest itself cloaked as economic conflict.

There have been many attempts to answer the question 'why do people work?' and a number of theories put forward. In particular, those of Maslow, Herzburg and McGregor have become widely known. It is beyond the scope of this book to examine the subject of motivation in detail but in terms of using the human factors paradigm it is very important to accept that if people's needs in this direction are not met then failures may be more likely to occur. In seeking to understand failure this subject area cannot be neglected even though the paradigm cannot be expressed in the same clear cut way that some of the others can.

12.5 **Human factors paradigm 5**

Group behaviour

The formal or informal work group is often the main source of social control in a system. It is therefore essential to examine the behaviour of groups within the system and the part they may have to play in contributing to, preventing or responding to failures. The way in which groups are likely to form within a system is also important because their formation is usually dictated by work patterns and by physical proximity rather than by job description, and this can lead to problems. For example, a lone quality control inspector working in the grinding shop of an engineering company may identify with the other workers in the grinding shop rather than with fellow inspectors who are scattered around the factory. This could obviously lead to a conflict of interests if the inspector feels unable to reject poor work because it was produced by his 'workmates'. It may also contribute to interdepartmental rivalry if one shop blames the poor quality of its work on the defects contained in the goods received from the previous process. If the inspectors were to see themselves as a group they would be in a better position to tackle such problems.

In general, if other factors are equal, the size of an immediate work group is negatively correlated with productivity, job satisfaction, regular attendance and industrial peace; in other words the smaller the group the higher the level of these variables is likely to be. Although a small group may have greater potential for improved productivity, the extent to which this potential is realised will depend upon the cohesiveness and goals of the group, and these factors must be taken into account when predicting group behaviour.

A cohesive work group is one whose members will stick closely to group norms. It has great potential for motivating employees to better (or poorer) performance, depending upon the goals of the group. Pressure is brought to bear on individuals to conform to the norms of the group by ostracising individuals who do not conform, and rewarding those who do, with acceptance, friendship and approval. Various studies have even shown that the values and customs of the group can be more important than cash benefits to the individuals within the group.

The activities of a small cohesive work group can be harnessed to support management's goals or to sabotage them. The goals of the group will be influenced by the reactions of the members of the group to their leader or supervisor and to the whole formal organisation within the system. They can also be influenced by the system's environment, for instance by a trade union. In essence, if a management wishes to change human behaviour within a system so as to avoid failure its best line of attack will be at the level of the work group.

As an example of the way in which knowledge of work groups has developed consider the following example. In 1961, a theory relating system objectives to group goal was put forward by Likert, specifying that:

The objectives of the entire organisation and of its component parts must be in satisfactory harmony with the relevant needs and desires of the great majority, if not all, of the members of the organisation and of the persons served by it.

The goals and assignments of each member of the organisation must be established in such a way that he is highly motivated to achieve them.

The methods and procedures used by the organisation and its sub-units to achieve the agreed upon objectives must be developed and adapted in such a way that the members are highly motivated to use these methods to their maximum potential.

The members of the organisation and the persons related to it must feel that the reward system of the organisation – salaries, wages, bonuses, dividends, interest payments – yields them equitable compensation for their efforts and contributions.

The theory was tested using data collected in a study conducted in 1955 and related to thirty-one geographically separated departments of a nationally based company. The departments carried out comparable work but varied in size from fifteen to fifty employees. All the analyses that were carried out gave support to the theory, which is now accepted widely. Just one example of the analyses will be highlighted here as an illustration of the findings.

Likert grouped the thirty-one departments into four clusters according to the degree to which the employees' and supervisors' responses to questionnaires conformed to a theoretical ideal of cohesive groups in which workers and supervisors have favourable attitudes towards each other.

The four clusters were made up as follows:

Cluster 1 Seven departments. High on cohesiveness. The workers indicated relatively high pride in their work groups, a strong sense of belonging to the group and favourable attitudes to other members of the group. At the same time, the workers and the supervisors indicated relatively favourable attitudes towards each other.

Cluster 2 Eleven departments. Relatively low on cohesiveness. The mutual attitudes were relatively favourable.

Cluster 3 Eleven departments. Low on cohesiveness and mutual attitudes unfavourable.

Cluster 4 Two departments. High on cohesiveness. Mutual attitudes unfavourable.

The average productivity of the departments in the different clusters was examined. The results are shown in figure 12.1.

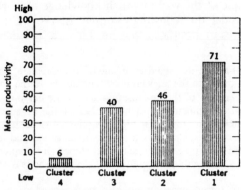

12.1   Mean productivity in each cluster

As predicted by the theory, the productivity of cluster 4 was particularly low. In the two departments which made up this cluster there was high group loyalty, but the relations between the groups and their supervisors and managers were relatively hostile. The powerful group forces were thus acting against the goals of the management and this resulted in low productivity.

If low productivity was being examined as part of a study of a systems failure, say in the event of the commercial collapse of a company, it would thus be as important to look at the groups within the system as well as considering technical difficulties, supply problems, poor quality and the like.

12.6 Human factors paradigm 6

Training

Poor or inadequate training can be a major contributor to systems failures. The results can range from catastrophic failure, as was the case at Three Mile Island, to a small but steady shortfall in performance levels, that may remain unnoticed.

This training paradigm takes the form of a generalised sequence of events that should take place in the development of any training programme. This sequence is shown in figure 12.2. It is necessary to check whether each stage has been carried out correctly and thus to identify any gaps in the procedures used at present. The analysis of the particular job must determine the inputs to the job from the rest of the system and the outputs that are required. Knowledge and skills can then be specified from a study of the processes by which the individual will make the transformation from input to output. The level of analysis here may vary according to the circumstances. It could range from a list of

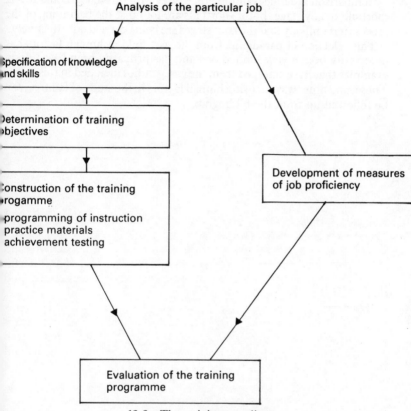

12.2 The training paradigm

tasks to the identification of specific activities such as sensing, discriminating, remembering and deciding. From this specification it should be possible to state in fairly precise terms the objectives of the training programme as a whole. These may just be concerned with the specific job or may include skills that are of a more general nature such as interpersonal or communication skills. The construction of the training programme involves the selection of specific subject matter to be used in the instruction, the drawing up of a timetable (in the loosest sense) and consideration of such matters as motivation of the trainee and achievement tests for each part of the programme; these in themselves may provide motivation as well as measuring progress. At the same time as these stages are being carried out, it is necessary to devise some method of measuring job proficiency at the end of the training period, so that the success or failure of the training can be gauged.

Comparison of actual training procedures with this model could reveal shortfalls at any stage, but if shortfalls are found at the beginning of the process it is unlikely that the later stages are being carried out effectively.

This selection of paradigms from the vast field of human factors has necessarily been a very limited one and has primarily been based upon examples that have emerged from the case studies included in this book. These, and other ways of using human factors in the study of failures, can be followed up from the bibliography.

13

Remedying, forecasting and preventing failure

So far, we have concentrated upon stories of past failures and shown how a systems approach could enable us to understand those failures. Admittedly the problems associated with the provision of low-fare public transport in South Yorkshire are still with us and some of the failures, such as the strike at Normansfield Hospital and a number of the shorter cases, could occur again but, nevertheless, the historical nature of the case study material could give rise to questions about the usefulness of the understanding that would be arrived at. There is a simple answer to such a challenge – an answer that is often used to justify the study of history in any context. It is that by learning about what has happened in the past we can place ourselves in a better position from which to influence what will happen in the future. In other words, by understanding how and why failures came about before, we hope to be able to avoid them in the future.

Before we go any further it is necessary to draw a clear distinction between the concepts of repair and remedy. After a failure has occurred as a result of the activities (or lack of activities) carried out within a system, a repair could be carried out that would return the system to the condition it was in before the failure took place. However, such a repair, which might be the replacement of a damaged piece of equipment, would provide no assurance whatsoever that a similar failure could not occur again. In order to achieve any such guarantee it would be necessary to carry out a remedy rather than a repair. The aim of a remedy would be not only to repair any damage but also to prevent future failure. Thus a remedy might involve not only the replacement of a damaged piece of equipment but also the insertion of, say, a missing link between two parts of the system or a mechanism for monitoring changes in the environment of the system. Such changes to the structure of the system would be suggested by the results of the comparisons between the situation and the paradigms.

Sadly, repairs rather than remedies often follow failures. The shortcomings of such actions should be obvious for they simply return the defective system to its previous working order. Our emphasis must be on prevention in all its various forms. These can be grouped into three main areas for convenience of discussion:

1. Preventing the same or similar failures occurring again in the situation that was examined (this is the area just outlined above);
2. Preventing the same or similar failures in similar systems;
3. Preventing failures that might happen but which have not done so yet either because the combination of events that would be necessary has not yet occurred or because the system does not exist yet.

We shall now look at each of these areas in greater detail.

Area 1 is the most straightforward: we use the knowledge gained from the study of the system, but with an important proviso: the repairs that were carried out after the failure may have (and probably will have) changed the system so that, given the same set of inputs again, it would now respond differently. It might not fail, it might not fail in the same way, or it might fail where otherwise it would not have.

The comparison process carried out as part of the systems approach should have highlighted areas where each system corresponds to paradigms corresponding to failure, and those where they differ from paradigms linked with success. It is then necessary to maximise the differences between the systems and the former and to minimise the difference between the systems and the latter.

Area 2 is an extension of the previous category. Sometimes one system will be very much like another, as is the case amongst accommodation rigs where one can resemble another in many respects, even though they may not both be of the same design. In other cases there may be great similarities between situations that, on the face of it, bear little superficial resemblance to each other. The benefits of comparing situations that are very alike are often realised but the opportunity to apply the lessons learnt from one failure to those cases with which it has a more tenuous connection is often lost. For example, a study of the failure of the search and rescue procedures after the collapse of the *Alexander L. Kielland* might start with an examination of similar rigs of the Pentagone design and then go on to the problems associated with rigs in general, but after this the lessons could be spread even further. They could be applied to accidents to ships and aircrashes at sea and then be extended even further to searches and rescues on land such as those which seek to help aircrash victims, lost walkers, fallen mountaineers and trapped pot-holers.

The procedure that is suggested is to select systems from the situation that has been identified as being similar and to use the same paradigms that were used to examine the relevent areas of the failure. This is not to say that other paradigms will not apply or that other areas cannot produce a failure; rather it is to stress that that which arises from experience should be applied first. Following the identification of potential failures, systems and paradigms, the comparison process proceeds as described for the study of an actual failure.

If we are to accept that in this imperfect world it is impossible to avoid all failure then the best line of defence against it would seem to be to concentrate firstly on those areas where failure would be most unacceptable. Before this can be done though, it is necessary to define what is 'unacceptable'. There can only be subjective definitions of such a concept, as is the case when we define both failure itself and the systems from which those failures emerge. Unfortunately, the willingness and ability to adopt such a strategy does not often go hand in hand with the authority to ensure that such a strategy is adopted. At best, the most we shall be able to achieve is to forecast potential failures in those areas where we have some authority or some influence.

To continue with the theme of forecasting we shall look at some work that has produced what is one of the most successful aids in this area to date. In the 1970s the sociologist, Barry Turner, examined the reports of official inquiries in areas such as transport and industrial accidents and picked out certain commonly-occurring features in the background or run-up to those events which sparked off the inquiries. To quote from Turner's book, he found that '. . . it can be tentatively suggested that the kinds of conditions which might very well provoke a disaster would be some combination of the factors set out below'. Area 3 lies here.

(Rather than repeat these pre-conditions in the form previously published, they are reordered here to show how they fall within the paradigms that were introduced in chapters 10, 11 and 12.)

1 The formal system

We would expect to find an organisational grouping of one or two large organisations and some smaller ones involved in a complex ill-defined and prolonged task. During the course of a project its goals are likely to shift. A characteristic task for the grouping is the design of a system which includes large or complex sites, to which the employees of a number of organisations have access, as does the public. Recognising hazards and taking action would call for the investment of time, money and energy in courses of action which would be difficult to justify within the organisation.

2 Control

Because of the prolonged nature of the task, the administrative machinery concerned with it is likely to undergo changes during the course of the project. Regulations relating to the task may be somewhat out of date, or may not be enforced stringently. Complaints from the public are usually treated in a fairly cursory manner, since they are felt to come from non-experts who do not understand fully the issues involved, and who do not have access to all the relevant information. Sometimes, with justification, it is pointed out that such complaints are made by unduly nervous cranks.

3 Communication
There would be a variety of information difficulties in the task and the members of the organisations concerned in it operate, in their official capacities at least, with stereotyped views of the public and its likely behaviour with regard to the project.

4 Engineering reliability
There will be ambiguities associated with the handling of the task; where signs of possible hazards emerge, some of them will be recognised and planned for but others will be neglected because they are not recognised by those operating with approved organisational stereotypes.

5 Human factors
Some of the parties in the project will change their roles in relation to task. By virtue of their organisational positions and professional or occupational background the individuals working in the area are preoccupied with some major issues relating to the task in hand, and they are reinforced in their preoccupations by organisational tradition and precedent. Some hazards will be neglected because of pressure of work, and most of the individuals concerned feel that quite probably a failure will not happen anyway.

To conclude, it is appropriate here to set out the ways our method of understanding failures produces results which can be fed into the designing of change. We recognise some contrasts that those responsible for setting about consideration of change might encounter. These are to do with the remit someone might have to take up, and the opportunities that are put into their hands or that they might arrange for themselves. Thus, a failure can be remedied directly, as would be the case when a comparison of a paradigm with something in the situation showed something to be missing. It might be a line of communication that could perhaps be simply inserted. In contrast to this, an indirect remedy involves something being done elsewhere in the situation. For example, South Yorkshire County Council failed to convince national government that the electorate saw free public transport as a worthwhile objective, one that should be financed from the rates. So rather than trying to whip up support for their theories, the council could tackle the failure by applying their efforts to actually running a free bus service on a small scale.

The next range of approaches to undertaking change has, at one extreme, those failures where we know what the objectives are, but need to decide how to achieve them. At the other extreme are failures where the objectives themselves can be challenged, so that wondering how to meet objectives becomes the second stage for consideration. Taking as an example the same case study as before, this represents the difference between on the one hand trying to make bus travel cheap or free and on the other hand opening up the discussion until it reaches the point at which there is an ideological choice. This might involve deciding between whether to allow people to live and work where they choose, then selling transport to them through fares and rates, compared to so constraining choice of home and work that transport needs are greatly reduced and can be met easily and cheaply.

So, although an attempt has been made here to look ahead and see the consideration of change as a process separate from understanding failure, it emerges that the consideration of change requires first an understanding of what prompts change, and the need for it, and what it will affect. Thus the activity continually finds itself back at understanding, and needing the approaches set out earlier in this book.

Bibliography

Chapter 1 **Failure**

Open University: TD 342 course *Systems Performance: Human Factors and Systems Failures*, 1976.
Unit 1 *Systems and Failures*.
Unit 2, 3 and 4 *The Hixon Analysis; Catastrophe and its preconditions*.
Unit 7/8 *Engineering Reliability Techniques*.
Unit 9/10 *Science Policy*.
Unit 13/14 *Mental Health Service Provision*.
Unit 15/16 *The Bay Area Rapid Transit System*.

Chapter 2 **The accident at Three Mile Island nuclear power station**

Lathrop, J. W., 'Planning for rare events: nuclear accident procedures and management', International Institute for Applied Systems Analysis, *Proceedings*, XIV, Pergamon Press, 1981.
Moss, T. H. R., Sills, D. C., (eds), 'The Three Mile Island Nuclear Accident: lessons and implications', *Annals of the New York Academy of Sciences*, CCCLXV, 1981.
Myrddin Davies, L., *The Three-Mile Island Incident*, Atomic Energy Technical Unit, Harwell, October 1979.
Three Mile Island: A report to the Commissioners and to the Public (The Rogovin Report), United States Nuclear Regulatory Commission Special Inquiry Group (M. Rogovin, director) USNRC Report NUREG/CR-1250-V, Washington, D.C., 1980.

Chapter 3 **The Humber Bridge**

Hull Daily Mail, 19 January 1966–26 April 1982.
The Humber Bridge Act (1959), HMSO, London.
Butler, D. E. and King, A., *The British General Election of 1966*, Macmillan, 1966.

Glen J. Haydon W., 'The Humber Bridge: the realisation of a dream', in Kinnersley, G. T. (ed), *Humberside Today and Tomorrow*, Treherne Publications (Humberside) Ltd., 1973.

Reed, B., *The Humberside Connection: How the Bridge was Built*, Home Publishing, Wallington, 1981.

'The Humber Bridge: The eighth wonder of the world', Aspinall Holdings, published as a supplement to the *Humberside and South Yorkshire Executive*, 1981.

Census of Population, 1981, OPCS.

Department of Employment Gazette, 1971–81.

Roads for the Future, HMSO, London, 1969 and 1970.

Leighton, M., 'Super-span' *Sunday Times* magazine, 10 May 1981.

Engineering the Humber Bridge, The Hillingdon Press, Uxbridge, Middlesex, 1981.

Humber Bridge, Expedite Graphic Ltd., London, 1981.

'Humber Bridge traffic ahead of forecasts', *New Civil Engineer*, 1 April 1982.

Humberside Structure Plan – Background Studies, 1976.

Humberside – A Feasibility Study, Central Unit for Environmental Planning, HMSO, 1969.

'Humber Bridge caisson – Howard sinks its problems', *Civil Engineering*, December 1976.

Chapter 4 **Crisis at Normansfield hospital**

National Health Service: report of the Committee of Inquiry into Normansfield Hospital, M. D. Sherrard (QC), Department of Health and Social Security, Cmnd 7357, HMSO, London, 1978.

Chapter 5 **The capsizing of the *Alexander L. Kielland* rig**

Norwegian public reports: *The Alexander L. Kielland accident*, from a commission appointed by royal decree of 28 March 1980, report presented to Ministry of Justice and Police, March 1981.

Uncontrolled blow-out on the Bravo platform on the Ekofisk Field on 22 April 1977, report to the Royal Norwegian Ministry of Justice and Police, 10 October 1977, from a commission appointed by royal decree of 26 April 1977.

Report of the Inquiry into the causes of the Accident to the Drilling Rig Sea Gem, Ministry of Power, Cmnd 3409, HMSO, 1967.

Offshore Safety, report of the committee (chairman Dr J. H. Burgoyne), presented to parliament by the Secretary of State for Energy, Cmnd 7866, HMSO, March 1980.

Chapter 6 **Buses in South Yorkshire**

Changing Directions, The Independent Commission on Transport, Coronet Books, 1974.

Thomson, J. M., *Modern Transport Economics*, Pergamon, 1974.

Gwilliam, K. M., Mackie, P. J., *Economics and Transport Policy*, George Allen and Unwin, 1975.

Public Expenditure to 1979–80, Cmnd 6393, HMSO, 1976.

Transport Policy: A Consultation Document, I and II, HMSO, 1976.

TUC Statements on Transport, 2nd edition, TUC Transport Industries Commission, 1975.

Barker, T. C., Savage, C. I., *An Economic History of Transport in Britain*, Hutchinson, 1974 (3rd edition).

Chapter 7 **Short studies**

Bignell, V. F., Peters, G., Pym, C., *Catastrophic Failures*, Open University Press, 1977.

Masefield, Sir Peter G., *To ride the storm: the story of the Airship R101*, William Kimber, 1982.

Report of the R101 Inquiry, Cmnd 3825, HMSO, March 1931.

Civil Aircraft Accident, Report of the court of inquiry into the accidents to Comet G-ALYP on 10 January 1954 and Comet G-ALYY on 8 April 1954, Ministry of Transport and Civil Aviation, HMSO, 1955.

Reed, A., *Britain's Aircraft Industry*, Dent, 1973.

Civil Aircraft Accident, report of the public inquiry into the causes and circumstances of the accident to Canadair C.4 G-ALHG which occurred at Stockport, Cheshire, on 4 June 1967, Board of Trade, HMSO, 1968.

Barlay, S., *Aircrash detective*, Hamish Hamilton, 1969.

Department of Trade, Accidents Investigation Branch. *Turkish Airlines DC-10 TC-JAV; Report on the Accident in the Ermenonville Forest, France, on 3 March 1974*, translation of the report published by the French Secretariat of State for Transport, Aircraft Accident Report 8/76, HMSO, 1976.

Godson, J., *The rise and fall of the DC-10*, New English Library, 1975.

Eddy, P., Potter, E., Page, B., *Destination disaster*, Hart-Davis, MacGibbon, 1976.

The Flixborough disaster, report of the Court of Inquiry, Department of Employment, HMSO, 1975.

Kennett, F., *The greatest disasters of the Twentieth Century*, Marshall Cavendish, 1975.

Rolls-Royce Limited; Investigation under Section 165(a) of the Companies Act 1948, report by R. A. MacCrindle and P. Godfrey, inspectors appointed by the Department of Trade and Industry, HMSO, 1973.

Rolls-Royce Limited and the RB 211 Aero-engine, Cmnd 4860, presented to parliament by the Secretary of State for Trade and Industry, HMSO, January 1972.

Chapters 8–10 **Systems**

Checkland, P., *Systems thinking, systems practice*, Wiley, 1981.
Kharbanda, O. P. and Stallworthy, E. A., *How to learn from project disasters*, Gower, 1983.
Open Systems Group (eds), *Systems behaviour*, Harper and Row, 1981.
Ramo, S., *Cure for chaos*, David McKay, New York, 1969.
Waddington, C. H., *Tools for thought*, Jonathan Cape, 1977.

Chapter 11 **Further paradigms for comparison**

Hammer, W., *Handbook of system and product safety*, Prentice Hall, 1972.
Lang, D. W., *Critical path analysis*, Hodder and Stoughton, 1977.
Lloyd, E., Tye, W., *Systematic safety*, Civil Aviation Authority, 1982.
Woodcock, A., Davis, M., *Catastrophe Theory*, Penguin, 1980.

Chapter 12 **Human factors paradigms**

Items referred to in the chapter:

Singleton, W. T., 'Current trends towards systems design', *Ergonomics for Industry*. 12, Ministry of Technology, 1966; reprinted in *Applied Ergonomics* II, 1971, 150–58.
Fitts, R. M., *Human Engineering for an Effective Air-Navigation and Traffic-Control System*, National Research Council, 1951.
Likert R., *New Patterns of Management*, McGraw-Hill, 1961.
Ellis H. D., 'The effects of cold on the performance of serial choice reaction time and various discrete tasks', *Human Factors* 24(5), 589–98, 1982.

Other items:

Brown, S. C., Martin, J. N. T., *Human Aspects of Man-made Systems*, Open University Press, 1977.
Gagne, R. M. (ed), *Psychological Principles in System Development*, Holt, Rinehart and Winston, 1966.
Chappanis, A., *Man-Machine Engineering*, Wadsworth, 1965.
Singleton, W. T., *Man–Machine Systems*, Penguin, 1974.
Brown, J. A. C., *The Social Psychology of Industry*, Pelican, 1954.
References can also be made to the following journals: *Applied Ergonomics, Ergonomics, Human Factors, Journal of Applied Psychology.*

Chapter 13 **Remedying, forecasting and preventing failure**

Turner, B. A., *Man-made disasters*, Wykeham, London, 1978.

Index